Oracle WebCenter 11g PS3 Administration Cookbook

Over 100 advanced recipes to secure, support, manage, and administer Oracle WebCenter

Yannick Ongena

BIRMINGHAM - MUMBAI

Oracle WebCenter 11*g* PS3 Administration Cookbook

Copyright © 2011 Packt Publishing

All rights reserved. No part of this book may be reproduced, stored in a retrieval system, or transmitted in any form or by any means, without the prior written permission of the publisher, except in the case of brief quotations embedded in critical articles or reviews.

Every effort has been made in the preparation of this book to ensure the accuracy of the information presented. However, the information contained in this book is sold without warranty, either express or implied. Neither the author, nor Packt Publishing, and its dealers and distributors will be held liable for any damages caused or alleged to be caused directly or indirectly by this book.

Packt Publishing has endeavored to provide trademark information about all of the companies and products mentioned in this book by the appropriate use of capitals. However, Packt Publishing cannot guarantee the accuracy of this information.

First published: July 2011

Production Reference: 1150711

Published by Packt Publishing Ltd.
32 Lincoln Road
Olton
Birmingham, B27 6PA, UK.

ISBN 978-1-849682-28-2

www.packtpub.com

Cover Image by Dan Anderson (Dan@CAndersonAssociates.com)

Credits

Author
Yannick Ongena

Reviewers
David Embrechts
Nelson Maia

Acquisition Editor
Rukhsana Khambatta

Development Editor
Rukhsana Khambatta

Technical Editors
Shreerang Deshpande
Dayan Hyames

Project Coordinator
Leena Purkait

Proofreader
Aaron Nash

Indexers
Monica Ajmera Mehta
Rekha Nair

Production Coordinator
Shantanu Zagade

Cover Work
Shantanu Zagade

About the Author

Yannick Ongena is an Enterprise 2.0 architect who has dedicated his career to specializing in Enterprise 2.0 portals. With over 5 years' experience in Oracle portal products like Oracle Portal and WebCenter, he has seen the evolution in enterprise portals. He was one of the first to receive the WebCenter Implementation Specialist certification.

Yannick is also dedicated to helping out the community. He is the founder of the WebCenter Enterprise Methodology Group, a top contributor in the WebCenter forums at OTN and a Enterprise 2.0 SIG leader for the Oracle Benelux User Group.

First of all, I want to thank my wife, Céline Croes, who needed a lot of patience while I was working on the book. Sorry for all the times you needed to do the dishes yourself.

I also would like to thank David Embrechts and Gerrit De Kepper from Contribute who gave me the opportunity to learn and specialize in WebCenter.

This book wouldn't be possible without the people from Packt Publishing. They really did a good job in helping me make this book as good as possible. First of all, many thanks to Rukhsana Khambatta who gave me the opportunity to write this book. I also want to thank Leena Purkait who coordinated the project. It was necessary to be reminded about the schedule sometimes...

I also thank Oracle for providing us with such a good product. I am glad I could write a book about such a product. This release is really a step forward in making WebCenter a fully mature product.

About the Reviewers

David Embrechts currently works as a senior software architect in Belgium for Contribute NV. David has over 15 years' experience as developer, architect, and technical manager in software development projects. He is currently the practice manager for the ADF and WebCenter development team within Contribute.

Nelson Maia was born in 1987, in São Paulo, Brazil. His first job was as a mathematics teacher in 2005. After that, he has been working with Java Technology. With proven experience in using the major Java frameworks in JEE applications, he has been working with Oracle technologies since 2007, including Oracle Portal, Oracle Application Server, Oracle WebLogic, and Oracle Enterprise Content Managent. Since 2010, he has been working as a Oracle WebCenter specialist. Among other certifications that he has obtained are Oracle WebCenter 11g Certified Implementation Specialist, Oracle Enterprise Content Management Certified Implementation Specialist, Oracle Application Server Administration I, Sun Certified Programmer for the Java Platform, Sun Certified Web Component Developer for the Java Platform, and BEA 8.1 Certified Developer.

> I would like to thank Yannick Ongena, the writer of this book, because he gave me an opportunity to work with him reviewing this WebCenter book. I'm very proud that I worked with him on this book.

www.PacktPub.com

Support files, eBooks, discount offers and more

You might want to visit `www.PacktPub.com` for support files and downloads related to your book.

Did you know that Packt offers eBook versions of every book published, with PDF and ePub files available? You can upgrade to the eBook version at `www.PacktPub.com` and, as a print book customer, you are entitled to a discount on the eBook copy. Get in touch with us at `service@packtpub.com` for more details.

At `www.PacktPub.com`, you can also read a collection of free technical articles, sign up for a range of free newsletters, and receive exclusive discounts and offers on Packt books and eBooks.

http://PacktLib.PacktPub.com

Do you need instant solutions to your IT questions? PacktLib is Packt's online digital book library. Here, you can access, read, and search across Packt's entire library of books.

Why subscribe?

- Fully searchable across every book published by Packt
- Copy and paste, print, and bookmark content
- On demand and accessible via web browser

Free access for Packt account holders

If you have an account with Packt at `www.PacktPub.com`, you can use this to access PacktLib today and view nine entirely free books. Simply use your login credentials for immediate access.

Instant Updates on New Packt Books

Get notified! Find out when new books are published by following `@PacktEnterprise` on Twitter, or the *Packt Enterprise* Facebook page.

Table of Contents

Preface	**1**
Chapter 1: Creating an Enterprise Portal with WebCenter	**7**
Introduction	7
Preparing JDeveloper for WebCenter	8
Creating a WebCenter portal	10
Managing pages	13
Changing the look and feel of your portal	17
Editing pages using the composer	19
Chapter 2: Consuming Portlets	**23**
Introduction	23
Building JSR 286 portlets in JDeveloper	24
Registering a portlet producer at design time	29
Registering a portlet producer at runtime	32
Consuming portlets at design time	33
Consuming portlets at runtime	36
Wiring two portlets together at design time	38
Wiring two portlets together at runtime	43
Contextual wiring of portlets using events	46
Chapter 3: Navigation Models and Page Hierarchies	**49**
Introduction	50
Creating a navigation model at design time	50
Creating a navigation model at runtime	52
Adding a folder to a navigation model	53
Adding a link to a navigation model	54
Adding content query to a navigation model	57
Adding a page hierarchy to a navigation model	59
Referencing a navigation model	61

Table of Contents

Adding a component to a navigation model	63
Adding a custom folder to a navigation model	64
Adding custom content to a navigation model	65
Changing the default start page of your portal	66
Filtering navigation resources based upon business logic	68
Exporting a navigation model	71
Importing an existing navigation model	73
Specifying the default navigation model	74
Managing the page hierarchy	75

Chapter 4: Managing the Resource Catalog — 79

Introduction	80
Creating a resource catalog at design time	80
Creating a resource catalog at runtime	82
Adding a folder to a resource catalog	84
Adding a link to a resource catalog	85
Adding another resource catalog to a resource catalog	87
Adding a component to a resource catalog	88
Adding a custom folder to a resource catalog	89
Adding custom content to a resource catalog	90
Adding resources to a catalog at runtime	91
Managing the Resource Library	93
Securing resource catalogs	95
Filtering resources based upon a role or other business logic	96
Selecting a resource catalog based upon business logic	100
Exporting a resource catalog	103
Importing a resource catalog	104

Chapter 5: Managing the Look and Feel of Your Portal — 107

Introduction	107
Creating a new template at design time	108
Creating a template at runtime	113
Creating a tree navigation	115
Enabling runtime editing of your template	118
Creating a new page style	121

Chapter 6: Integrating Content with Document Services — 125

Introduction	125
Preparing UCM for a remote connection	126
Creating a connection to a content server	128
Creating a content driven navigation model	130
Displaying a single content item with the content presenter	133
Displaying multiple content items with the content presenter	137

Creating a content presenter template for a single item	140
Creating a content presenter template for multiple items	144
Using the document service taskflows	148

Chapter 7: Discussions and Wiki Services — 153

Introduction	153
Creating a connection to the discussion service	154
Adding discussion forums to your portal	156
Creating forums	160
Creating topics	162
Adding announcements to your portal	163
Creating an announcement	166
Creating a wiki document	167
Editing a wiki document	168

Chapter 8: Organizing and Finding Content — 171

Introduction	171
Creating a connection for the link and tagging services	172
Enabling tagging functionality to pages	176
Showing related content	179
Showing a tag cloud	182
Linking content	185
Linking to a document	187
Linking to a discussion	190

Chapter 9: Using Polls and Surveys — 193

Introduction	193
Creating a connection for the poll services	194
Creating a poll	197
Adding a poll to a page	200
Managing sections	202
Managing questions	204
Scheduling a poll	209
Analyzing the results	211
Creating a poll template	212
Applying a template to a poll	214

Chapter 10: Integrating External Content and Applications — 217

Introduction	217
Registering an external application in JDeveloper	218
Register an external application at runtime	220
Adding an external application to your portal	222
Integrating external content with the WebClipping portlet	227

Table of Contents

Registering the Omniportlet	230
Integrating external content with the Omniportlet	232

Chapter 11: WebCenter Spaces — 239

Introduction	239
Creating a discussion and announcement service connection	240
Creating a document service connection	242
Registering external Applications	245
Registering a portlet producer	247
Creating a group space	248
Enabling additional pages	252
Creating subspaces	253
Creating lists	254
Creating a space template	257
Exporting group spaces	259
Importing group spaces	261

Chapter 12: Securing Your WebCenter Portal — 263

Introduction	263
Securing pages with the page hierarchy	264
Securing pages at runtime	266
Using Oracle Identity Directory as an identity store	269
Enabling SSL for a WebCenter portal application	273
Securing taskflows	278

Chapter 13: Managing WebCenter Portal Applications — 281

Introduction	281
Creating a connection to an application server	282
Deploying a WebCenter Portal Application	283
Undeploying an application	286
Managing connections in the Enterprise Manager	287
Propagating changes from a staging environment to a production environment	289
Viewing log messages in the Enterprise Manager	293
Monitoring the performance of an application	296

Chapter 14: WebCenter Analytics and Activity Graph — 301
Introduction — 301
Registering a WebCenter Portal application to the Analytics collector — 302
Manually running the Gathering Engine — 304
Scheduling the Gathering Engine — 306
Creating a connection to the activities schema in JDeveloper — 307
Using the WebCenter Analytics taskflows — 309
Creating your own analytics report — 314
Showing an activity stream on your portal — 319

Index — 323

Preface

WebCenter has changed a lot since the last release. A lot of new features have been introduced. We will try to cover all these features. In the first section, the navigation model, the resource model, and the newly supported JSR 286 standard are covered.

The second section will show you how you can build content-driven portals with the document services. You will also see how to build wikis and integrate the forum services as well as linking items together and allowing the users to find the content they really want.

The last section covers the administration tasks like managing the application in the enterprise manager. You will also see how you can use the WebCenter Analytics and Activity Graph to find out what sections of your portal are popular. You will also see how you can use this information to guide the user to the information they might want.

What this book covers

Chapter 1, Creating an Enterprise Portal with WebCenter, gives a brief overview of the new WebCenter portal template.

Chapter 2, Consuming Portlets, focuses on the uses of the newly supported JSR 286 standard to build and consume portlets in WebCenter.

Chapter 3, Navigation Models and Page Hierarchies, describes the creation and management of navigation models to guide the user through your portal.

Chapter 4, Managing the Resource Catalog, describes the creation and management of different resource catalogs to add components during runtime editing of your pages.

Chapter 5, Managing the Look and Feel of your Portal, shows the building templates and styles to provide a unique look and feel for your portal.

Preface

Chapter 6, Integrating Content with Document Services, describes how to use the full functionality of the Content Server to build content-driven portals.

Chapter 7, Discussions and Wiki Services, describes the use of the Wiki and Discussion services to build collaborative portals.

Chapter 8, Organizing and Finding Content, describes how to link items together and allow the users to find content they really want to see.

Chapter 9, Using Polls and Surveys, shows how to build polls to allow users to give their opinions.

Chapter 10, Integrating External Content and Applications, describes the integration of other applications into your own portal.

Chapter 11, WebCenter Spaces, shows how to build collaborative environments and integrate the different services for a feature-rich environment.

Chapter 12, Securing Your WebCenter Portal, describes the functioning of the security model of WebCenter.

Chapter 13, Managing WebCenter Portal Applications, explains the use of the Enterprise Manager to manage your WebCenter portals.

Chapter 14, WebCenter Analytics and Activity Graph, lets you analyze the use of your portals and use the analytics to give the users the information they want.

What you need for this book

The focus of this book is on Oracle WebCenter Admin 11g R1; you will only need the following software or IDE:

- JDeveloper 11.1.1.5 or JDeveloper 11.1.2
- Some chapters and recipes require a full installation of the WebCenter Suite

 JDeveloper 11.1.2 is not compatible with WebCenter yet, so in order to complete the recipes of this book, please use JDeveloper 11.1.1.5.

Who this book is for

If you are a WebCenter administrator who wants to keep yourself updated with the newer version, and learn all the important and advanced aspects of administering WebCenter, then this book is for you.

You would need to have WebCenter installed and basic knowledge of administering WebCenter would be required.

Conventions

In this book, you will find a number of styles of text that distinguish between different kinds of information. Here are some examples of these styles, and an explanation of their meaning.

Code words in text are shown as follows: " The header is displayed in a `panelBorderLayout`."

A block of code is set as follows:

```
<?xml version='1.0' encoding='UTF-8'?>
<jsp:root xmlns:jsp="http://java.sun.com/JSP/Page" version="2.1"
  xmlns:f="http://java.sun.com/jsf/core"
  xmlns:h="http://java.sun.com/jsf/html"
```

When we wish to draw your attention to a particular part of a code block, the relevant lines or items are set in bold:

```
<jsp:directive.page contentType="text/html;charset=UTF-8"/>
<af:pageTemplateDef var="attrs">
  <af:panelGroupLayout id="pnlAll">
  <af:panelGroupLayout id="Pnlheader" layout="vertical">
```

Any command-line input or output is written as follows:

```
keytool -importcert -trustcacerts -alias webcenter_portal -file
webcenter_portal.cer -keystore cacerts -storepass welcome1
```

New terms and **important words** are shown in bold. Words that you see on the screen, in menus or dialog boxes for example, appear in the text like this: "By clicking the **Page Properties** button, you can modify the **Display options** of the page and add page parameters".

[Warnings or important notes appear in a box like this.]

[Tips and tricks appear like this.]

Reader feedback

Feedback from our readers is always welcome. Let us know what you think about this book—what you liked or may have disliked. Reader feedback is important for us to develop titles that you really get the most out of.

To send us general feedback, simply send an e-mail to feedback@packtpub.com, and mention the book title via the subject of your message.

If there is a book that you need and would like to see us publish, please send us a note in the **SUGGEST A TITLE** form on www.packtpub.com or e-mail suggest@packtpub.com.

If there is a topic that you have expertise in and you are interested in either writing or contributing to a book, see our author guide on www.packtpub.com/authors.

Customer support

Now that you are the proud owner of a Packt book, we have a number of things to help you to get the most from your purchase.

Downloading the example code

You can download the example code files for all Packt books you have purchased from your account at http://www.PacktPub.com. If you purchased this book elsewhere, you can visit http://www.PacktPub.com/support and register to have the files e-mailed directly to you.

Errata

Although we have taken every care to ensure the accuracy of our content, mistakes do happen. If you find a mistake in one of our books—maybe a mistake in the text or the code—we would be grateful if you would report this to us. By doing so, you can save other readers from frustration and help us improve subsequent versions of this book. If you find any errata, please report them by visiting `http://www.packtpub.com/support`, selecting your book, clicking on the **errata submission form** link, and entering the details of your errata. Once your errata are verified, your submission will be accepted and the errata will be uploaded on our website, or added to any list of existing errata, under the Errata section of that title. Any existing errata can be viewed by selecting your title from `http://www.packtpub.com/support`.

Piracy

Piracy of copyright material on the Internet is an ongoing problem across all media. At Packt, we take the protection of our copyright and licenses very seriously. If you come across any illegal copies of our works, in any form, on the Internet, please provide us with the location address or website name immediately so that we can pursue a remedy.

Please contact us at `copyright@packtpub.com` with a link to the suspected pirated material.

We appreciate your help in protecting our authors, and our ability to bring you valuable content.

Questions

You can contact us at `questions@packtpub.com` if you are having a problem with any aspect of the book, and we will do our best to address it.

1
Creating an Enterprise Portal with WebCenter

With the new release of WebCenter, you have the ability to create rich enterprise portals without needing to code a lot.

In this chapter, I will explain how to set up, create, and build such a portal application.

In this chapter, you will learn about:

- Preparing JDeveloper for WebCenter
- Creating a Webcenter portal
- Managing pages
- Changing the look and feel of your portal
- Editing pages using the composer

Introduction

An enterprise portal is a framework that allows users to interact with different applications in a secure way. There is a single point of entry and the security to the composite applications is transparent for the user.

Each user should be able to create their own view on the portal. A portal is highly customizable, which means that most of the work will be done at runtime. An administrator should be able to create and manage pages, users, roles, and so on. Users can choose whatever content they want to see on their pages so they can personalize the portal to their needs.

In this chapter, you will learn some basics about the WebCenter Portal application. Later chapters will go into further details on most of the subjects covered in this chapter. It is intended as an introduction to the WebCenter Portal.

Preparing JDeveloper for WebCenter

When you want to build WebCenter portals, JDeveloper is the preferred IDE. JDeveloper has a lot of built-in features that will help us to build rich enterprise applications. It has a lot of wizards that can help in building the complex configuration files.

Getting ready

You will need to install JDeveloper before you can start with this recipe.

JDeveloper is the IDE from Oracle and can be downloaded from the following link: http://www.oracle.com/technetwork/developer-tools/jdev/downloads/index.html. You will need to download JDeveloper 11.1.1.5 **Studio Edition** and not JDeveloper 11.1.2 because that version is not compatible with WebCenter yet. This edition is the full-blown edition with all the bells and whistles. It has all the libraries for building an ADF application, which is the basis for a WebCenter application.

How to do it...

1. Open JDeveloper that was installed.
2. Choose Default Role.
3. From JDeveloper, open the **Help** menu and select **Check for updates**.
4. Click **Next** on the welcome screen.
5. Make sure all the **Update Centers** are selected and press **Next**.
6. In the available Updates, enter WebCenter and select all the found updates.
7. Press **Next** to start the download.
8. After the download is finished, you will need to restart JDeveloper.

You can check if the updates have been installed by opening the **About** window from the **Help** menu. Select the **Extensions** tab and scroll down to the WebCenter extensions. You should be able to see them:

Chapter 1

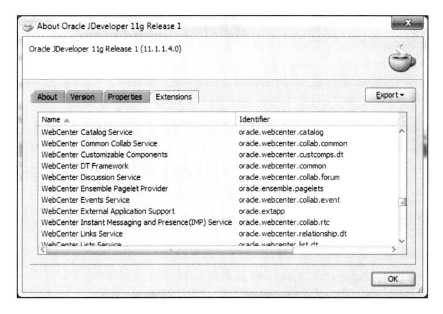

How it works...

When you first open JDeveloper, you first need to select a role. The role determines the functionality you have in JDeveloper. When you select the default role, all the functionality will be available.

By installing the WebCenter extensions, you are installing all the necessary jar files containing the libraries for the WebCenter framework.

JDeveloper will have three additional application templates:

- Portlet Producer Application: This template allows you to create a producer based upon the new JSR286 standard.
- WebCenter Portal Application: Template that will create a preconfigured portal with ADF and WebCenter technology.
- WebCenter Spaces Taskflow Customizations: This application is configured for customizing the applications and services taskflows used with the WebCenter Spaces Application. The extensions also include the taskflows and data controls for each of the WebCenter services that we will be integrating in our portal.

Creating an Enterprise Portal with WebCenter

Creating a WebCenter portal

In this release of WebCenter, we can easily build enterprise portals by using the WebCenter Portal application template in JDeveloper. This template contains a preconfigured portal that we can modify to our needs. It has basic administration pages and security.

Getting ready

For this recipe, you need the latest version of JDeveloper with the WebCenter extensions installed, which is described in the previous recipe.

How to do it...

1. Select **New** from the **File** menu.
2. Select **Application** in the **General** section on the left-hand side.
3. Select **WebCenter Portal Application** from the list on the right.
4. Press **OK**.

The **Create WebCenter Portal Application** dialog will open. In the dialog, you will need to complete a few steps in order to create the portal application:

1. Application Name: Specify the application name, directory, and application package prefix.
2. Project Name: Specify the name and directory of the portal project. At this stage, you can also add additional libraries to the project.
3. Project Java Settings: Specify the default package, java source, and output directory.
4. Project WebCenter settings: With this step, you can request to build a default portal environment. When you disable the *Configure the application with standard Portal features* checkbox, you will have an empty project with only the reference to the WebCenter libraries, but no default portal will be configured. You can also let JDeveloper create a special test-role, so you can test your application.
5. Press the **Finish** button to create the application.

You can test the portal without needing to develop anything. Just start the integrated WebLogic server, right-click the portal project, and select **Run** from the context menu.

When you start the WebLogic server for the first time, it can take a few minutes. This is because JDeveloper will create the WebLogic domain for the integrated WebLogic server. Because we have installed the WebCenter extensions, JDeveloper will also extend the domain with the WebCenter libraries.

How it works...

When the portal has been started, you will see a single page, which is the Home page that contains a login form at the top right corner:

When you log in with the default WebLogic user, you should have complete administration rights.

The default user of the integrated WebLogic server is weblogic with password weblogic1. When logged in, you should see an **Administration** link. This links to the **Administration Console** where you can manage the resources of your portal like pages, resource catalogs, navigations, and so on.

In the Administration Console you have five tabs:

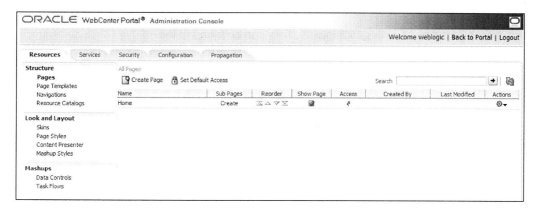

> - Resources: In this tab, you manage all the resources of your portal. The resources are divided into three parts:
>   - **Structure**: In the structure, you manage the resources about the structure of your portal, such as pages, templates, navigations, and resource catalogs.
>   - **Look and Layout**: In the look and layout part, you manage things like skins, styles, templates for the content presenter, and mashup styles.
>   - **Mashups**: Mashups are taskflows created during runtime. You can also manage data controls in the mashup section.

- **Services**: In the services tab, you can manage the services that are configured for your portal.
- **Security**: In the security tab, you can add users or roles and define their access to the portal application.
- **Configuration**: In this tab, you can configure default settings for the portal like the default page template, default navigation, default resource catalog, and default skin.
- **Propagation**: This tab is only visible when you create a specific URL connection. From this tab, you can propagate changes from your staging environment to your production environment. Read *Chapter 13* to learn more about the propagation tab.

There's more...

The WebCenter Portal application will create a preconfigured portal for us. It has a basic structure and page navigation to build complex portals.

JDeveloper has created a lot of files for us.

Here is an overview of the most important files created for us by JDeveloper:

Templates

The default portal has two page templates. They can be found in the `Web Content/oracle/Webcenter/portalapp/pagetemplates` folder:

- `pageTemplate_globe.jspx`: This is the default template used for a page
- `pageTemplate_swooshy.jspx`: This is the same template as the globe template, but with another header image

You can of course create your own templates. This will be covered in *Chapter 5*.

Pages

JDeveloper will create four pages for us. These can be found in the `Web Content/oracle/Webcenter/portalapp/pages` folder:

- `error.jspx`: This page looks like the login page and is designed to show error messages upon login.
- `home.jspx`: This is an empty page that uses the globe template.
- `login.jspx`: This is the login page. It is also based upon the globe template.

Resource catalogs

By default, JDeveloper will create a default resource catalog. This can be found in the `Web Content/oracle/Webcenter/portalapp/catalogs` folder.

In this folder, you will find the **default-catalog.xml** file which represents the resource catalog. When you open this file, you will notice that JDeveloper has a design view for this file. This way it is easier to manage and edit the catalog without knowing the underlying XML. *Chapter 4* covers recipes about the resource catalog.

Another file in the catalogs folder is the **catalog-registry.xml**. This is the set of components that the user can use when creating a resource catalog at runtime.

Navigations

By using navigations, you can allow users to find content on different pages, taskflow, or even external pages.

By defining different navigation, you allow users to have a personalized navigation that fits their needs.

By default, you will find one navigation model in the `Web content/oracle/Webcenter/portalapp/navigations` folder: **default-navigation-model.xml**. It contains the page hierarchy and a link to the administration page. This model is not used in the template, but it is there as an example. You can of course use this model and modify it, or you can create your own models.

You will also find the **navigation-registry.xml**. This file contains the items that can be used to create a navigation model at runtime.

Chapter 3 covers the recipes about the navigations.

Page hierarchy

With the page hierarchy, you can create parent-child relationships between pages. It allows you to create multi-level navigation of existing pages. Within the page hierarchy, you can set the security of each node. You are able to define if a child node inherits the security from its parent or it has its own security.

By default, JDeveloper will create the **pages.xml** page hierarchy in the `Web Content/oracle/Webcenter/portalapp/pagehierarchy` folder. This hierarchy has only one node, being the Home page.

Managing pages

One of the most important features for an administrator of a portal is managing the pages. Without pages, you won't have any place to put your content on.

This recipe will show you how you can manage the pages of your portal.

Creating an Enterprise Portal with WebCenter

Getting ready

For this recipe, you need a WebCenter Portal application. You will also need to start the Portal application.

We will use the default WebCenter Portal Application as an example in this recipe.

How to do it...

1. Go to the **administration** section on the portal by logging in as an administrator.
2. Select **Pages** from the **Structure** section in the **Resource** tab. You should be able to see a table with the existing pages:

3. Press the **Create Page** button. This will open the dialog to create a new page.

In the create page popup, you will need to specify the following fields:

- **Page Name**: The name of your page. This will be used in the navigation and to list the page in the Pages list.
- **Page Template**: You can specify a specific template for your page or use the Application Page Template, which will use a default template.
- **Page Style**: The page style specifies how the content will be divided on your page:

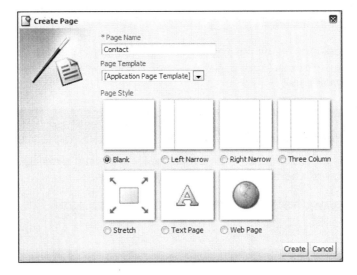

When you press the **Create** button, the popup closes and you see the page in the list.

In the list, there is a **Show Page** checkbox. When this checkbox is selected for a page, the page will show up in the navigation. If this checkbox is not enabled, you can access the page by linking to the page or specifying the URL of the page in the browser. The page will however not be visible in a navigation model when you add a page hierarchy. You will need to manually create a link from another page to that page.

When you want to secure your page instead of using the visible attribute, you need to specify specific security settings in the page hierarchy, which is described in *Chapter 3*.

There's more...

Move the page

Once the page has been created, you want to put the page in the correct hierarchy of your portal. In WebCenter, you can assign a parent page to each page. By default, the **ROOT** is the parent of each page. The root is not a real page. It is the parent node for each newly created page:

1. Click on the actions icon on the page you want to move and select **Move Page** from the context menu.
2. Browse to the location where you want to put the page.
3. Select the node you want as a parent for the page.
4. Press the **OK** button.

You will see that the column Sub Pages of the parent node will have an icon telling you that there are child nodes. Click on it to see the child pages.

Securing the pages

When you create a page, the security will be inherited from the parent. The inheritance is a property so it means that when you modify the security on the parent, it will be propagated to all of its children who use inheritance.

You can modify this behaviour by setting the security. This can be done by clicking the actions button and selecting the **Set Access** from the context menu.

At the top of the popup, you can specify the Access Method:

- Delegate Security: Specify the security on the page yourself
- Inherit Parent Security: Inherit the security rules from the parent page

Creating an Enterprise Portal with WebCenter

When you have specified the delegate security, the list of access rules is populated based upon the rules of the parent. From this point on, you can add your own roles and modify the security:

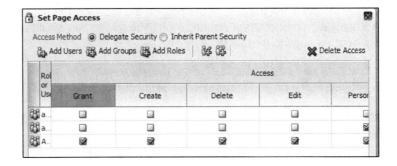

You can add both users and roles and need to specify what actions they can perform on the page.

Following access rules can be granted:

- Grant: Allows the user/role to grant access to other users/roles
- Create: Allows users/roles to create subpages
- Delete: Allows the user/role to remove the page
- Edit: Allows the user/role to customize the page
- Personalize: Allows the user to personalize preferences of the portlet put on the page
- View: Allows the user/role to view the page

Page actions

There are some other actions you can perform on the pages from the actions context menu:

- Edit page: This is a link to the actual page. You will enter the page in edit mode. This will be explained in another recipe.
- Copy page: This action will copy your page. You will first be asked to enter a name for the new page.
- Delete page: This will completely removes the pages from the system. No recovery is possible!
- About this page: This opens a dialog that shows some information about the page such as the name, created by, date created, last modified, and direct URL.

Changing the look and feel of your portal

The default template from the WebCenter portal application is a good start, but you want to have a portal with a look and feel that matches the house style of your company. In this recipe, I will show how to build your own page template.

A page template describes the default skeleton of your portal. In a template, you define where to put the header, footer, navigation, and other common content. You also define where the content area should be.

Getting ready

For this recipe you only need a WebCenter Portal Application in JDeveloper.

How to do it...

1. In JDeveloper, right-click on the Portal project and select **New** from the context menu.
2. In the left menu, select **JSF** from the **Web Tier**.
3. Select **JSF Page Template** from the list on the right.
4. Press **OK**.
5. Enter a file name for your template.
6. Enter the full **Directory** or browse to the directory you want to put the template in.
7. Enter a **Page Template Name**. This name is used in the drop-down list of templates when you create a new JSPX in JDeveloper.
8. You can use a **Quick Start Layout** by selecting the checkbox. When you click the browse button, you can choose more default layouts to base your template on. This will create a very basic skeleton for you to work with.
9. In the Facet Definitions part, you should at least create one facet for the content. A facet is a placeholder for content that will be created on the actual page. It is a region you can define where the page that uses the template has the ability to edit the content. To use this template at runtime, you need to create at least one facet definition called "content", which will be used when you create a new page at runtime.
10. In the **attributes** tab, you can define parameters that a page can pass to the template.
11. Press **OK** to create the template.

 If you want to use the template in a WebCenter application, it is important you create it in the /oracle/Webcenter/portalapp folder.

How it works...

When you have created the template without using a quick start layout, the code of the template should look something like this:

```xml
<?xml version='1.0' encoding='UTF-8'?>
<jsp:root xmlns:jsp="http://java.sun.com/JSP/Page" version="2.1"
          xmlns:f="http://java.sun.com/jsf/core"
          xmlns:h="http://java.sun.com/jsf/html"
          xmlns:af="http://xmlns.oracle.com/adf/faces/rich">
  <jsp:directive.page contentType="text/html;charset=UTF-8"/>
  <af:pageTemplateDef var="attrs">
    <af:xmlContent>
      <component xmlns=
        "http://xmlns.oracle.com/adf/faces/rich/component">
        <display-name>company_template</display-name>
        <facet>
          <description>The actual content of the page
            </description>
          <facet-name>content</facet-name>
        </facet>
      </component>
    </af:xmlContent>
  </af:pageTemplateDef>
</jsp:root>
```

> **Downloading the example code**
> You can download the example code files for all Packt books you have purchased from your account at http://www.PacktPub.com. If you purchased this book elsewhere, you can visit http://www.PacktPub.com/support and register to have the files e-mailed directly to you.

The definition of the template can be found between the `af:xmlContent` tags. In this tag, display name, facets, and attributes are defined.

At this point, you don't have an actual page template, only the definition.

The actual page template comes before the `af:xmlContent` tag. In the listing below, you can see a very basic template with a header group and the actual content facet:

```xml
<?xml version='1.0' encoding='UTF-8'?>
<jsp:root xmlns:jsp="http://java.sun.com/JSP/Page" version="2.1"
          xmlns:f="http://java.sun.com/jsf/core"
          xmlns:h="http://java.sun.com/jsf/html"
```

```
            xmlns:af="http://xmlns.oracle.com/adf/faces/rich">
  <jsp:directive.page contentType="text/html;charset=UTF-8"/>
  <af:pageTemplateDef var="attrs">
    <af:panelGroupLayout id="pnlAll">
      <af:panelGroupLayout id="Pnlheader" layout="vertical">

      </af:panelGroupLayout>
      <af:panelGroupLayout id="pnlContent" layout="vertical">
        <af:facetRef facetName="content"/>
      </af:panelGroupLayout>
    </af:panelGroupLayout>
    <af:xmlContent>
      <component
        xmlns="http://xmlns.oracle.com/adf/faces/rich/component">
        <display-name>company_template</display-name>
        <facet>
          <description>The actual content of the
            page</description>
          <facet-name>content</facet-name>
        </facet>
      </component>
    </af:xmlContent>
  </af:pageTemplateDef>
</jsp:root>
```

As you can see, we have a `panelGroupLayout` for the header and one for the content. In the content group, we have a reference to the content facet. This area will be made available for the consumer of the template. All the rest is off limits and cannot be modified. All page templates need to have the `<af:facetRef    facetName="content"/>` to work fine.

In the template, you would add taskflows for navigation, company logo, tag line, and other things you would like to see on your portal.

Editing pages using the composer

A portal isn't a portal unless you have the ability to make customizations at runtime. That's why WebCenter has the **Composer component**. It lets you add taskflows, portlets, or other components to a page. Using the composer, you are also able to change the layout of the content.

By letting users create their own page, you can let them design a custom dashboard. With the composer component, they can select which components to add on their dashboard.

Creating an Enterprise Portal with WebCenter

Getting ready

For this recipe you need a WebCenter Portal Application with a default admin page.

How to do it...

1. Log in as an administrator to your portal application.
2. Go to the administration page.
3. Select the **Resources** tab and select **Pages** from the structure section.
4. Click on the actions icon on the page you want to edit and select **Edit** from the context menu:

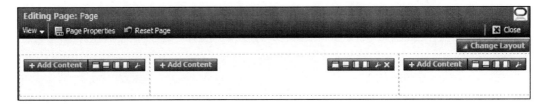

Each area of the layout has some buttons that control the layout.

In the left-hand side of each area, you find the **Add content** button. This opens the resource catalog so you can add components to the area.

In the top left corner of each area, you will find six buttons:

- Add a tab or set: This allows you to add tabs in an area. Each tab can have its own components:

- Add box above, below, left, and right. These buttons let you add a box at the side corresponding to the button. This box has the same features as any other area.
- Edit: With the edit button, you can set the properties of those boxes like the style and the allowed actions.
- Delete: With the delete button, you can delete the box and its content.

We will now add some components and show what we can do with them:

1. Click the **Change Layout** button in the top right corner.
2. Select the **Two-Column** layout. The layout should look like the layout in the image above.

3. Press the Add Content button in the first area. This will open the resource catalog.
4. Open the Web Development folder and click on the add link from the Moveable Box component. This is a component were you can also add new content.
5. Close the resource catalog.
6. Repeat steps 3 through 5 for the second area.

   At this point your page should look like this:

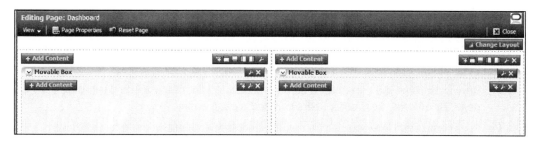

   When you hover over the **Movable Box** title bar, you see the cursor change to the cross icon. This means that you can drag the box to another area.

7. Drag the movable box from the first area to the second area or even inside the movable box of the second area. Each portlet that you will add will have this behaviour by default. In this way, users can rearrange the portlets to their own choosing. The difference between a movable box and a box is that in a moveable box the user can rearrange their portlets, and in a box just the editor of the page can rearrange the portlets.

How it works...

Everything you do in the composer can be seen as customization. Every customization you do is stored in the MDS on top of the real page. The MDS stored the delta of each page. This means that your changes are stored as an XML file that will be applied on the original page. Even the page bindings have a representation in the MDS. When a portlet has parameters, these bindings are stored in the page bindings so when you add portlets, the MDS needs to store the delta in its repository so it can apply the changes.

When you reset the page to its original value, the delta will be removed from the MDS and you see the original page.

The MDS (Metadata Services) is a repository used by WebCenter to store metadata. The integrated WebLogic server in JDeveloper stores the metadata in a file-based repository. When you install a standalone WebLogic server, the MDS will be stored in the database. The MDS repository is an XML-based repository. By using the XML features of the latest Oracle database, the performance of the MDS is really great.

Creating an Enterprise Portal with WebCenter

There's more...

When you want to put the page back to its original state, you can use the **Reset Page** button. This will remove everything from your page and bring it back to its original state.

By clicking the **Page Properties** button, you can modify the **Display options** of the page and add page parameters.

The page properties have following options:

- Page Name: The page name will be used to display the title of the page in the browser window.
- Description: Specify a description about the page.
- Keywords: Here you can enter a comma-separated list of keywords describing the page. By entering keywords, users can find a page easily.
- Page template: Here you can change the look-and-feel of the page by selecting the template.
- Background color: Specify the background color of your page.
- Background image: Specify the image you want to use as a background for your page.
- Other CSS: In this text field, you can enter additional styles that need to be applied to your page.

2
Consuming Portlets

In this chapter, you will learn about:

- ▶ Building JSR 286 portlets in JDeveloper
- ▶ Registering a portlet producer at design time
- ▶ Registering a portlet producer at runtime
- ▶ Consuming portlets at design time
- ▶ Consuming portlets at runtime
- ▶ Wiring two portlets together at design time
- ▶ Wiring two portlets together at runtime
- ▶ Contextual wiring of portlets using events

Introduction

One of the most important tasks you will have as an administrator is to manage portlets in your application. Portlets are the building blocks of an Enterprise 2.0 portal. It will allow you to turn a regular application into composite applications. By developing portlets instead of regular web applications, you allow other platforms to integrate custom build functionality into a single environment.

WebCenter supports the JSR 286 portlet standard. This standard describes how a portlet and its consuming portal can interact. All portlets in WebCenter are remote. This means that we need WSRP (Web Service for Remote Portlet) to access the portlets from within our portlet. The reason for this is that we can easily scale the server where we deploy the portlets. By having remote portlets, you also have a loosely coupled link between the portlet and portal server.

Building JSR 286 portlets in JDeveloper

JDeveloper is Oracle's integrated development environment. It allows you to build complex applications from the complete Fusion Middleware stack.

JDeveloper contains a template for building a portlet producer.

A portlet is the building block of your portal. It allows you to create your own functionality and include it into your portal.

With WebCenter, you can make use of the ADF Rich faces technology to build good looking, user friendly portlets. It also allows you to make use of the complete ADF stack like the data controls and business components so you can build your portlets based upon the MVC methodology.

Getting ready

Before you can start on this recipe, you need a working version of the latest JDeveloper with the WebCenter extensions installed.

How to do it...

First we will create the portlet producer:

1. Create a new application by pressing *Ctrl+ N*. This will open up the new gallery.
2. From the left menu, select **Applications** from the **General** section.
3. In the right pane, select **Portlet Producer Application**.
4. Press **OK** to create the application.
5. Enter an application name, directory, and prefix package.
6. Press **Next** to enter the finalization setting of the application.
7. Specify the default package of the application, source folder, and output folder. The output folder will contain the compiled java files.
8. After pressing **Finish**, JDeveloper will create the folder structure for our portlet producer.

We will now create a portlet:

1. Press *Ctrl + N* to open the New Gallery.
2. Select **Portlets** from the **Web Tier**.
3. Select **Standards-based Java Portlet (JSR286) portlet** from the right pane.
4. Press **OK** in order to open the **Create JSR286 Java Portlet** wizard.

5. Specify the general information about the portlet like the name, class, package, and language.
6. In the next step, we can specify additional portlet information. Most of that information will be used in the resource catalog:
    - Display name: The name the user will see for the portlet in the RC
    - Portlet title: Used in the header when the portlet is displayed on the screen
    - Short title: Not used in the RC
    - Description: More information about the portlet
    - Keywords: Comma-separated list for entering keywords that can help the user to find the portlet
7. Select a mode.
8. Specify the JSP or JSPX page.
9. Press the Add button to add available modes to the selected list:

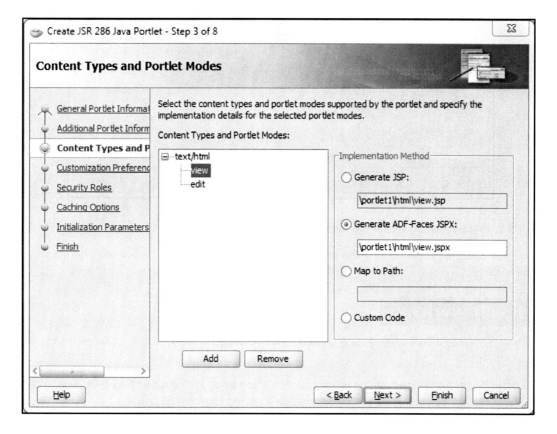

Consuming Portlets

10. Specify the personalization parameters so users can personalize the behavior of the portlet. JDeveloper will also add the necessary input fields to the page specified for the edit mode in the previous step. Each parameter has a name and a default value (which can be empty). You also have the ability to translate the parameter in case your portal supports localization. By default, there is the **Portlet Title**. This is a mandatory parameter from WebCenter when you enable edit mode. This is not a part of the J JSR286 standard!

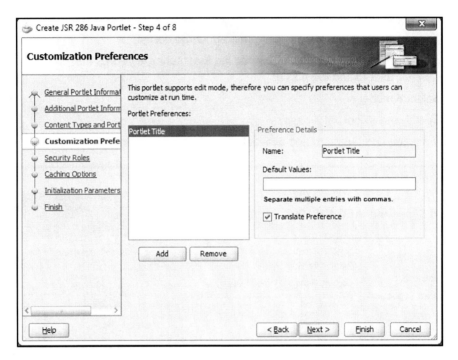

11. Press **Finish** to create the portlet.

Now you can start implementing the portlet by editing the JSP or JSPX page and generated java classes.

How it works...

When you create a Portlet producing application, JDeveloper will add additional libraries to your classpath.

By default, you will notice that JDeveloper has selected **Java, JSP and Servlets** and WebCenter Portlet Creation Service. These technologies are required for creating portlets.

If you are planning on using ADF portlets, you don't need to specify the ADF libraries. The necessary libraries will be added when we specify an ADF portlet in the create portlet wizard.

Chapter 2

The third step of the wizard is one of the most important steps. There, you need to specify the actual JSP file for each portlet mode. By default, JDeveloper will enable 2 modes. The view mode is a mandatory one and the edit mode. The last one is used to personalize the portlet. In the list, you can select a specific mode and ask JDeveloper to create a JSP or a JSPX page. When you select JSPX, JDeveloper will automatically import the ADF libraries so you can use the ADF rich faces components in your portlets. You can also specify additional modes and their corresponding page. Oracle provides some extra modes like help, about, preview and print. In order to add other modes, you need to press the **Add** button and add available modes to the selected list.

After we have finished the wizard, JDeveloper will create the files needed for the portlet.

First of all there is the **portlet.xml**. This file contains the actual portlet definition. You can have only one `portlet.xml` in your application. If you add additional portlets, the entries will be added to the `portlet.xml`. As you can see, all the information we entered during the wizard is available in the `portlet.xml`:

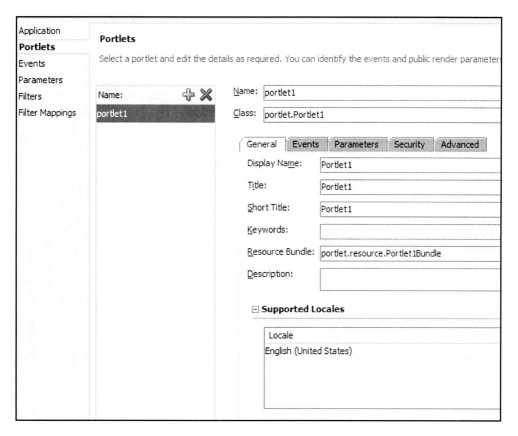

— [27] —

JDeveloper will also create the JSP or JSPX pages we have defined in step 3. You will also find a reference to those pages in the `portlet.xml` where they are linked to a portlet mode.

The actual `portlet` class will also be generated. This can be found in the package defined in the first step and will be found in the `portlet.xml` in the **portlet-class** entry. As described by the JSR286 standard, this class must extend the `GenericPortlet`. When you have selected a JSP page as your portlet, this class will actually extend the `GenericPortlet`, but when you have selected a JSPX page, the class will extend the `ADFBridgePortlet` which contains the logic to implement ADF Portlets. The `ADFBridgePortlet` will extend the `GenericPortlet`, so using JSPX pages will not violate the standard.

Based upon the standard, the `portlet` class will implement the **processAction** and **render** methods. The `render` method is called every time the portlet is rendered on the screen. The `processAction` is called when the contents of a form inside the portlet is submitted to the server.

There's more...

Creating new portlets is one thing; a second thing is that you can turn existing ADF applications into portlets. By using the ADF portlet bridge, we can easily turn existing taskflows or individual JSPX pages into portlets. This can be done by right-clicking on the taskflow or JSPX page you want to migrate and selecting the **create portlet entry** from the context menu. This will initialize the same wizard as discussed in this recipe.

In the case you are migrating taskflows, all the navigational and input parameters will be turned into public render parameters.

There are also some additional steps for creating a portlet that are mostly not as important as the others:

- ▶ Security roles: This step enables you to map available J2EE roles to your portlet. WebCenter does not use J2EE roles, so in most cases you won't need this step.
- ▶ Caching options: By defining caching on your portlet, you can gain performance. When your portlet is not static, it is not recommended to use caching.
- ▶ Initialization parameters: Here we can specify additional initialization parameters. In most cases, you won't add them in this step, but add them directly to the `portlet.xml`.

Registering a portlet producer at design time

Before you can consume portlets in your application, you first need to register the producer to your application.

There are two types of producers in WebCenter. First, there is a **WSRP producer**. This producer is based upon the WSRP standard (Web Service for Remote Portlets). The standard describes how to expose portlets to a consuming application by calling web services over HTTP(S) using the SOAP protocol. There are two versions of the WSRP standard. The first one is a basic one that maps to the JSR168 standard. The second and newly created standard is mapping of the JSR286 standard which allows inter-portlet communication using both parameters and events. Oracle WebCenter supports both WSRP1.0 and WSRP2.0.

A second type of producers is the legacy type producers from Oracle Portal. This is called a **PDK portlet producer**. PDK is the Oracle Portlet Development Kit for Oracle Portal. The PDK allows the creation of portlets using java. These portlets are not based upon the JSR 168 or 286 standard, so when you create PDK portlets, you can only use them in Oracle Portal or in WebCenter, but not in other J2EE portals.

Getting ready

As an example, we will register the default portlet producer containing some example portlets coming with WebCenter. In order to use it, you need to have a working version of WebCenter 11g or start the integrated WebLogic server in JDeveloper with the WebCenter extensions installed. You should be able to access the following URL if you are using the integrated WLS: `http://localhost:7101/wsrp-tools/`

In this recipe, we will register a WSRP producer. Before registering the producer, you need to know the endpoint of the producer. Normally, when you deploy a portlet using JDeveloper, you will find the links to both the WSRP1.0 and WSRP2.0 endpoint by browsing to the context root of your application.

You will always need an endpoint when registering a producer. You will receive such an URL from other parties, or other applications will expose functionality by WSRP producers, or you will need to find the endpoint yourself when deploying producers.

As an example, we will register the WSRP tools that are deployed by default on a WebLogic server when installing WebCenter. The method described here will also be used when you need to find the endpoint of portlets that you have deployed.

Consuming Portlets

The context root of the WSRP tools web application is: `/wsrp-tools`. When you browse to that page (`http://localhost:7101/wsrp-tools/`), you will find information about the available portlets in the producer:

ORACLE WebCenter Portlets

WSRP Producer Test Page

Your WSRP Producer Contains the Following Portlets:

Portlet Name (Minimum WSRP Version)

- Parameter Display Portlet (2.0)
- Parameter Form Portlet (2.0)

Container Configuration

Persistent Store Type: File
Value obtained from environment entry java:comp/env/oracle/portal/wsrp/server/persistentStore

File Store Root: C:\Oracle\Middleware11gRC4_2\jdeveloper\portal\portletdata
Value obtained from environment entry java:comp/env/oracle/portal/wsrp/server/fileStoreRoot

Use Java Object Cache: false
Value obtained from environment entry java:comp/env/oracle/portal/wsrp/server/enableJavaObjectCache

Container Version

Implementation version: 11.1.1.4.0

WSDL URLs

WSRP v1 WSDL
WSRP v2 WSDL

SOAP Monitor

SOAP Monitor

At the bottom, you can find the links to the WSRP WSDLs. If you are using inter-portlet communication, then you are obliged to use WSRP 2.0. Otherwise, you can choose, but we recommend using WSRP 2.0 in case you upgrade your portlet so it uses IPC functionality.

The default format of the WSRP URL is:

▶ `http://<server>:<port>/<context root>/portlets/wsrp2?WSDL`

The endpoint of the WSRP tools on an integrated WLS in JDeveloper is the following:

▶ `http://localhost:7101/wsrp-tools/portlets/wsrp2?WSDL`

How to do it...

1. Right-click the **Connections** folder from the **Application Resources** and select **New Connection, WSRP Producer** from the context menu. This will open the Register WSRP Producer wizard.
2. Name your provider. The name is important because users will see this as a folder in the resource catalog, so be sure you give it a meaningful name. If you have multiple projects in your application, you will also need to specify the project where you want to register the producer to. This needs to be a web project containing the JSPX files.
3. Specify the **WSDL URL**. This is the endpoint of the producer you want to use.
4. In case your server is behind a proxy server, you can configure the proxy settings by entering the proxy host and port.
5. When you click **Next**, JDeveloper will connect to the endpoint and parse the WSDL file to see if it correct. This can take a few seconds.
6. Specify a timeout interval in seconds. This is the maximum time the application will wait for a response from the producer. If the producer has not responded within the interval, the user will receive a message that the portlet is not available.
7. In the next step, you can configure security between the producer and the consuming application. Based upon the type of security, the authorization will also be parsed to the portlets. More about this can be found in *Chapter 8, WebCenter and Security*.
8. In the last step, you can specify the keystore used to authenticate the user to your portlets.
9. Press the **Finish** button. JDeveloper will request the information from your provider about the portlets.

When this is finished, you will see the producer in your connections in the **Application resources**. You can open the producer like a normal folder. This way, you can see a list of the portlets available in the producer. If you have registered the WSRP tools, you will see two portlets as shown in following image:

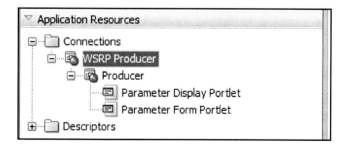

Now you are ready to consume the portlets that are available in the producer.

All producers you have registered are automatically available in the resource catalog.

Consuming Portlets

How it works...

When registering a producer, JDeveloper will read the WSDL endpoint of your WSRP producer. This endpoint contains all the information about the individual endpoints of the web services to access the portlets. The services are used to request the available portlets and to call the portlets.

You will also have additional files in the `/WEB-INF/wsdl` folder of your web project. This folder contains the necessary XSD's to validate the WSDL's. It will also incorporate some basic WSRP interfaces.

See also

The next recipe shows how to add a producer at runtime.

Registering a portlet producer at runtime

Most of the tasks that can be done in design time can also be done in runtime with the WebCenter Portal Application.

In this recipe, we will add a standard WSRP2.0 producer to our portal at runtime.

Getting ready

As an example, we will register the default portlet producer containing some example portlets coming with WebCenter. In order to use it, you need to have a working version of WebCenter 11g or start the integrated WebLogic server in JDeveloper with the WebCenter extensions installed. You should be able to access the following URL if you are using the integrated WLS: `http://localhost:7101/wsrp-tools/`

How to do it...

1. Go to the administration page of your portal. Open the **Services** tab.
2. Select **Portlet Producers** from the list on the left.
3. Press the **Register** button.
4. Enter a producer name.
5. Select **WSRP producer**.
6. Enter the **WSDL URL**.
7. In case you want to use a proxy, enter the **host** and **port**.
8. Press the **OK** button to register the producer.

Register Portlet Producer

Name and Type
- *Producer Name: WSRPTools
- Producer Type: ⦿ WSRP Producer ○ Oracle PDK-Java Producer ○ Pagelet Producer

Portlet Producer URL
- *WSDL URL: http://localhost:7101/wsrp-tools/portlets/wsrp2?WSDL
- Use Proxy? ☐
- Proxy Host:
- Proxy Port:

Advanced Configuration
Specify additional (optional) information.
- Default Execution Timeout (Seconds):

Security
Select the token profile used for authentication with this WSRP producer.
- Token Profile: None

How it works...

When you register a producer during runtime, the connection will be stored in the MDS repository.

See also

The next recipe shows how to add a producer at design time.

Consuming portlets at design time

Once you have registered a producer, you can start consuming portlets. When using portlets at design time, you can just drag and drop the portlet on a JSPX page.

By using portlets at design time, you have the ability to use portlets as reusable modules. The difference between using regular modules or taskflows and portlets is that you can stick to a standard. You are not bound to the framework. You also can make use of the personalization functionality of portlets without needing a complete portal environment.

Getting ready

Before you can start with this recipe, you will need to have a WebCenter portal application with a registered producer in it.

Consuming Portlets

How to do it...

1. Drag a portlet from a producer in the application resources to your page.
2. Select **ADF Rich Portlet** from the context menu

How it works...

You will notice that when you drop the portlet to a page, the portlet will not display as it is. You will see the message **[Portlet content Will Appear Here]**. Once you run the page, the real portlet content will be rendered.

When you drop a portlet to your page, there are two important things you should know about.

When you view the code of your portlet in the JSPX page, you will notice that the portlet is defined in the page bindings instead of the JSPX page. You can see this because the **value** of the portlet has a value that refers to the page bindings:

```
<adfp:portlet value="#{bindings.ParameterFormPortlet1_1}"
                        id="portlet1"/>
```

As you will notice, the real definition of the portlet is stored in the **page bindings**. When you open the page definition, you see the entry in the **executable** part.

> The page definition can be opened from the bindings tab of a JSPX or JSFF. At the top, you can find a link to the page definition file. In this way, you can view and change the source of the page definition.

You will notice that for each personalization parameter, there will be a corresponding variable in the **variableIterator** in the bindings. The actual parameter in the portlet is bound to those page parameters. In this way, you can set the parameters of the portlets by setting the page parameters.

The portlet entry in the bindings will also hold the definition such as the `portletInstance` which is a URL representation of the path to the portlet:

```
<executables>>
    <variableIterator id="variables">
      <variable Name="ParameterFormPortlet1_1_parameter1"
                Type="java.lang.Object"/>
      <variable Name="ParameterFormPortlet1_1_parameter2"
                Type="java.lang.Object"/>
      <variable Name="ParameterFormPortlet1_1_parameter3"
                Type="java.lang.Object"/>
    </variableIterator>
```

```xml
<portlet id="ParameterFormPortlet1_1"
         portletInstance="/oracle/adf/portlet/WSRP_Tools/ap/
         Ei1default_842aee7f_012c_1000_8001_c0a84101299e"
         class="oracle.adf.model.portlet.binding.PortletBinding"
         retainPortletHeader="false"
         xmlns="http://xmlns.oracle.com/portlet/bindings">
  <parameters>
    <parameter name="parameter1"
               pageVariable="ParameterFormPortlet1_1_parameter1"/>
    <parameter name="parameter2"
               pageVariable="ParameterFormPortlet1_1_parameter2"/>
    <parameter name="parameter3"
               pageVariable="ParameterFormPortlet1_1_parameter3"/>
  </parameters>
  <events>
    <event name="ParameterFormPortlet1_1_Event"
           eventType="ParametersChange"/>
  </events>
</portlet>
</executables>
```

As you can see from this example, the portlet I have added is the `ParameterFormPortlet`. It has three parameters, so we have the corresponding entries in the `variableIterator`.

The portlet also defines an **event** called `ParametersChange`. This event can be used to communicate with other portlets.

There's more...

The following table shows some of the most used attributes that can be assigned to the portlets. You can add these attributes in the code or by using the **property inspector**:

Attribute	Description
Title	Specifies the title of the portlet.
Width	Specifies the width of the portlet.
Height	Specifies the height of the portlet.
partialTrigger	By using a partialTrigger, you can refresh the portlet based upon events from other components or portlets.
	partialTrigger is often used with inter-portlet-communication.
DisplayHeader	Boolean that specifies if you want to show a header.
DisplayShadow	Boolean that let you display a shadow on the portlet.
DisplayScrollBar	Boolean that enabless a scrollbar in the portlet.

Attribute	Description
RenderPortletInFrame	If this attribute is set to true, the portlet will be rendered in an iframe instead of inline. When you create ADF portlets or use an upload form, the portlet will always render in an iframe, no matter what the value of this attribute is.
Rendered	Boolean that specifies if you want to render the portlet or not
DisplayActions	▶ always: Action icons will be displayed in the title bar ▶ onHover: Action icons will only be displayed when you hover over the title bar

All these attributes can also be bound to properties in a managed bean. When using the property inspector, you can make use of the expression builder. This way you can browse thru the available managed beans and select the desired property.

See also

Later on in this chapter, you can find a recipe on how to wire portlets together using parameters or events.

The next recipe shows how to add portlets at runtime.

Consuming portlets at runtime

Once you have registered a producer in JDeveloper, all those portlets will be made available in the resource catalog. Each provider will have its own folder containing the portlets.

Getting ready

For this recipe, you will need to have a WebCenter portal. You also need to register a producer to your application. This can be done at runtime or design time. For explanation, see the previous recipes.

How to do it...

1. Log in to your portal with an administrator.
2. Go to the administration page.
3. Select **Pages** from the **Resources** tab.
4. Select **Edit** from the action of the Home page.
5. Press the **Add Content** button to show the resource catalog.

6. Select **Providers**.
7. Select a provider.
8. When you have found the portlet you want to add, you only need to press the **Add button** on the right of the resource catalog:

9. Close the resource catalog.

How it works...

When you add a portlet to your page at runtime, a runtime customization will be added to the MDS. This customization is a delta of the page compared to the original JSPX. When the page gets rendered, all the deltas found in the MDS for the current page will be checked and added as a layer on top of the normal page.

The MDS will also hold an entry for the delta on the page bindings because all the parameters and events are managed in the page bindings.

There's more...

When you click on the pencil button on the top-right corner of the portlet as shown in following image, this will open the property inspector for the portlet:

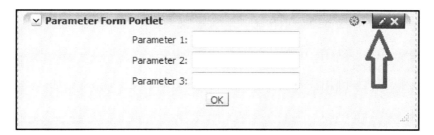

Consuming Portlets

The properties popup will have following tabs:

- **Parameters**: This tab contains the navigation parameters which can be used for inter-portlet-communication. Do not confuse these parameters with the personalization parameters defined in the `portlet.xml`.
- **Display Options**: In this tab, you can find different properties that change the display of the portlet, for example, the background, display actions, header, and so on.
- **Style**: This tab contain some basic CSS properties and a textarea were you can enter custom CSS that will be applied to your portlet.
- **Content Style**: The styles defined in this tab will be applied to the content of your portlet.
- **Events**: In case your portlet has defined events in the `oracle-portlet.xml`, those events can be managed in this tab. This will also be used for inter-portlet-communication.

See also

In this chapter, you will also see how to wire portlets together at runtime.

Wiring two portlets together at design time

Interoperability is very important in modern portals. This is a feature that is not possible with the JSR168 standard. That's one of the reasons why the Java community came up with a new portlet standard: JSR286 or the portlet 2.0 standard. This new standard described how you can create portlets that have the possibility to communicate with each other.

Getting ready

For this recipe, you need a WebCenter application with a producer registered that has at least two portlets that are prepared for inter-portlet-communication.

If you don't have such portlets, you can register the WSRP Tools to your application. This is explained in the *Registering a portlet producer* recipe earlier in this chapter. This producer has a parameter form and a parameter display portlet. In this recipe, we will send the values from the parameter form to the display portlet.

If you are using the integrated WebLogic server, make sure it has been started before continuing with this recipe.

How to do it...

1. Drag and drop the parameter forms portlet to a page.
2. Drag and drop the parameter display portlet to a page.

How it works...

If you have ever worked with WebCenter PS2, then you might know that it can be quite a hassle to wire two portlets together. With the implementation of the JSR 286 standard, all the difficulties are gone. WebCenter will wire portlets completely automatically. You don't need to tamper with page parameters anymore. There is only one constraint and that is that you will need to have parameters with the same name. If the first portlet and the second portlet both use a parameter with the same name, WebCenter will automatically pass the value from one portlet to the other.

There's more...

By default, you don't need to do anything special to wire portlets together. Suppose that you want to wire portlets together that do not share a parameter, then you need to use the same technique as the previous versions of WebCenter. In this technique, you need to configure page parameters and bind them to the parameters of the portlets.

When you have added the parameter forms portlet and the parameter display portlet, the source of your page may look something like this:

```
<af:group id="g1">
  <adfp:portlet value="#{bindings.ParameterFormPortlet1_1}"
      id="portlet1"/>
  <adfp:portlet value="#{bindings.ParameterDisplayPortlet1_1}"
      id="portlet2"/>
</af:group>
```

When you look at the bindings of the page, the **executables** look like this:

```
<executables>
    <variableIterator id="variables">
      <variable Name="ParameterFormPortlet1_1_parameter1"
                Type="java.lang.Object"/>
      <variable Name="ParameterFormPortlet1_1_parameter2"
                Type="java.lang.Object"/>
      <variable Name="ParameterFormPortlet1_1_parameter3"
                Type="java.lang.Object"/>
      <variable Name="ParameterDisplayPortlet1_1_parameter1"
                Type="java.lang.Object"/>
```

Consuming Portlets

```xml
        <variable Name="ParameterDisplayPortlet1_1_parameter2"
                 Type="java.lang.Object"/>
        <variable Name="ParameterDisplayPortlet1_1_parameter3"
                 Type="java.lang.Object"/>
    </variableIterator>
    <portlet id="ParameterFormPortlet1_1"
portletInstance="/oracle/adf/portlet/WSRP_Tools/ap/Ei1default_
842aee7f_012c_1000_8001_c0a84101299e"
class="oracle.adf.model.portlet.binding.PortletBinding"
retainPortletHeader="false"      xmlns="http://xmlns.oracle.com/
portlet/bindings">
 <parameters>
  <parameter name="parameter1"
pageVariable="ParameterFormPortlet1_1_parameter1"/>
  <parameter name="parameter2"                   pageVariable="Parame
terFormPortlet1_1_parameter2"/>
  <parameter name="parameter3"
                      pageVariable="ParameterFormPortlet1_1_
parameter3"/>
  </parameters>
  <events>
    <event name="ParameterFormPortlet1_1_Event"
             eventType="ParametersChange"/>
  </events>
 </portlet>
 <portlet id="ParameterDisplayPortlet1_1"
portletInstance="/oracle/adf/portlet/WSRP_Tools/ap/Ei2default_
94761da2_012c_1000_8003_c0a8410114e8"
         class="oracle.adf.model.portlet.binding.PortletBinding"
retainPortletHeader="false"
xmlns="http://xmlns.oracle.com/portlet/bindings">
<parameters>
  <parameter name="parameter1"
         pageVariable="ParameterDisplayPortlet1_1_parameter1"/>
<parameter name="parameter2"
         pageVariable="ParameterDisplayPortlet1_1_parameter2"/>
   <parameter name="parameter3"
         pageVariable="ParameterDisplayPortlet1_1_parameter3"/>
</parameters>
<events>
  <event name="ParameterDisplayPortlet1_1_Event"
       eventType="ParametersChange"/>
  </events>
</portlet>
</executables>
```

As you can see, each parameter of each portlet has an entry in the **variableIterator**. These entries are called **page parameters** because we can access those parameters in the page scope. You can reference them from inside your JSPX page.

Each portlet has an entry with a node for each of their parameters. These parameters are linked to the page parameters created in the `variableIterator` above.

In order to wire two portlets together, we only need to change the referenced page variable from the display portlet so it will use the page parameter of the form portlet:

1. Remove the page parameters called **parameterDisplayPortlet1_1_parameter1, parameterDisplayPortlet1_1_parameter2**, and **parameterDisplayPortlet1_1_parameter3**.
2. Use the following code for the parameters part of the ParameterDisplayPortlet1_1 portlet:

The removed code was:

```
<portlet id="ParameterDisplayPortlet1_1"
         portletInstance="/oracle/adf/portlet/
WsrpPortletProducer0/ap/Ei2default_04ca821d_012e_1000_8001_
ac140281d517"
         class="oracle.adf.model.portlet.binding.
PortletBinding"
         retainPortletHeader="false"
         listenForAutoDeliveredPortletEvents="true"
         listenForAutoDeliveredParameterChanges="true"
         xmlns="http://xmlns.oracle.com/portlet/bindings">
    <parameters>
      <parameter name="parameter2"
         pageVariable="ParameterDisplayPortlet1_1_parameter2"/>
      <parameter name="parameter1"
         pageVariable="ParameterDisplayPortlet1_1_parameter1"/>
      <parameter name="parameter3"
         pageVariable="ParameterDisplayPortlet1_1_parameter3"/>
    </parameters>
    <events>
      <event eventType="ParametersChange"
             name="ParameterDisplayPortlet1_1_Event"/>
    </events>
  </portlet>

<parameters>
  <parameter name="parameter1"
      pageVariable="ParameterFormPortlet1_1_parameter1"/>
  <parameter name="parameter2"
      pageVariable="ParameterFormPortlet1_1_parameter2"/>
  <parameter name="parameter3"
      pageVariable="ParameterFormPortlet1_1_parameter3"/>
</parameters>
```

Consuming Portlets

You don't need to modify the parameters of the parameter form portlet because this is the portlet that will be sending the parameters. It is important that the portlet which will send the values and the portlet that is receiving the values are linked to the same page parameters. The **pageVariable** part of each parameter should match.

Now both parameters will use the same page parameters. This means that when the first portlet changes the values of the page parameter, the second parameter can read the new values. In order to notify the second parameter, we need to set a **partialTrigger** on the second portlet. This way the portlet will be notified when the first portlet changes the values of the page parameters:

3. In the page source of your page, add a `partialTrigger` to the display portlet so it listens to the forms portlet. You can use following snippet for it:

    ```
    <adfp:portlet value="#{bindings.ParameterDisplayPortlet1_1}"
        id="portlet2" partialTriggers="portlet1"/>
    ```

When you run the page, you will see that the parameter form portlet has three input fields and the parameter display portlet has three output fields.

When you enter a value for each parameter and press the **OK** button, you should see that the output fields of the display portlet are updated with the entered values:

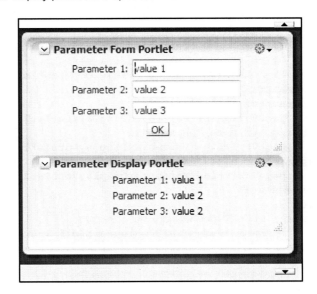

When you develop ADF portlets, it is important to know that it is only possible to set navigation parameters when using full submit. When you are trying to use partial submits, you don't have a reference to the portlet context and it's not possible to set its parameters. When you do a partial submit, the portal will not notice the state change and will not update portlets wired to it.

See also

The next recipe will show how to wire portlets together at runtime.

Wiring two portlets together at runtime

Wiring two portlets at runtime is not that hard. It is easier than when you would wire two portlets in design time. The same technique as at design time is used, but a lot will be done by the composer for us.

When you add portlets at runtime, WebCenter will also wire portlets together that share the same parameter, so you don't need to do anything for them. However, when you want to wire portlets together that do not share the same parameter, we need to wire it manually, which is described in this recipe.

Getting ready

For this recipe, we will need a WebCenter portal application that has a producer registered with at least two portlets that are enabled for inter-portlet-communication.

In this recipe we will use the WSRP tools as an example.

How to do it...

1. Log in to your portal application with an administrator.
2. Go to the administrator page.
3. Select **Pages** from the **Resource** tab.
4. Select **Edit** from the home page in order to edit the page.
5. Add both the parameter form and display portlet.

Consuming Portlets

6. Your page should look something like the image below:

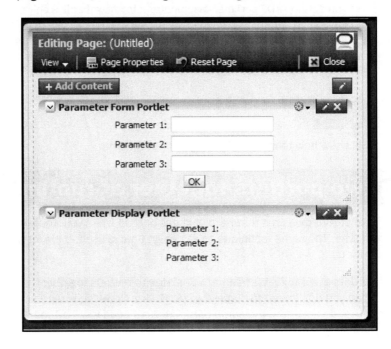

7. Open the properties window of the parameter display portlet by clicking on the pencil button.

8. The first tab lists the parameters exposed by the portlet. We will bind those parameters to the parameters of the form portlet. You can do this by using the **expression builder**. Next to the input field, click on the small arrow and select **expression builder** from the context menu.

9. At the top of the builder, select **Choose a value**. In the first dropdown list, select **page parameter**.

10. From the second dropdown list, select the parameter that needs to be bound with the parameter of the display portlet. The page parameter will have the portlet id in their name, an underscore, and the name of the parameter defined in the `oracle-portlet.xml`.

    The **Parameters** tab of the display portlet should look something like this:

    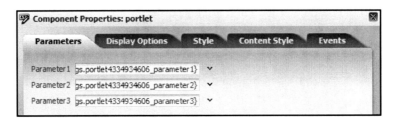

11. The next thing to do is to set the partial trigger on the display portlet. Before we do that, we first need to copy the ID of the parameter form portlet. This can be found in the **Display Options** tab in the properties window of the parameter form portlet as shown in following image:

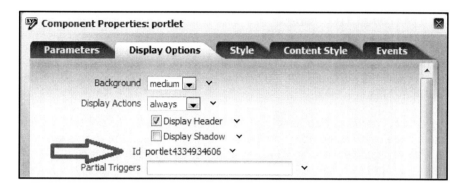

12. Copy the ID to the clipboard.
13. Open the properties window from the display portlet and select the **Display Options** tab.
14. Paste the ID from the parameter form portlet in the **Partial Triggers** field and press the **OK** button.
15. Close the composer by clicking the close button in the top right corner.

Test if it works by entering some values in the parameters field in the forms portlet and press the **OK** button. If everything went well, you should see the values in the display portlet.

How it works...

By assigning the page parameters to the display portlet, we link the output from the forms portlet to the input of the display portlet. This means that when we press the **OK** button in the forms portlet, the page parameters will be updated. By using a partial trigger on the display portlet, we can register the portlet as a listener to the forms portlet. When the forms portlet changes state, the display portlet will be notified and update itself. Because of this update, the display portlet will request the new values of the page parameter. This is how inter-portlet-communication works!

See also

In the previous recipe we explained how to wire two portlets in design time.

Consuming Portlets

Contextual wiring of portlets using events

A portlet can define an event that can be triggered from the portlet. Other components can register to listen on those events. When the events trigger, the portlets will be notified of the event so they can handle it accordingly.

A big advantage on this technique is that an event has a payload. This payload is a collection of objects. These objects can be of any type. When you wire portlets using parameters, the types of the parameters are limited. If you don't know how many parameters will be passed, then the event technique is ideal.

As with the wiring of portlets, WebCenter will automatically register the portlets to events from other portlets if the event name from both portlets are the same. If the events are not the same, you will need to do the wiring manually, which is described in this recipe.

Getting ready

For this recipe you need a WebCenter portal application with a registered producer that has at least two portlets which are event-enabled.

How to do it...

1. Log in to your portal application with an administrator.
2. Go to the administrator page.
3. Select **Pages** from the **Resource** tab.
4. Select **Edit** from the home page in order to edit the page.
5. Add both the parameter form and display portlet.
6. Open the properties window of the display portlet by clicking the pencil button on the portlet.
7. Open the last tab. This will show the available events on the page. Each event that has been defined by a portlet on a page will be listed in the **Events** list.
8. Select the event with the parameter forms ID in the name.
9. Select the only available action in the **action** list.
10. Enable the **Enable action** checkbox.
11. In order to pass the values to the portlet, we need to map the parameters from the payload sent with the event to the parameters of the receiving portlet. Because the payload is a collection, we can access the individual parameters by calling their names.

When everything is configured correctly, it should look something like this:

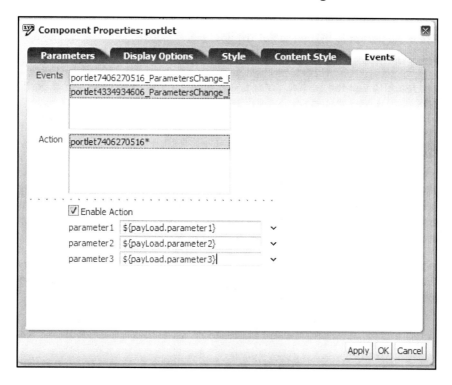

The portlet is now registered as a listener to the event fired by the forms portlet. We also need to set the partial trigger of the display portlet so it will be refreshed when the forms portlet fires the event:

1. In order to set the partial trigger, you first need to copy the ID of the forms portlet.
2. The ID can be found in the **Display options** tab in the properties of the portlet as shown in following image:

3. Copy it to the clipboard.
4. Open the **Display Options** tab of the display forms.
5. Paste the portlet ID in the **Partial Trigger** field.
6. Press **OK** to close the properties window.

Now you are ready to test the portlet. Enter some values in the parameter forms portlet and press the **OK** button. You should see the values appear in the display portlet.

How it works...

By registering the display portlet as a listener to the forms portlet, it will be notified when the forms portlet triggers the event. The event will pass the payload through to the display portlet. This payload holds the parameters we entered in the forms portlet. By linking the individual parameters of the payload to the parameters of the display portlet, we have access to the new values.

By using a partial trigger, the portlet gets notified at the exact same moment that the event triggers. Without the partial trigger, the display portlet will receive the notification when the render procedure of the display portlet is called.

3
Navigation Models and Page Hierarchies

In this chapter, you will learn about:

- Creating a navigation model at design time
- Creating a navigation model at runtime
- Adding a folder to a navigation model
- Adding a link to a navigation model
- Adding content query to a navigation model
- Adding a page hierarchy to a navigation model
- Referencing a navigation model
- Adding a component to a navigation model
- Adding a custom folder to a navigation model
- Adding custom content to a navigation model
- Changing the default start page of your portal
- Filtering navigation resources based upon business logic
- Exporting a navigation model
- Importing an existing navigation model
- Specifying the default navigation model
- Managing the page hierarchy

Navigation Models and Page Hierarchies

Introduction

A navigation model defines the elements and hierarchy of a navigation. It allows you to control which elements are added and specify the metadata for those resources.

In WebCenter, you can have different navigation models. This way you can customize the model for specific needs. For example, you can create a navigation model for people who are working in the Finance department and a completely different model for people from the HR department.

Navigation models can have links to pages, external links, links to external applications, portlets, taskflows, and so on. You can include almost every resource in a navigation model.

WebCenter lets you manage navigation models both at design time and runtime. This way, it is very easy for administrators who manage the portal to edit the navigation models.

Creating a navigation model at design time

By default, JDeveloper will create a standard navigation model for you. You can find it in the `Web Content/oracle/Webcenter/portalapp/navigations` folder. Each navigation model you create should be placed in that folder!

In this recipe, we will create an empty navigation model so you can use it to add components explained in the following recipes.

Getting ready

For this recipe, you need a WebCenter Portal Application. You can look back at *Chapter 1* for the recipe on how to create a new WebCenter Portal application.

How to do it...

1. In JDeveloper, press *Ctrl + N* to open the **New Gallery** popup.
2. Select **Portal** in the list on the left in the **Web Tier** section.
3. Select **Navigation** from the list on the right.
4. Press **OK**.
5. Specify a filename, for example, `hr.xml`.
6. Specify a directory. You can leave this filled in with the default.
7. Check the **Create as a portal resource** if you wish to use the navigation model on your pages. If you uncheck this, the navigation model can only be used as a reference in other models.
8. Press **OK**.

How it works...

A navigation model is nothing more than an XML file:

```xml
<?xml version="1.0" encoding="windows-1252" ?>
<navigationDefinition visible="${true}" id="hr"
            xmlns="http://xmlns.oracle.com/adf/rcs/catalog">
  <contents xmlns="http://xmlns.oracle.com/adf/rcs/catalog"/>
  <schema resourceBundle="oracle.adf.rc.attribute.nls.AttributeBundle"
          xmlns="http://xmlns.oracle.com/adf/rcs/catalog">
    <descriptor labelKey="TITLE.PROMPT_KEY" searchable="true"
                endUserVisible="true" attributeId="Title"
                shortLabelKey="TITLE.SHORT_PROMPT_KEY"
                               multivalue="false"
                xmlns="http://xmlns.oracle.com/adf/rcs/catalog"/>
    ...
  </schema>
</navigationDefinition>
```

The **navigationDefinition** tag holds the metadata attributes of a navigation model like the `id` and `visible` attribute. You can also add a `name` and `description` attribute, but these aren't mandatory.

The **contents** tag is the part where the actual components of our model will be defined. When you create a navigation model, the part will be empty because we haven't added any component to it.

There's more...

A navigation can also have lots of attributes that describe the navigation model. You can add these attributes by opening your navigation model and press the plus sign in the **navigation attributes** section. You will get a list of available attributes:

Atribute	Description
Title	Title of the navigation model.
AccessKey	Shortcut for use with the *Alt* key on your keyboard to access the model.
Description	Description of the navigation model.
IconURI	URI of the icon used for the navigation model.
Subject	Keywords used for searching.
Target	Specifies the target of the navigation resources. This can be: ▸ _blank: opens resource in new window. ▸ _parent: opens resource in parent window. ▸ _self: opens resource in same window. This is the default.
Tooltip	Text that shows when a user hovers over the navigation resources.

Navigation Models and Page Hierarchies

See also

The next recipe shows how you can add a navigation model at runtime.

The recipes after that will show you how you can add different resources to your navigation model.

Creating a navigation model at runtime

Lots of administrators will not have access to JDeveloper, but they will need to manage navigation models. In WebCenter, you can easily create and manage navigation models at runtime.

In this recipe, we will show how you can add navigation models at runtime.

Getting ready

For this recipe, you need a WebCenter Portal application.

How to do it...

1. Run your portal application.
2. Log in as an administrator.
3. Go to the **administration** page.
4. Select **Navigations** from the **Resource tab**.
5. Press the **Create** button.
6. Specify a name, for example, **hr**.
7. Specify a description, for example, **Navigation model for HR users**.
8. Leave **copy from** empty. In this list, you can select an existing navigation model so the newly created model will copy the content from the selected model.
9. Press the **Create** button:

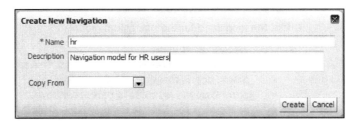

The navigation model is now created and you can add components to it.

How it works...

When you add a navigation model at runtime, an XML file will be generated in the background. The navigation model will be stored in the MDS. You can request the path to the actual xml file by selecting **Edit properties** from the Edit menu when you select a navigation model. In the properties window, you will find a field called Metadata file. This is the complete directory to the actual XML file.

There's more...

Even at runtime, you can modify the actual XML representation of the navigation model. This allows you to be completely flexible. Not everything is possible at runtime, but when you know what XML to add, you can do so by modifying the XML of the navigation model. This can be done by selecting **Edit Source** from the Edit menu. This way you will get the same XML representation of a navigation model as in JDevleoper.

See also

The next few recipes will show how to add different types of resources to your navigation model.

Adding a folder to a navigation model

A folder is the simplest resource you can add to your navigation model. It does not link to a specific resource. A folder is only intended to organize your navigation model in a logical way.

In this recipe, we will add a folder for the HR resources.

Getting ready

We will add the folder to the default navigation model so you only need the default WebCenter Portal application for this recipe.

How to do it...

1. Open `default-navigation-mode.xml` from `Web Content/oracle/Webcenter/portalapp/navigations`.
2. Press the **Add** button and select **Folder** from the context menu.
3. Specify an `id` for the folder. The `id` should be unique for each resource over the navigation model.
4. Specify an expression language value for the **Visible** attribute.

How it works...

Adding a folder to a navigation model will add a folder tag to the XML with the metadata specified:

```xml
<folder visible="#{true}" id="hr">
  <attributes>
    <attribute isKey="false"
      value="folder" attributeId="Title"/>
  </attributes>
  <contents/>
</folder>
```

The `folder` tag has a `contents` tag as a child. This means that when you add a resource to a folder, these will be added as a child to the `contents` tag.

There's more...

You can also add a folder at runtime to a navigation model. This is done by selecting your navigation model and selecting **Edit** from the Edit menu. From the Add menu, you can select **Folder**. You are able to add the `id`, `description`, `visible` attribute and `iconUrl`.

Adding a link to a navigation model

A link in a navigation model is more than just a link as you would expect. A link in a navigation model can be a lot of things. It can be a link to an external application, page, taskflow, portlet, and so on.

You can also specify to render the link in a specific page template. This way you can add links to taskflows or external pages but still keep the look and feel of your portal.

Getting ready

For this recipe, you need a WebCenter Portal application.

How to do it...

1. Open `default-navigation-mode.xml` from `Web Content/oracle/Webcenter/portalapp/navigations`.
2. Press the **Add** button and select **Link** from the context menu.
3. Specify an `id` for the link. This must be unique within the navigation model.

4. Specify the type of link:
    - External link: Creates a link to an external page.
    - External application: Creates a link to an external application. This way when the user has configured a username and password for this application, the user will be automatically logged on to the application.
    - Page: Creates a link to a JSP or JSPX page from within your project.
    - Taskflow: Creates a link to a taskflow from your application or resource palette.
    - Portlet: Creates a link to a portlet from a provider that has been registered to your application.
    - Content: Creates a link to content from a content repository.
    - Other: Creates a link to any type of component as long as you specify the Factory Class.
5. Specify Factory Class: When you have specified Other as the link type, you will need to specify the factory class that is responsible for instantiating the resources. When you have selected another type, the factory class will be greyed out.
6. Specify the URL. In most cases, you can use the magnification glass next to the URL field. This is contextually bound to the type of link. Based upon the selected type, you are able to select the resource from a popup.
7. Specify whether or not to render the URL in a page template or just redirect to the URL.
8. Specify an expression language value for the `visible` attribute
9. Specify a value in the `Title` attribute because this value will be used when displaying the link.

How it works...

When you add a link to a navigation model, a `url` tag will be added to the XML:

```
<url visible="#{true}"              factoryClass="oracle.Webcenter.
portalframework.sitestructure.rc.AdfPageResourceFactory" id="url8"
url="page://oracle/Webcenter/portalapp/pages/home.jspx">
  <attributes>
    <attribute isKey="false" value="my Page" attributeId="Title"/>
    <attribute isKey="false" value="false"
      attributeId="Redirect"/>
    </attributes>
</url>
```

Navigation Models and Page Hierarchies

The `url` tag contains the basic information about the link like the `id`, `visible` attribute and **factoryClass**. It will also contain the actual URL. Based upon the type, the `url` can have a different format. For example, a link to a portlet will start with `portlet://` while a link to a taskflow will start with `taskflow://`. In the example above, the `url` contains a link to a page from a project.

It is best that you use the popup to select a resource instead of entering the URL by yourself because in most cases it can be a very complex one.

An `url` also has a set of attributes. These contain additional attributes, for example, the `title` and the attribute that is responsible for redirecting the link or displaying it on the same page.

When you specify a specific template to render the URL, an additional parameter will be added to the `url` tag. This parameter will contain the path to the template that will be used to render the URL:

```
<url visible="#{true}"        factoryClass="oracle.Webcenter.
portalframework.sitestructure.rc.AdfPageResourceFactory" id="url8"
url="page://oracle/Webcenter/portalapp/pages/home.jspx">
   ...
  <parameters>
    <parameter id="pageTemplate">/oracle/Webcenter/portalapp/
pagetemplates/pageTemplate_globe.jspx</parameter>
  </parameters>
</url>
```

When you create a link to a taskflow or a portlet, than this template will be used to render the taskflow or portlet in. At first sight, it does not seem logical to link to a taskflow or a portlet, but in fact, it can be very useful. In some cases, you will create a page with only one component on it and you should add that page to your navigation. By using a link to a taskflow or portlet, you don't need to create pages for each taskflow or portlet. This way, it gives greater flexibility in designing the look and feel of your portal.

This technique is also used to show a portlet or taskflow in full page mode. When you have a page with multiple components on it, it can be useful to provide a link to a page with only one taskflow or portlet so it will be rendered bigger.

There's more...

You can also add a link to a navigation model during runtime. This is done by editing a navigation model and selecting **link** from the add menu. During runtime, you don't need to specify the type, but you can also use a popup to select the resource for the URL. Based upon the selected URL, the `factory` class will automatically be populated:

Adding content query to a navigation model

By adding content query to a navigation model, you are able to add a dynamic folder that contains links to all the content matching the query you provide.

This way, you don't need to add a link each time content is added. It is also dynamically generated, so when a new content item matches the query, it will be added to the model.

Getting ready

Before you begin with this recipe, you need a WebCenter portal application with a connection to content repository. It will only work with a connection to a content server or Oracle portal repository.

How to do it...

1. Open `default-navigation-mode.xml` from `Web Content/oracle/Webcenter/portalapp/navigations`.
2. Press the `Add` button and select **Content Query** from the context menu.
3. Specify an `id` for the content query. The id should be unique for each resource over the navigation model.
4. Select a **Repository** by opening the popup by clicking on the magnification glass.
5. This will only show the content repositories that are available for content queries. A connection to a local file system will not work
6. Enter the **query** that needs to match.
7. Enter an expression language value for the `visible` attribute.
8. Check the **Insert Folder Contents** if you want the navigation model to include the child contents in case the query will return folders.
9. Specify a **title** in the Content Query Attributes. This will be used to display the root element of the query in the navigation model.

How it works...

When you add a content query to your navigation model, a custom folder will be added to the model. A custom folder is a folder that needs a `factory` class and that will populate the contents of the folder during runtime based upon the parameters of the folder. Content query is a specific type of custom folder where some parameters are preset for us:

```
<customFolder visible="#{true}"
  factoryClass="oracle.Webcenter.content.model.rc.ContentListFactory"
  id="MyContent" insertFolderContents="true">
  <attributes>
    <attribute isKey="false"
      value="contentQuery" attributeId="Title"/>
  </attributes>
  <parameters>
    <parameter id="datasourceType">
      dsTypeQueryExpression
    </parameter>
    <parameter id="datasource">
      connectionName=LocalCS#dCollectionId=10
    </parameter>
  </parameters>
</customFolder>
```

The `customFolder` contains the information like the `visible` and `id` attributes, as well as the `insertFolderContents` attribute that will include the child items in case an item is a folder.

As you can see from the snippet above, the data source and query are stored in a parameter called **datasource**. The first value holds the name of the connection and then the query.

The query you can enter depends on the type of repository. For the correct syntax of the query, you should see the manual of the repository you are using because it is not WebCenter specific.

There's more...

You can also add a content query to a navigation model at runtime. This can be done by editing a navigation model at runtime and selecting **Content query** from the add menu.

In the popup, you can specify the `name`, `description`, `visible`, and `query string` attributes.

Chapter 3

The **Query String** you enter at runtime needs to be prefixed with the connection name:

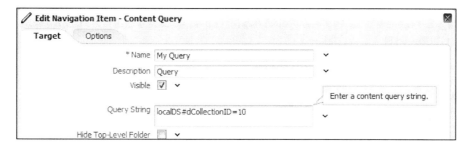

Adding a page hierarchy to a navigation model

Often you want to add pages to your navigation model. With adding a page query, you can do this by selecting a node from a page hierarchy. A WebCenter application can only have a single page hierarchy but by using the page query, you can select a specific node from the hierarchy to add to your navigation.

Getting ready

For this recipe, you need a WebCenter portal application.

How to do it...

1. Open `default-navigation-mode.xml` from `Web Content/oracle/Webcenter/portalapp/navigations`.
2. Press the `Add` button and select **Page Query** from the context menu.
3. Specify an `id` for the page query. The `id` should be unique for each resource over the navigation model.
4. **Scope** can be empty. This is not used for regular WebCenter applications. Each application should have only one scope.
5. Specify the **path** to the XML file containing the page hierarchy.
6. Specify the **page template** that will be used to display the pages so they fit the look and feel of your portal.
7. Specify the **page skin** that will be used to display the content of the pages.
8. Specify the page visibility. With this field, you can specify to only show the visible pages, show the hidden pages, or show all the pages.
9. Specify an expression language value for the **visible** attribute.
10. Check the **Insert folder contents** checkbox if you want to include the child nodes.

Navigation Models and Page Hierarchies

How it works...

Adding a page hierarchy to your navigation model is also adding a `customFolder` with specific parameters:

```
<customFolder visible="#{true}"
 factoryClass="oracle.Webcenter.page.view.rc.PageServiceContextFactory
" id="pageQuery" insertFolderContents="true">
 <attributes>
   <attribute isKey="false"
     value="pageQuery" attributeId="Title"/>
 </attributes>
 <parameters>
   <parameter id="path">
     /oracle/Webcenter/portalapp/pagehierarchy/pages.xml
   </parameter>
 </parameters>
</customFolder>
```

The path to the page hierarchy is a parameter called `path`.

The path can also contain a JSPX or JSP page. When you enter a JSPX or JSP page as the path, it will be matched with the page hierarchy of the application. The selected page will be the root node of the page hierarchy that will be included in the navigation model.

There's more...

You can also add a page query to a navigation model during runtime. This can be done by editing a navigation model in runtime and selecting page query from the add menu.

In the popup, you can add the properties of the page query like the `name`, `description`, and `visible` attribute. You also need to specify the path. For this you can use a popup and select the page you want from the page hierarchy:

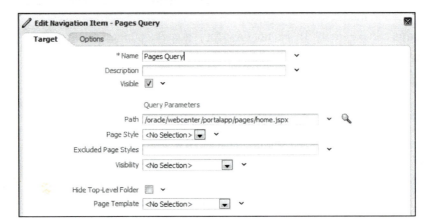

Referencing a navigation model

When you have multiple and complex navigation models, it can come in handy to have special navigation models that will be included in other models. This improves the reusability of navigation models.

Adding navigation models to a navigation model will only include a pointer to an existing model. This way when the referenced model changes, the changes will also be shown in the models that use the changed model and thus helps reuse the model.

Getting ready

For this recipe, you need a WebCenter portal application.

How to do it...

First we will create a new navigation model that will be referenced in the default model:

1. In JDeveloper, press *Ctrl + N* to open to **New Gallery**.
2. Select **Portal** in the list on the left in the **Web Tier** section.
3. Select **Navigation** from the list on the right.
4. Press **OK**.
5. Specify a filename, for example, `referenceModel.xml`.
6. Specify a directory. You can leave this filled in with the default.
7. Uncheck the **Create as a portal resource** because we don't want to use it as a model in our portal. We only want to use it as a reference, so we don't want to expose it to our portal as a resource.
8. Press **OK.**

We will add a few external links to the navigation model that we will reference:

1. Open `referenceModel.xml`.
2. Press the **Add** button and select **Link** from the context menu.
3. Specify **Google** for the `id`.
4. Select **External Link** as the type.
5. Enter `http://www.google.be` as the URL.
6. Enter **Google** for the `title` attribute.
7. Press the **Add** button and select Link from the context menu.
8. Specify **bing** for the `id`.

9. Select **External Link** as the type.
10. Enter `http://www.bing.com` as the URL.
11. Enter **Bing** for the `title` attribute.

The navigation model should look something like this now:

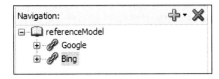

Now we can add this navigation model to the default navigation model:

1. Open `default-navigation-model.xml`.
2. From the Add menu, select Navigation.
3. Specify an `id`.
4. Select the correct XML for the referenced navigation model in the path field. You can use the browse button to select the navigation model.
5. Specify an expression language value for the `visible` attribute.
6. Specify a title, for example, **Search Engines**.

When you run the application, you should something like in the image below:

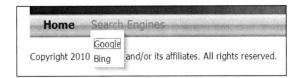

How it works...

When you add a reference to a navigation model, an `includeNavigation` tag will be added to the XML:

```
<includeNavigation visible="#{true}" scope="/" id="navigation"
          navigationId="/oracle/Webcenter/portalapp/navigations/
referenceModel.xml">
  <attributes>
    <attribute isKey="false"
      value="Search Engines" attributeId="Title"/>
  </attributes>
</includeNavigation>
```

The `includeNavigation` tag contains all the information needed to reference another navigation model. It contains the attributes for the `id` and `navigationId`. The `navigationId` is the path to the XML representing the referenced navigation model.

It is also important to know that it will only include a reference to the navigation model. The actual content will be added at runtime. This means that when the navigation model specified in the `navigationId` attribute changes, the changes will also be seen in the navigation models that use the referenced model.

There's more...

You can also add a reference to a navigation model during runtime. This can be done by editing a navigation model at runtime and selecting **Navigation Reference** from the add menu.

At runtime, you will be able to select the available navigations that you want to reference instead of specifying a path to an XML file. This means that you can only select those navigation models that are made available as a portal resource.

Adding a component to a navigation model

You can also add components to your navigation models. These components will be shown on a full page. This can be useful when you develop custom ADF Faces components. For example, when you have a calendar component. This can be useful to show the component as a link so that it will show up on an empty page.

Getting ready

For this recipe, you need a WebCenter portal application.

How to do it...

1. Open `default-navigation-mode.xml` from `Web Content/oracle/Webcenter/portalapp/navigations`.
2. Press the **Add** button and select **Component** from the context menu.
3. Specify an `id` for the component. The `id` should be unique for each resource over the navigation model.
4. Specify a Component factory. You can use **oracle.adf.rc.component.XmlComponentFactory** in order to add ADF components or other components available in JSPX pages.
5. Specify an expression language value for the `visible` attribute.

Navigation Models and Page Hierarchies

6. Specify a `title` that will be shown in the navigation.
7. From the component Parameters, press the **Add** sign and select XML. This will add a parameter were you need to enter the XML representation of your component.

How it works...

When you add a component to a navigation model, a component tag will be added to the XML:

```xml
<component visible="#{true}" id="component"
  factoryClass="oracle.adf.rc.component.XmlComponentFactory">
  <attributes>
    <attribute attributeId="Title" isKey="false"
      value="component"/>
  </attributes>
  <parameters>
    <parameter id="xml">&lt;cust:panelCustomizable id="#"
       xmlns:cust="http://xmlns.oracle.com/adf/faces/customizable"/
&gt;</parameter>
  </parameters>
</component>
```

The most important part is the parameter with the id `xml`. This will contain the XML representation of the component as if you would add the component to a JSPX page. This can be complex and can also contain nested components. You should also specify the namespace for each component because you don't have a header to specify the namespaces.

Adding a custom folder to a navigation model

A custom folder is a folder where the content will be populated during runtime. You need to provide a context factory that is responsible for populating the content. Depending on the factory, you can have additional parameters. Each context factory should implement the **oracle.adf.rc.component.ComponentFactory** interface.

Getting ready

For this recipe, you need a WebCenter portal application.

How to do it...

1. Open `default-navigation-mode.xml` from `Web Content/oracle/Webcenter/portalapp/navigations`.
2. Press the **Add** button and select **Custom folder** from the context menu.
3. Specify an `id` for the custom folder. The `id` should be unique for each resource over the navigation model.
4. Specify a path from the MDS. This should remain empty.
5. Specify the Initial context factory.
6. Specify an expression language value for the `visible` attribute.
7. Enter a `title` to display the root folder in the navigation model.

How it works...

When you add a custom folder to your navigation model, a `customFolder` tag will be added to the XML:

```
<customFolder visible="#{true}" id="customFolder"
factoryClass="oracle.Webcenter.content.model.rc.CustomFolderContextFac
tory"  path="">
      <attributes>
         <attribute attributeId="Title" isKey="false"
value="customFolder"/>
      </attributes>
 </customFolder>
```

The actual content of the folder will be populated at runtime. When the navigation model is called, the factory will be called to request the actual content of the folder.

Adding custom content to a navigation model

Custom content is almost the same as a custom folder. Instead of an initial context factory, you need to provide a content provider which needs to implement the **oracle.adf.rc.spi.plugin.catalog.CustomContentProviderV2** interface.

Getting ready

For this recipe, you need a WebCenter portal application.

Navigation Models and Page Hierarchies

How to do it...

1. Open `default-navigation-mode.xml` from `Web Content/oracle/Webcenter/portalapp/navigations`.
2. Press the **Add** button and select **Custom content** from the context menu.
3. Specify an `id` for the custom content. The `id` should be unique for each resource over the navigation model.
4. Specify the Content Provider.
5. Specify an expression language value for the `visible` attribute.
6. Enter a `title` to display the root folder in the navigation model.

How it works...

When you add custom content to a navigation model, a `customContent` tag will be added to the XML with the metadata of the custom content:

```
<customContent contentProviderClass="com.oracle.ensemble.interop.
adf.EnsembleContentProvider"    id="ensembleContentProvider"
visible="true">
  <attributes>
       <attribute attributeId="Title" isKey="false" value="ensembleCo
ntentProvider"/>
      </attributes>
</customContent>
```

A custom content is also like a custom folder, meaning that the content will be populated at runtime. The difference with a custom folder is that when the provider does not return any content, the folder will not be shown. When you have a custom folder that does not provide content, the folder will be shown in the navigation model, but it will be empty. With a custom content, the folder will not be there unless there is actual content.

Changing the default start page of your portal

When you don't use the default navigation model or you have removed the page hierarchy element from the default model, then you might notice that you cannot start the portal. When you create a WebCenter portal application, the wizard will create an `index.html` file, which contains a redirect to the home page that is configured in the page hierarchy. When you either remove the home page from the page hierarchy or remove the page hierarchy from your navigation model, the redirect fails and you get a 404 page not found error. This is of course not the behaviour that we want.

In this recipe, I will show how you can modify the `index.html` so it redirects to an existing page.

Getting ready

For this recipe, you need a WebCenter Portal application.

How to do it...

1. Open the `index.html` file from the Web Content folder.
2. On line 5 replace the following code:

   ```
   <meta http-equiv="refresh" content="0;url=./faces/pages_home" />
   ```

   With the following code:

   ```
   <meta http-equiv="refresh" content="0;url=./faces/myPage" />
   ```

3. Run the portal project.

How it works...

Changing the default home page is very simple, but you need to know what to do. There is a big difference in the way you can redirect in a WebCenter application than in another application.

As you can see, the default redirect states `/faces/pages_home`. This is not really a redirect to a page. In fact, you are telling WebCenter to redirect to the `home` node inside the `pages` folder. The syntax of the redirect always refers to the navigation model. By default, the navigation model contains the page hierarchy. That node has the id pages. Because the page hierarchy contains a `home` node, you can refer to the home page by adding `pages_home` after the faces URL.

So suppose you have added a page at the first level of your navigation model with the ID `myPage`, you would have to use the following code in the `index.html`:

```
<meta http-equiv="refresh" content="0;url=./faces/myPage" />
```

If `myPage` would get dropped in a folder called `myPages`, then you would need the following code:

```
<meta http-equiv="refresh" content="0;url=./faces/myPages_myPage" />
```

Filtering navigation resources based upon business logic

When you have a complex navigation model, it is possible to filter specific resources based upon custom code. This way you can show or hide specific resources based upon your custom code.

Filtering resources is done by specifying a filter on the navigation model. The filter should implement the `CatalogDefinitionFilter` interface.

In this recipe, we will show how to filter the default catalog based upon custom code. We will first add to empty folders. One folder will be shown when we are not logged in and the other will be shown when the user has been authenticated.

Getting ready

For this recipe, we will need a WebCenter portal application.

How to do it...

First we will add the folders to the navigation model:

1. Open the `default-navigation-model.xml`.
2. Click the **Add** button and select **Folder** from the context menu.
3. Enter **anonymous** for the `id`.
4. Enter **Anonymous** for the `title` attribute.
5. Select the default-navigation-model root element.
6. Click the **Add** button and select **Folder** from the context menu.
7. Enter **authenticated** for the `id`.
8. Enter **Authenticated** for the `title` attribute.

After this, the default navigation model should look something like this:

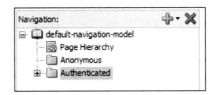

Now we need to create the filter:

1. Press *Ctrl + N* to open the New Gallery.
2. Select **Java** in the left menu.
3. Select **Java Class** in the right menu.
4. Class Name: `NavigationFilter`.
5. Package: `portal`.
6. Implements: Add `CatalogDefinitionFilter`.

Use the following code for the `includeInCatalog` method:

```java
public boolean includeInCatalog(CatalogElement element,
  Hashtable hashtable)
{
    ADFContext ctx = ADFContext.getCurrent();
    SecurityContext sCtx = ctx.getSecurityContext();
    boolean authenticated = sCtx.isAuthenticated();
    if(catalogElement.getId().equals("anonymous"))
        return ! authenticated;
    if(catalogElement.getId().equals("authenticated"))
        return authenticated;
    return true;
}
```

In the next step, we need to specify the filter on the navigation model:

1. Open the `default-navigation-model.xml`.
2. Select the root element.
3. Enter `portal.NavigationFilter` in the **navigation filter** field. You can find the class by clicking on the **browse** button and enter the name of the class. This will only show the classes that implement the correct interface for the filter.

When you run the portal, you will see that the `anonymous` folder will only show up when you are not logged in. As soon as you log in, the `authenticated` folder will show up.

How it works...

For every resource in the navigation model, the `includeInCatalog` method is called. The method returns a Boolean specifying whether or not to display the element in the navigation model.

Navigation Models and Page Hierarchies

In the example above, we have checked if the user has been authenticated to our portal, but in fact you can write whatever code you want in the filter:

```
public boolean includeInCatalog(CatalogElement element,
  Hashtable hashtable)
{
    ADFContext ctx = ADFContext.getCurrent();
    SecurityContext sCtx = ctx.getSecurityContext();
    boolean authenticated = sCtx.isAuthenticated();
    if(element.getId().equals("anonymous"))
        return ! authenticated;
    if(element.getId().equals("authenticated"))
        return authenticated;
    return true;
}
```

In our filter, we first get the necessary context to request if the user has been authenticated or not. This is stored in the `securityContext` of the `ADFContext`. Once we have a reference to the context, we can easily check the status of the user.

The next line checks if the `id` of the element is anonymous or authenticated, and based upon that returns the correct Boolean. When the `id` is anonymous, we need to return the opposite of the authenticated Boolean because we want to show that element when authenticated is false.

As a last line, we need to return true. This is because all the elements will pass the filter and if we don't provide a default value, those elements we don't check will not be shown in the navigation model and this is something we don't want.

Filters are used when you have complex logic to check whether or not to include the element in the model. When the logic is not that complex, you can easily use the `visible` attribute and bind it to a method in a managed bean.

There's more...

The example from this recipe can easily be done in another way. You can use the `visible` attribute on both the `authenticated` and `anonymous` folder. Because the logic we use to show this folder can easily be done by using expression language, we don't actually need a filter to achieve this.

In order to change it, use the following steps:

1. Open the `default-navigation-model.xml`.
2. Select the authenticated folder.

3. Enter the following expression in the `visible` attribute:

   `#{securityContext.authenticated}`

4. Select the anonymous folder.

5. Enter following expression in the visible attribute:

   `#{!securityContext.authenticated}`

Now you can remove the filter from the navigation model and we will have the exact same functionality.

It's not easy to know when to use a filter or when to use the `visible` attribute. It all depends on the complexity of the rules and the size. If you have lots of elements with the same rules, it is easy to write a filter because you have all the rules in a single class. If you add elements, you can easily modify the filter.

When you have just a few elements that need rules, it is better to use the `visible` attribute because it will give better performance this way. The filter will be called for each and every component, so the logic will be executed for each component which can cause bottlenecks. That's why you should be careful when using the filter.

Exporting a navigation model

In an environment where you do a lot at runtime, you need to have a method to export your work to other environments. In most cases you will have a development, test, and production environment. It would be a lot of work if you would recreate your navigation models on each environment. That's why WebCenter lets you export an existing navigation model so you can easily transport it to another environment.

In this recipe, we will show you how you can export a navigation model.

 Notice that you can't export the default navigation model! You can only export your own navigation models.

Getting ready

For this recipe, you need a WebCenter portal application.

How to do it...

First we will create a navigation model based upon the default navigation model:

1. Log in to your portal as an administrator.
2. Go to the **administration** page.

Navigation Models and Page Hierarchies

3. From the **Resource** tab select **Navigations**.
4. Press the **Create** button.
5. Enter **myModel** for the name.
6. Select Default Navigation in the **Copy From** field.
7. Press **Create**:

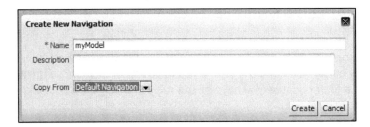

The navigation model will now be created and it will contain all the elements currently available in the default navigation model.

We now can export this model:

1. Select **myModel** in the list of navigation models.
2. Press the **Download** button.
3. Specify an archive name. It must end with `.ear` because the export will be an `ear` file.
4. Press the **Download** button.
5. Once the archive has been created, you can choose to download it or save it to the server.

 Make sure you have disabled a popup blocker or added the domain of the portal as a trusted site or you will not be able to download the `ear` file.

How it works...

When you download the `ear` file, it only contains a `mar` file. Inside that `mar` file, all the needed files and structures from the MDS will be stored in order to restore the navigation model in another environment.

In another portal, you can upload the `ear` file so the navigation model will also be available there.

See also

The next recipe will show you how you can import an existing navigation model.

Importing an existing navigation model

When you have exported a navigation model, you want to keep it as a backup or you want to import it into another environment so you won't need to create the navigation model from scratch.

This recipe will show you how you can import a navigation model into your portal application.

Getting ready

For this recipe, you will need a WebCenter application and you also need to do the previous recipe in order to have an export of an existing navigation model.

How to do it...

1. Log in to your portal as an administrator.
2. Go to the **administration** page.
3. From the **Resource** tab select **Navigations**.
4. Press the **Upload** button.
5. Select **On Local File System**.
6. Press the **browse** button and select an `ear` file with a navigation model export.
7. Press **Upload**.

When the upload has been completed, you should see the message **Resource uploaded successfully** and the navigation model should appear in the list.

How it works...

When you upload an `ear` file, the contents of the file will be read by the portal. Because we have pointed it to an export of a navigation model, all the files are there to identify the navigation model. All the files from the MDS that describe the navigation model are included in the `ear` file.

There's more...

You can also import resources into JDeveloper. This is done in a similar way as shown in this recipe:

1. In JDeveloper, right-click on your portal project and select **Import portal resources**.
2. Press the **browse** button and select an `ear` file.
3. Press the **OK** button.

Specifying the default navigation model

When your portal has multiple navigation models, you want to specify which one is the default. This is done in the `adf-config.xml` configuration file.

Getting ready

For this recipe, you need a WebCenter portal application.

How to do it...

1. In JDeveloper, open the **adf-config.xml** file. It can be found in the `Application resources` in the `Descriptors/ADF META-INF` folder.
2. Open the source tab.
3. Look for the following code:

   ```
   <portal:adf-portal-config>
     <portal:preferences>
       <portal:preference  id="oracle.Webcenter.portalapp.navigation.model"
                           desc="Default Navigation Model"
   value="/oracle/Webcenter/portalapp/navigations/default-navigation-model.xml"
   resourceType="navigation" display="true"/>
   ```

4. Change the `value` attribute to the path of the navigation model you want to use as a default.

How it works...

When the portal starts, it will read the preferences from the `adf-config,xml`. Based on that, the navigation model specified in the `portal:preferences` tag will be used as a default.

There's more...

The navigation model you specify in the `adf-config.xml` is a first layer of preferences. You can also specify the default navigation model at runtime. These settings will overwrite the settings of the `adf-config.xml` so it is important to know that when you have specified a navigation model at runtime, the settings in the `adf-config.xml` will be ignored.

The following steps describe how to define the default model at runtime:

1. Log in to your portal as an administrator.
2. Go to the **administration** page.
3. Select the **configuration** tab.
4. Select the default navigation from the list.

Modifications you do on this page will be stored automatically as soon as you change a value. There is no need for a save button.

Managing the page hierarchy

A page hierarchy describes where each page of your portal is in relation to another page. It is a parent-child relationship where each page can have different child pages.

The page hierarchy also defines the security for each page. You can specify security for each node or you can also let each node inherit the security from its parent.

Page hierarchies are used in combination with navigation models in order to create a user-friendly navigation.

A WebCenter application can only have a single page hierarchy, but the navigation model can have multiple references to the page hierarchy with each reference another entry point. This way you use the page hierarchy in a dynamic way.

In this recipe, we will show you how to add a page to the page hierarchy and manage the security on it.

Getting ready

For this recipe, you need a WebCenter portal application.

Navigation Models and Page Hierarchies

How to do it...

First we will create a new JSPX page based upon a default template:

1. Press *Ctrl + N* to open the **New Gallery**.
2. From the left menu, select **JSF** from the **Web Tier**.
3. From the right menu, select **JSF Page**.
4. Press the **OK** button.
5. File Name: myPage.jspx.
6. Directory: `public_html\oracle\Webcenter\portalapp\pages`.
7. Check the **Create as XML document** checkbox.
8. Select **Oracle Three Column Layout** as page layout.
9. Press the **OK** button.

We don't need to modify anything on the page. We only created it so we can add it to the page hierarchy.

Now we can add the page to the page hierarchy:

1. Open `pages.xml` from the `Web content/oracle/Webcenter/portalapp/pagehierarchy` folder.
2. Select the **Root** element.
3. Press the **Add** button.
4. Browse to the newly created page and select it.
5. Press the **Open** button.
6. Select `myPage` from the hierarchy.

Now you have added the page to the hierarchy and you can see its properties. You can also modify the security or set the page as invisible by unchecking the `Visible` checkbox.

How it works...

The page hierarchy is a simple XML file containing all the pages in the correct places:

```xml
<?xml version="1.0" encoding="windows-1252" ?>
<pagesDef xmlns="http://xmlns.oracle.com/Webcenter/page"
          xmlns:xsi="http://www.w3.org/2001/XMLSchema-instance"
          xsi:schemaLocation="http://xmlns.oracle.com/Webcenter/page/pagesDef.xsd">
   <pageDef contentMRef="/oracle/Webcenter/portalapp/pages/home.jspx"
          hidden="false" shared="false" hasSubPages="false" id="home"/>
   <pageDef contentMRef="/oracle/Webcenter/portalapp/pages/myPage.jspx"
          hidden="false" shared="false" hasSubPages="false" id="myPage"
          overridePolicy="false"/>
</pagesDef>
```

Each page is defined by a `pageDef` tag. This tag contains the `contentMRef` attribute which points to the path of the page.

When the page has sub pages, the `hasSubpages` attribute will be set to true. Once a page has subpages, it will have its own page hierarchy, so each page hierarchy only has one level of pages. All the other levels will be added by including the other page hierarchies.

There's more...

You can easily use the drag and drop method to organize the page hierarchy.

For example, suppose that we want our page `myPage.jspx` should be a child node of the Home page. This can be done by dropping `myPage` from the page hierarchy on the `Home` node in the hierarchy.

4
Managing the Resource Catalog

In this chapter, you will learn about:

- Creating a resource catalog at design time
- Creating a resource catalog at runtime
- Adding a folder to a resource catalog
- Adding a link to a resource catalog
- Adding another resource catalog to a resource catalog
- Adding a component to a resource catalog
- Adding a custom folder to a resource catalog
- Adding custom content to a resource catalog
- Adding resources to a catalog at runtime
- Managing the resource library
- Securing resource catalogs
- Filtering resources based upon a role or other business logic
- Selecting a resource catalog based upon business logic
- Exporting a resource catalog
- Importing a resource catalog

Introduction

A resource catalog is the repository that contains the resources you can add on a page, taskflow, or template. It can contain taskflows, portlets, content, and so on. All these components can be organized in folders.

A WebCenter application can have multiple catalogs. You can create complex business logic that will decide which catalog to use. Each component can also be filtered based upon your own logic. All these topics will be covered in this chapter.

Managing the resources that are available in a catalog will be an important task for an administrator. That's why it is important you should be able to do this at runtime without needing to redeploy the application.

With the resource manager in WebCenter, you have the ability to manage almost every aspect of the resource catalog. In this chapter, you will learn all you need to know how to manage resource catalogs.

Creating a resource catalog at design time

A WebCenter Portal Application will have a default resource catalog. Most of the time you will need different catalogs so different types of users can have a different set of components.

Getting ready

For this recipe, you will need a WebCenter portal application.

How to do it...

1. In JDeveloper, press *Ctrl + N* to open the **New Gallery**.
2. From the left menu, select **Portal** from the **Web Tier**.
3. In the list on the right, select **Application Resource Catalog**.
4. Press **OK**.
5. Enter the File Name.
6. Enter the directory. You should put the catalogs in the `oracle/Webcenter/portalapp/catalogs/` folder.
7. Check the **Create as a Portlet Resource** checkbox if you want the catalog is to be available at runtime. If you uncheck this option, you will create a resource catalog that should be used as a reference in another catalog.
8. Press **OK** to create the catalog.

When the catalog has been created you see the design view of the catalog. From here, you can set the properties of the catalog and manage the components:

1. Specify the `id` of the catalog. Each catalog should have a unique `id`.
2. Specify a catalog filer. By using a catalog filter, you can filter the components defined in the catalog based upon some business logic.
3. Specify an expression language value for the `visible` property.

How it works...

The resource catalog is an XML file describing the resources that are made available for runtime editing of pages, taskflows, and templates.

The XML of an empty resource catalog looks like following snippet:

```xml
<?xml version="1.0" encoding="windows-1252" ?>
<catalogDefinition id="admin-catalog" visible="${true}"
                   xmlns="http://xmlns.oracle.com/adf/rcs/catalog"
                   definitionFilter="">
  <contents xmlns="http://xmlns.oracle.com/adf/rcs/catalog"/>
  <schema resourceBundle="oracle.adf.rc.attribute.nls.AttributeBundle"
          xmlns="http://xmlns.oracle.com/adf/rcs/catalog">
    <descriptor endUserVisible="true" shortLabelKey="TITLE.SHORT_PROMPT_KEY"
                labelKey="TITLE.PROMPT_KEY" searchable="true" multivalue="false"
                attributeId="Title"
                xmlns="http://xmlns.oracle.com/adf/rcs/catalog"/>
    <descriptor endUserVisible="true" shortLabelKey="DESCRIPTION.SHORT_PROMPT_KEY"
                labelKey="DESCRIPTION.PROMPT_KEY" searchable="true"
                multivalue="false" attributeId="Description"
                xmlns="http://xmlns.oracle.com/adf/rcs/catalog"/>
    <descriptor endUserVisible="true" shortLabelKey="SUBJECT.SHORT_PROMPT_KEY"
                labelKey="SUBJECT.PROMPT_KEY" searchable="true"
                multivalue="false" attributeId="Subject"
                xmlns="http://xmlns.oracle.com/adf/rcs/catalog"/>
    <descriptor endUserVisible="true" shortLabelKey="TOOL_TIP.SHORT_PROMPT_KEY"
                labelKey="TOOL_TIP.PROMPT_KEY" searchable="false"
                multivalue="false" attributeId="ToolTip"
                xmlns="http://xmlns.oracle.com/adf/rcs/catalog"/>
    <descriptor endUserVisible="false" shortLabelKey="ICON_URI.SHORT_PROMPT_KEY"
                labelKey="ICON_URI.PROMPT_KEY" searchable="false"
                multivalue="false" attributeId="IconURI"
```

Managing the Resource Catalog

```
            xmlns="http://xmlns.oracle.com/adf/rcs/catalog"/>
    </schema>
</catalogDefinition>
```

The **catalogDefinition** holds the ID of the catalog and the `visible` property. The actual content of the catalog comes in the **contents** tag. In the example above, it is empty.

Below the contents, you will find some descriptors. These are properties that are made available to all resources we will add to the catalog as well as the catalog itself. The catalog has the following descriptors:

- Title: Label that will be used to display the resource in the catalog
- Description: The description will also be shown in the resource catalog
- Subject: Keywords that will be used when the user search for resources in the catalog
- Tooltip: Text that will be shown when the user hovers over the folder in the catalog
- IconURI: Icon that will be used instead of the default folder icon

These properties will be added as an attribute after the `catalogDefinition`. The following snippet shows how to add the title:

```
<catalogDefinition id="admin-catalog" visible="${true}"
    xmlns="http://xmlns.oracle.com/adf/rcs/catalog"
    definitionFilter="">
  <attributes>
    <attribute isKey="false" value="My Title" attributeId="Title"/>
  </attributes>
  <contents xmlns="http://xmlns.oracle.com/adf/rcs/catalog"/>
  ...
```

See also

Later in the chapter, you will also see how to populate the resource catalog and apply a Catalog Filter.

Creating a resource catalog at runtime

Creating a resource catalog at runtime allows you to create catalogs without needing to redeploy your application. This way, developers can concentrate on developing the portal without needing to know which resource catalogs you want to create.

Getting ready

For this recipe, you will need a WebCenter portal application.

How to do it...

1. Log in as an administrator to the portal.
2. Go to the **administration** page.
3. Open the **Resources** tab.
4. Click on **Resource Catalogs** in the left menu.
5. Press the **Create** button.
6. Enter a name for the resource catalog.
7. Enter a description.
8. If you want to copy the contents of another catalog, you can specify that catalog in the **Copy from** field.
9. Press the **Create** button.

You are now able to add components to the resource catalog.

How it works...

When you add a resource catalog at runtime, an XML file will also be created, but it will be stored in the MDS. You can find the properties of the catalog by selecting the catalog in the list and selecting **Edit properties** from the edit menu:

Managing the Resource Catalog

In this popup, you can see the Internal ID. This is a GUID generated by the system. This is used for internal purposes.

The path to the Metadata file can also be found. When you want to edit this file, you can do so by selecting the resource catalog in the table and selecting **Edit source** from the **edit** menu.

There's more...

You can also create a resource catalog at runtime by uploading an `ear` file. This can be done by clicking the **Upload** button in the overview of resource catalogs. In the popup, you can choose to upload an `ear` file from your local file system or by specifying the path of the `ear` file on the server. You can also download the resource catalog, import in JDeveloper, and make some modifications that you need.

See also

Later on in this chapter, you will see how to populate the resource catalog with resources.

Adding a folder to a resource catalog

A folder allows you to organize the content of a resource catalog in a logical way. This way, you can group content together so users can easily find the resources they want.

Getting ready

For this recipe, you will need a WebCenter portal application.

How to do it...

1. In JDeveloper, open the **default-catalog.xml** file from the `Web Content/oracle/Webcenter/portalapp/catalogs` folder.
2. Click on the **Add** button (green plus sign) and select **Folder** from the context menu.
3. Enter an `id` for the folder.
4. Enter a value for the `visible` property. This should be expression language. This way you can bind the visible attribute of the folder to a managed bean and bind it to some business logic from your beans.
5. Enter a meaningful value for the **Title** attribute in the **Folder Attributes**.

A folder can have additional attributes. When you press the **add** button in the Folder Attribute section, you are able to select the following additional attributes:

- **Description**: Specify a description that will appear in the resource catalog below the title.
- **Subject**: Specify a subject for the folder. This can help users find a specific folder.
- **Tooltip**: Specify the tooltip that will appear when the user hovers over the folder in the resource catalog
- **IconURI**: Specify the URI for the icon that will be used for the folder.

How it works...

When you add a folder, a `folder` tag will be added to the XML of the resource catalog:

```xml
<folder id="myFolder" visible="#{true}">
  <attributes>
    <attribute isKey="false" value="MyFolder"
      attributeId="Title"/>
    <attribute isKey="false" value="/images/adminIcon.png"
      attributeId="IconURI"/>
  </attributes>
  <parameters/>
  <contents/>
</folder>
```

This example shows an empty folder. The content of the folder will be added between the `contents` tag. You can also have a `folder` tag in the `contents` tag so you can create subfolders.

The example also shows how to add a custom icon for your folder.

Adding a link to a resource catalog

A link can be lots of things in a resource catalog. It can be a taskflow, portlet, content, or custom component.

Getting ready

For this recipe, you need a WebCenter portal application.

Managing the Resource Catalog

How to do it...

1. In JDeveloper, open the **default-catalog.xml** file from the `Web Content/oracle/Webcenter/portalapp/catalogs` folder.
2. Select the folder were you want to place the link.
3. Click on the **Add** button and select **Link** from the context menu.
4. Enter an **id** for the link.
5. Select the **type** for the link:
   - Taskflow: Add an existing taskflow to the resource catalog.
   - Portlet: Add a portlet from a registered producer.
   - Content: Add a file or folder from a content repository.
   - Other: Add a custom component. You will need to provide the `factory` class for this.
6. Enter the **URL** or use the **browse** button next to the field to select the resource you would like to add.
7. Enter a value for the **visible** property. You can use expression language here to bind the value to some business logic.
8. Enter a value for the **title** attribute in the URL attributes.

How it works...

When you add a link to a resource catalog, a `url` tag will be added to the XML:

```
<url id="mailTF"
  factoryClass=
  "oracle.Webcenter.portalframework.sitestructure.rc.TaskFlowResource
Factory"
     visible="#{true}"          url="taskflow://oracle/Webcenter/
collab/mail/view/jsf/regions/mini-view-definition.xml#mail-mini-view">
    <attributes>
      <attribute isKey="false" value="Mail"
        attributeId="Title"/>
      <attribute isKey="false" value="/images/mailIcon.png"
        attributeId="IconURI"/>
    </attributes>
</url>
```

This example shows how to add the mail taskflow to your catalog. As you can see, there is no attribute defining the type. You specify the type in the design tab to preset the `factoryClass`. When you select **Taskflow**, **Portlet** or **Content** as a type, the **factoryClass** will automatically be set.

You will also find the type in the prefix of the **URL** attribute.

There's more...

You can also add taskflows, portlets, or content from a repository by dragging them into your resource catalog. The URL and type filed will be automatically filled in accordingly.

Adding another resource catalog to a resource catalog

You can add an existing resource catalog to your catalog. This way, it improves the reusability. When you have multiple and complex resource catalogs, it can be useful to split resource catalogs. When you have lots of components that occur in each resource catalog, it is good practice to create a new resource catalog with only those resources and then add a reference to the catalog.

Getting ready

For this recipe, you need a WebCenter portal application.

How to do it...

1. In JDeveloper, open the **default-catalog.xml** file from the `Web Content/oracle/Webcenter/portalapp/catalogs` folder.
2. Click on the **Add** button and select **Resource Catalog reference** from the context menu.
3. Enter an **id** for the resource catalog.
4. Enter a **path** to the XML file for the resource catalog. You can also use the browse button next to the path field to select the XML file.
5. Enter a **title** in the Catalog Attributes section.

How it works...

When you add a resource catalog, an `includeCatalog` tag will be added to the XML:

```
<includeCatalog scope="/" id="mycatalog"                    catalogId=
"/oracle/Webcenter/portalapp/catalogs/mycatalog.xml"
    visible="#{true}">
    <attributes>
       <attribute attributeId="Title" isKey="false"
          value="mycatalog"/>
    </attributes>
</includeCatalog>
```

Managing the Resource Catalog

This snippet will add a pointer to an existing catalog. The path to the catalog is defined in the `catalogId` attribute.

When you add a resource catalog to another resource catalog, you actually add a reference to it, meaning that the content will be merged at runtime. This also means that when you add resources to the catalog, they will also be shown in the catalog that references the catalog.

This has the advantage that when you modify the referenced catalog, the changes will reflect to each catalog that has added the modified catalog as a reference.

There's more...

You can add existing resource catalogs by dragging the XML file into your resource catalog. The path field will be populated with the path of the dropped catalog.

Adding a component to a resource catalog

You can easily add custom components to a resource catalog. For example you can add ADF Faces components to a resource catalog. This can be done by adding the XML representation of the component to your resource catalog.

This recipe will show you how to add the `panelCustomizable` to the resource catalog.

Getting ready

For this recipe, you will need a WebCenter portal application.

How to do it...

1. In JDeveloper, open the **default-catalog.xml** file from the `Web Content/oracle/Webcenter/portalapp/catalogs` folder.
2. Select the folder where you want the component to be added.
3. Click on the Add button and select **Component** from the context menu.
4. Enter an **id** for the component.
5. Enter the **Component factory** that will create the instances of the component. You can also use the browse button to look for the class. This will open a popup where you can search through all the classes available in the classpath of the application. You can only select classes that implement the **oracle.adf.rc.component.ComponentFactory** interface.

    When you want to add a component by its XML representation, you need to use the **oracle.adf.rc.component.XmlComponentFactory** factory.

6. Enter a value for the **visible** property. This can also be an expression language value so you can bind it to some business logic.

7. In the Component parameters section, add the xml parameter and specify the following value:

   ```
   <cust:panelCustomizable id="#" xmlns:cust="http://xmlns.oracle.
   com/adf/faces/customizable"/>
   ```

How it works...

When you add a component to the resource catalog, a component tag will be added to the XML:

```
<component visible="#{true}" id="component"
 factoryClass="oracle.adf.rc.component.XmlComponentFactory">
<attributes>
  <attribute attributeId="Title" isKey="false"
    value="component"/>
</attributes>
<parameters>
  <parameter id="xml">&lt;cust:panelCustomizable id="#"
    xmlns:cust="http://xmlns.oracle.com/adf/faces/customizable"/&gt;</parameter>
</parameters>
</component>
```

This snippet shows how to add the panel customizable component to the resource catalog. As you see, the factoryClass is the **oracle.adf.rc.component.XmlComponentFactory.** This is a build in factory that can be used to include components based upon their XML notation.

This factory requires a parameter for the xml component. When you want to add the component, you need to provide the xmlns namespace as well. You can also add nested components, but then you need to provide the namespace for each component.

Adding a custom folder to a resource catalog

A custom folder is a special kind of folder. You can't put content into the folder. The custom folder is a folder that uses a context factory to populate the folder at runtime. This means that the content of the folder is completely dynamic.

Getting ready

For this recipe, you need a WebCenter portal application.

Managing the Resource Catalog

How to do it...

1. In JDeveloper, open the **default-catalog.xml** file from the `Web Content/oracle/Webcenter/portalapp/catalogs` folder.
2. Click on the Add button and select **Custom Folder** from the context menu.
3. Enter an **id** for the custom folder.
4. Enter the **MDS folder** in the **path** field. This field can remain empty.
5. Enter an initial context factory that will populate the folder at runtime. These factories should implement the **oracle.adf.rc.spi.plugin.catalog.CustomContentProviderV2** interface.

   You will need to use the **custom Folder Parameters** section to specify additional parameters depending on the selected factory.
6. Enter a value for the **visible** property. This can be an expression language value so you can bind it to some business logic.

How it works...

When you add a custom folder to your resource catalog, a `customFolder` tag will be added to the XML of the catalog:

```
<customFolder visible="#{true}" id="customFolder"
factoryClass="oracle.Webcenter.content.model.rc.CustomFolderContextFac
tory"  path="">
     <attributes>
        <attribute attributeId="Title" isKey="false"
value="customFolder"/>
     </attributes>
  </customFolder>
```

This snippet shows how to add a custom folder that adds all the available connections to a content repository to your catalog. Therefore we use the built-in `factoryClass` **CustomfolderContextFactory**.

Adding custom content to a resource catalog

Custom content is like a custom folder. The content will also be provided at runtime. The difference between a custom content folder and a custom folder is that a custom content is based upon a content provider while the custom folder requires an initial context factory. Another difference is that when the custom content does not provide any content at runtime, the folder will not show in the resource catalog. A custom folder will always be available in the catalog, even when the folder is empty.

Getting ready

For this recipe, you need a WebCenter portal application.

How to do it...

1. In JDeveloper, open the **default-catalog.xml** file from the `Web Content/oracle/Webcenter/portalapp/catalogs` folder.
2. Click on the Add button and select **Custom content** from the context menu.
3. Enter an **id** for the custom content.
4. Enter the Content Provider. This class should implement the **oracle.adf.rc.spi.plugin.catalog.CustomContentProviderV2** interface. You will need to use the **custom content parameter** section to specify additional parameters depending on the selected factory.
5. Enter a value for the **visible** property. This can be an expression language value so you can bind it so some business logic.

How it works...

When you add a custom content folder to your resource catalog, a `customContent` tag will be added to the XML:

```
<customContent contentProviderClass="com.oracle.ensemble.interop.
adf.EnsembleContentProvider"        id="ensembleContentProvider"
visible="true">
  <attributes>
        <attribute attributeId="Title" isKey="false" value="ensembleCo
ntentProvider"/>
    </attributes>
</customContent>
```

This snippet shows how to add custom content. It uses a built-in provider that will add all the registered pagelet providers. When there aren't any providers, you won't see the `ensembleContentProvider` folder in the catalog.

Adding resources to a catalog at runtime

Adding resources to a catalog at runtime can be quite easy. The best way to do it is by using the library. When you add resources at runtime, you can add resources from a predefined library. This can be any type of resource: taskflows, portlets, content, connections, pagelets, and so on.

This recipe will show you how to use this library at runtime editing of a catalog.

Managing the Resource Catalog

Getting ready

For this recipe, you will need to start a WebCenter portal application.

How to do it...

1. Log in to your Portal Application.
2. Go to the administration page.
3. Click on **Resource Catalogs** on the **Resources** tab.
4. Select a catalog that has been created during runtime. If there isn't one, create a new one.
5. Select **Edit** from the **Edit** menu.
6. Select **Add from Library** from the **Add** menu.
7. Select a folder from the list on the left.
8. Select the resource in the list on the right.
9. Enter the name you want the resource to have in the catalog at the bottom left of the popup.
10. Press the **Add** button.

How it works...

The resource catalog is an actual XML file. When you create it at runtime, the XML file will be created in the MDS. All resources that you add in the catalog will be added to the XML in the MDS.

You can view the actual XML contents of the resource catalog by selecting it in the overview of the catalogs and selecting **Edit Source** from the **edit** menu.

There's more...

At runtime, you can also do more than just edit resources from the library. You can also add folders and custom components:

- Folder: This will add a folder to your catalog so you can organize and group resources in a logical way.
- Component: This will allow you to add components based upon their XML representation. It will use the `XmlComponentFactory` to add the component.

Component

1. Select **Component** from the **Add** menu.
2. Enter a meaningful name for the component.
3. Enter an optional description that will be shown in the catalog.
4. Enter the XML in the textarea. This is the same as adding the component to a JSPX page. You would also have to add the namespace of the component. For example, the snippet below shows how to add an ADF outputText to the resource catalog:

   ```
   <af:outputText id="#" xmlns:af="http://xmlns.oracle.com/adf/faces/rich"/>
   ```

The id of the component must be # so it can be replaced when using the component on a page.

Edit components

Some attributes or parameters can only be changed when the resource has already been added to your catalog. In order to edit a resource, select the component and press the edit button. This will open the **Edit Resource Catalog Item** popup.

The first tab is the **Target** tab. This contains the details about the resource. Depending on the type of resource, you will find a different field set in the tab.

The second tab is the **Attributes** tab. In this tab, you can add the optional attributes like description, subject, icon, and so on. The available attributes can be selected by clicking the down arrow next to the attribute name field.

Depending on the type, you will see a third tab. In this tab, you are able to specify parameters required for the component. When you add a taskflow, you will most likely have this tab because taskflows can have input parameters. These parameters will be mapped in the last tab.

See also

The next recipe will show you how to modify the `catalog-definition.xml` which represents the repository that is used to populate the library for adding components at runtime.

Managing the Resource Library

The Resource Library is the library you will see when you add resources to a catalog at runtime and select **Add from Library** from the add **menu**. In fact, that library is a special kind of resource catalog. It can't be used as a resource catalog and is specially designed to populate the library.

Managing the Resource Catalog

Getting ready

For this recipe, you need to have a WebCenter portal application.

How to do it...

1. Open the default resource library. It can be found in the `/oracle/Webcenter/portalapps/catalogs` folder and is named **catalog-registry.xml**. This is a regular resource catalog that is not defined as a portal resource, so you can't use it as an actual resource catalog unless for the library or as a reference in another catalog. Editing of this file is just the same as a regular catalog because it is a catalog.
2. Add or remove components.

How it works...

When the library requests the components, it will read the property from the `adf-config.xml` file and get the contents from the specified catalog.

The resource library is a regular resource catalog, so you can treat it as a normal resource catalog. You can add folders, components, links, or any other resources. You can follow the other recipes on how to add components to the catalog.

There's more...

You can also specify another resource catalog that acts as the library. The catalog that is used is defined in the `adf-config.xml` file which can be found in the `ADF META-INF` folder in the Application resources as shown in the image below:

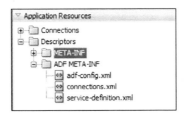

1. Open **adf-config.xml** by double clicking it in JDeveloper.
2. Open the source view by clicking the **source** tab.
3. Configuration of the resource catalog can be found between the **rcs:adf-rcs-config** tags. Inside that tag, you will find the configuration for the catalog, navigation, and security manager. By default it will look like this:

```
<rcs:adf-rcs-config>
  <rcs:rcs-config>
    <rcs:catalog-config default-scope="/"
                       default-registry="/oracle/Webcenter/
portalapp/catalogs/catalog-registry.xml"/>
    <rcs:navigation-config default-scope="/"
                       default-registry="/oracle/Webcenter/
portalapp/navigations/navigation-registry.xml"/>
    <rcs:security-manager class-name="oracle.Webcenter.
portalframework.genericsiteresources.internal.security.
CatalogSecurityManager"/>
  </rcs:rcs-config>
</rcs:adf-rcs-config>
```

4. The catalog that will be used as a library is defined in the **rcs:catalog-config** tag as the **default-registry** attribute. This contains the path to the resource catalog.

Securing resource catalogs

By specifying security on a resource catalog, you can allow other administrators to manage the resource catalog. Specifying which components are shown based upon the users is not done in the security, but in the filter which will be shown in another recipe.

Getting ready

For this recipe, you need a WebCenter portal application.

How to do it...

1. Log in to your portal application.
2. Go to the administration page.
3. Click on **Resource Catalog** from the menu on the left.
4. Select the resource catalog for which you want to specify security.
5. Select **Security settings** from the **edit** menu.

The security settings popup will show where you can specify the security. By default, each resource catalog will use the **Application Permissions**. These permissions are defined in the `jazn-data.xml` in JDeveloper.

When you want to make exceptions from those settings, you can select **Use Custom Permissions**.

Managing the Resource Catalog

You can add both users or roles and grant the **Manage** and/or **Update** rights:

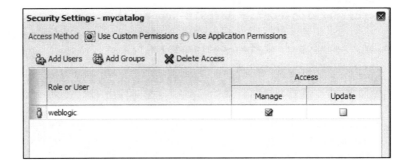

When you press the **Add User** or **Add Groups** button, a popup will open where you can query the integrated **LDAP** of the **WebLogic server** where your application is deployed.

How it works...

When you specify custom permissions on a resource catalog, the customizations are also stored in the MDS.

See also

Later in this chapter, you can see how we can specify a filter for a resource catalog and how to write a resource selector. Both can contribute to implementing security on resource catalogs.

Filtering resources based upon a role or other business logic

It often happens that a large portion of a resource catalog is applicable for most of your users, but a few components have special rules. You could create different catalogs for this, but it is a lot of work and not easy to maintain. Therefore, you can write a filter that will check whether or not the resource should be shown in the catalog.

For example, you have a catalog with a lot of components and some user roles have their own folder with custom components. The HR and Finance role each have their own folder. When a user from the HR department uses the catalog, he does not need to see the finance folder.

In the filter, we will check to see if the user is from department HR or Finance and based upon that the correct folder should be shown.

Chapter 4

Getting ready

For this recipe, you will need a WebCenter portal application.

The application should also have an HR and Finance role. In the code of the book, you can find a sample application with these roles predefined. The default catalog in this sample will also include an HR and Finance folder.

How to do it...

First we will create the filter:

1. Press *Ctrl + N* to open the New Gallery.
2. Select **Java** in the left menu.
3. Select **Java Class** in the right menu.
4. Class Name: DepartmentCatalogFilter.
5. Package: portal.
6. Implements: Add CatalogDefinitionFilter:

Managing the Resource Catalog

7. Press **OK**.
8. Use the following code for the includeInCatalog method:

```
public boolean includeInCatalog(CatalogElement catalogElement,
  Hashtable hashtable)
{
  ADFContext aDFContext = ADFContext.getCurrent();
  boolean isHR =
    aDFContext.getSecurityContext().isUserInRole("HR");
  boolean isFinance =
    aDFContext.getSecurityContext().isUserInRole("Finance");
      if(catalogElement.getId().equals("HR"))
        if(isHR)
          return true;
        else
          return false;
      if(catalogElement.getId().equals("Finance"))
        if(isFinance)
            return true;
        else
            return false;
      return true;
}
```

When the filter has been created, we can specify the filter on the resource catalog:

1. Open **default-catalog.xml**. It can be found in the `Web Content/oracle/Webcenter/portalapp/catalogs` folder.
2. Select the root folder (Default Portal Catalog).
3. Enter **portal.DepartmentCatalogFilter** as Catalog Filter.

When adding content with an HR user, you will notice that the HR folder is visible and the Finance role isn't. When logging in with a finance user, you will see the finance folder but not the HR folder.

You can write whatever business logic you want in the filter.

How it works...

The interface we implement (**CatalogDefinitionFilter**) has only one method: `includeInCatalog`. This method will be invoked for each and every resource that is included in the resource catalog. The method returns a Boolean saying whether or not to include the resource in the catalog:

```
ADFContext aDFContext = ADFContext.getCurrent();
boolean isHR =
```

```
        aDFContext.getSecurityContext().isUserInRole("HR");
    boolean isFinance =
        aDFContext.getSecurityContext().isUserInRole("Finance");
```

These lines may look straightforward if you have experience with ADF applications. By using this code, we can easily check if a user is in a specific role. The **isUserInRole** from the **SecurityContext** will return true if the user is in the specific role:

```
            if(catalogElement.getId().equals("HR"))
```

The `catalogElement` is a parameter of the method. It contains all the information about the resource that is invoking the method.

The following methods are available with the `catalogElement`:

- `getId`: Returns the Id of the resource
- `getDescription`: Returns the description of the resource
- `getParentFolder`: Returns the parent folder of the current resource

As a last statement, we return true. This is needed because we need to provide a return value for each resource, even if it is not one of those we want to filter. That's why we need to provide a default value.

There's more...

Instead of using a `CatalogDefinitionFilter`, you can also use an expression language value that sets the `visible` property of each resource. This can be set from the properties in the overview of the resource catalog. The default value is `#{true}`, but you can set any value you want.

For example, if we want to achieve the same as shown in this recipe but without using a filter, we could write the following expression in the `visible` property of the HR folder:

```
#{securityContext.userInRole['HR']}
```

This snippet will return true if the user is in the HR role, so the HR folder will be shown:

```
#{securityContext.userInRole['Finance']}
```

This above expression will be used in the `visible` property of the Finance folder and will only result in true if the user is a member of the Finance role.

This can be done for easy expressions, but if you want to include complex business logic, than you will use a filter instead of this method.

Managing the Resource Catalog

See also

If you want to use different resource catalogs instead of using a filter, then read the following recipe. This will show you how to select a resource catalog based upon some business logic.

Selecting a resource catalog based upon business logic

When different groups of users require different resource catalogs, then you need to write a catalog selector. This is a class that will return the name of the catalog that should be used. You can write whatever code you want to determine the catalog. Often you will select the catalog based upon the role a user is in.

In this recipe, I will show you how to create a selector where we have a default catalog for most of the users. But when someone from the HR or Finance departments logs in, they get their own catalog.

Getting ready

In the code of this book, you will find an application that has the requirements for this recipe. It has a default catalog, one for the HR and one for the finance department. The application is also configured, so it has both the HR and Finance role.

How to do it...

Create the Resource Selector Class:

1. In JDeveloper press *Ctrl + N* to open the New Gallery.
2. Select **Java** from the list left.
3. Select **Java Class** from the list on the right.
4. Class Name: CustomResourceSelector
5. Package: portal
6. Extends: java.lang.Object
7. Implements: **oracle.adf.rc.model.config.ResourceCatalogSelector**

Chapter 4

8. Press the **OK** button.
9. Use the following code for the getCatalogName methode:

```
public String getCatalogName(Map map) {
    ADFContext ctx = ADFContext.getCurrent();
    SecurityContext sCtx = ctx.getSecurityContext();
    boolean isHR = sCtx.isUserInRole("HR");
    boolean isFinance = sCtx.isUserInRole("Finance");
    if(isHR)
       return "hrCatalog";
    if(isFinance)
       return "financeCatalog";
    return "default";
}
```

Managing the Resource Catalog

When the class has been created, we need to configure the portal so it will use our class instead of the default selector. This is done in the `adf-config.xml`:

1. Open **adf-config.xml** from the **Application Resources | ADF META-INF** folder:

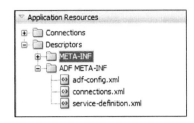

2. Replace the following code:

```
<rcv:rcv-config>
    <rcv:default-catalog catalog-name="/oracle/Webcenter/portalapp/catalogs/default-catalog.xml"/>
    <rcv:catalog-selector class-name="oracle.Webcenter.portalframework.sitestructure.rc.PortalCatalogSelector"/>
</rcv:rcv-config>
```

With:

```
<rcv:rcv-config>
    <rcv:default-catalog catalog-name="/oracle/Webcenter/portalapp/catalogs/default-catalog.xml"/>
    <rcv:catalog-selector class-name="portal.CustomResourceCatalog"/>
</rcv:rcv-config>
```

How it works...

You can test the application with following steps:

1. Run the portal application.
2. Log in with **hrUser** and password **hrUser123**.
3. Go to the **administration** page.
4. Select the **Home** page and select **Edit** from the actions menu.
5. Press an **Add Content** button.

You should normally see the HR resource catalog because you are logged in with a user that has the HR role.

Now we will log in with the finance user:

1. Log out from the portal.
2. Log in with **financeUser** and password **financeUser123**.
3. Go to the **administration** page.
4. Select **Home** page and select **Edit** from the actions menu.
5. Press the **Add Content** button.

You should now see a different resource catalog. This is because you are logged in with a user that has the finance role instead of the HR role.

The `ResourceCatalogSelector` interface has only one method: `getCatalogName`. This method is responsible for selecting the catalog. This is done by returning the name of the catalog that needs to be shown.

When pressing the Add Content button from the Composer, this method is called to see what catalog needs to be fetched.

In the code of the method, we get the `SecurityContext` from the `ADFContext`. This way we can check if the user is in a specific role as shown in the snippet below:

```
ADFContext ctx = ADFContext.getCurrent();
SecurityContext sCtx = ctx.getSecurityContext();
boolean isHR = sCtx.isUserInRole("HR");
```

The return is the name attribute from the resource catalog. You can find it in the source of a resource catalog:

```
<catalogDefinition id="DefaultCatalog" visible="#{true}"
  name="default"
    ...                       xmlns="http://xmlns.oracle.com/adf/rcs/
catalog">
```

Exporting a resource catalog

When you are working with large projects, you will have different environments like development, test, and production. When you create a resource catalog at runtime, you often want to have the same catalog on all the environments.

You could recreate the catalog on each environment, but this is time consuming and not a good method. You could easily forget resources or do something wrong. That's why you have the ability to export and import catalogs. This way, you can easily migrate a catalog from one environment to another.

Managing the Resource Catalog

Getting Ready

For this recipe, you will need to have a WebCenter Portal application and create a resource catalog at runtime.

How to do it...

1. Log in to your portal application.
2. Go to the **administration** page.
3. Select **Resource Catalog** from the **resources** tab.
4. Select the resource catalog you want to export.
5. Press the **Download** button.
6. Enter a name for the earEAR file.
7. Press the **Download** button.
8. Select **Download File** or **Save to server**.

How it works...

The generated EAR file contains the necessary files for creating the resource catalog. It contains the XML file defining the catalog.

Importing a resource catalog

When you have exported a resource catalog, you can easily import it into another environment so you don't need to create the resource catalog from scratch in every environment.

In this recipe, you will see how to import a resource catalog.

Getting ready

For this recipe, you need a WebCenter portal application. You also should do the previous recipe in order to have an exported resource catalog.

How to do it...

1. Log in to your portal application.
2. Go to the Administration page.
3. Select **Resource Catalog** from the **resources** tab.
4. Press the **Upload** button.
5. Press the **Browse** button and select the EAR file that contains the exported resource catalog.
6. Press the **Upload** button.

When the upload has been completed, you should see the message **Resource uploaded successfully** and the navigation model should appear in the list.

How it works...

When you upload an ear file, the contents of the file will be read by the portal. Because we have pointed it to an export of a resource catalog, all the files are there to identify the resource catalog. All the files from the MDS that describe the resource catalog are included in the ear file.

There's more...

When you have exported a resource catalog, you can also import it into JDeveloper. This way you can finetune a resource catalog created at runtime and use the features provided at design time:

1. In JDeveloper, right-click on your portal project and select **Import portal resources**.
2. Press the **browse** button and select an ear file.
3. Press the **OK** button.

5
Managing the Look and Feel of Your Portal

In this chapter, you will learn about:

- Creating a new template at design time
- Creating a new template at runtime
- Creating a tree navigation
- Enabling runtime editing of your template
- Creating a new page style

Introduction

The look and feel of your portal is the signature of your portal. How a web application looks is often more important than what it does. People will decide in just a few seconds whether or not to stay on a website. That's why the looks of a portal are very important. A very good portal with lots of interesting features but with an ugly interface will not have much success with a big audience.

In this chapter, you will learn some techniques on how to create your own custom look and feel. You will learn how to create templates and skins so your portal has a uniform look and feel.

Creating a new template at design time

A page template is a skeleton for your pages. It defines the look and feel for your page. In a template you can define the header, footer, navigation, and other general parts. You define everything in a template except for the content. A template contains a definition for the content region but it does not contain the content itself.

By using a template, you can easily reuse the look and feel. It also enables you to have a uniform layout over the complete portal, which is a very good thing.

In this recipe, we will create a simple template with a header that shows the name of the company. Below the header, we will add the navigation and a link to the administration page. The administration link will only be shown when the user has been authenticated and has the administrator role. The template will be based upon the default template available in the WebCenter portal application. This way, you can learn the basics on how to create a WebCenter portal template. The difference between the default template and this one is that this one is a stretch layout.

In the *How it works...* section, I will break down the code for the template into several parts so you know how everything works.

Getting ready

For this recipe, you need a WebCenter portal application.

How to do it...

1. In JDeveloper, press *Ctrl + N* to open the **New Gallery**.
2. In the list on the left, select **JSF**.
3. In the list on the right, select **JSF Page Template**.
4. Press **Ok**.
5. Specify a **File Name** for your template.
6. Specify the directory. If you want to use the template at runtime, you should put the template in the `public_html/oracle/webcenter/portalapp/pagetemplates` folder.
7. Specify a name for the template. This will be used in the list of templates when you create a new page.
8. By enabling the **Use a Quick Start Layout**, you can use a predefined layout with regions that can match your template.
9. In the **Facet Definitions** section, press the **Add** button.
10. Replace **facet1** with **content**.
11. Press OK.

The template file will now be created and you can start editing it. A template is a regular JSPX page with some additional code, but you can treat it like a regular JSPX page and thus edit it like one.

In the code accompanying this book, you can find the template for this recipe. You can copy/paste the source code from that template to the template you just created.

How it works...

In the template, we will use different parts like a navigation, login/logout link, administration link, and so on.

The most used parts are included in the template attached with the code of this chapter. I will discuss them here so you can learn how to modify the template to fit your needs.

When you take a look at the structure of the template, it exists out of some `panelGroupLayout`s that put the components in a vertical order. Inside those `panelGroupLayout`s, we use other `panelGroupLayout`s to group other components together or to define regions in our template.

The header is displayed in a `panelBorderLayout`. The `panelBorderLayout` allows us to position some content at the end of the panel. That's where we will put the logout link:

```
<af:panelBorderLayout id="pt_pgl1"
                      rendered="#{!composerContext.inEditMode
or attrs.isEditingTemplate}"
                      inlineStyle='background-image:
url(#{facesContext.externalContext.requestContextPath}/images/globe.
png);'>
```

As you can see, the header will not be shown when we edit the page. This is set in the rendered attribute. The `composerContext.inEditMode` will return true if we are in edit mode.

The background image is also set in this panel. This image will only be used for the header.

In order to position the logout link at the right of the panel, we need to use the end `facet`:

```
<f:facet name="end">
```

Within that `facet`, we group the components together by using a `panelGroupLayout`. In our template, we have only added a single component to the end `facet`, being the logout link:

```
<af:commandLink id="pt_glnk4" text="Logout"
  action="#{o_w_s_l_LoginBackingBean.doLogout}"
  rendered="#{securityContext.authenticated}"
  inlineStyle="font-size:small; color:White;"/>
```

Managing the Look and Feel of Your Portal

The action is bound to a bean that handles the logout.

The rendered attribute is also used so the logout link will only be displayed when the user is authenticated. This can be checked with the `securityContext.authenticated` expression.

After the header, we specify a `panelGroupLayout` with a horizontal layout that will be used for the navigation.

The navigation exists out of each element from the navigation model and a link to the administration page. The last one will only be shown when the user is an administrator.

First we loop the elements from the navigation model:

```
<af:forEach var="node" varStatus="vs"
items="#{navigationContext.defaultNavigationModel.
listModel['startNode=/, includeStartNode=false']}">
  <af:goLink id="pt_gl1" text="#{node.title}"
    destination="#{node.goLinkPrettyUrl}"
    targetFrame="#{node.attributes['Target']}"
    inlineStyle="font-size:small;#{node.selected ? 'font-
    weight:bold;' : ''}"/>
  <af:spacer id="sp1" width="20px"/>
</af:forEach>
```

The items of the navigation model are stored in the `navigationContext.defaultNavigationModel.listModel['startNode=/']`.

Each node contains the information we need to create the link. The following attributes can be used:

- `node.title`: Title of the resource we link to
- `node.goLinkPrettyUrl`: Actual URL that needs to be used in the action attribute so the `goLink` will point to the correct page
- `node.attributes['Target']`: Specifies the target of the link
- `node.selected`: Will return true if the current page is the page where the node points to

After each node, we put a spacer component with a width of 20px. Otherwise the `goLinks` will be glued together.

When we have looped each node, we can add the administration link:

```
<af:goLink id="pt_glnk1" text="Administration"
                      destination="/admin"
   rendered="#{securityContext.userInRole['Administrator']}"
   inlineStyle="font-size:small;"/>
```

The administration link should point to /admin.

The rendered attribute is used to make sure only the administrators can see this link. This is done by checking the `securityContext.userInRole['Administrator']` expression. The Administrator role is a predefined role in a WebCenter portal application.

After the navigation, we can define the region that will be used for the content. This must be the content facet:

```
<af:facetRef facetName="content"/>
```

After the actual template, you need to define the different facets available in the template and the name of the template. Normally this is added by JDeveloper when you use the **Create Template wizard**:

```
<af:xmlContent>
<component xmlns="http://xmlns.oracle.com/adf/faces/rich/component">
  <display-name>corporateTemplate</display-name>
  <facet>
      <facet-name>content</facet-name>
  </facet>
</component>
</af:xmlContent>
```

There's more...

There are some more sections you can use in your template that I will be discussing here.

Before you are logged in, you need to enter the username and password. This can also be added to your template. A login form needs to be added as a subform. By using the `rendered` parameter, you can make sure the form will only be shown when the user is not logged in:

```
<af:subform id="pt_sf1" defaultCommand="pt_logincb"
   rendered="#{!securityContext.authenticated} and
   attrs.showLogin">
 <af:panelFormLayout id="pt_pfl1">
   <af:panelLabelAndMessage id="pt_plam1" label="User Name"
     styleClass="NoLabelWrap"
     labelStyle="font-size:small;color:white;">
        <af:inputText id="pt_it1" simple="true"
           value="#{o_w_s_l_LoginBackingBean.userName}"
           columns="15"/>
   </af:panelLabelAndMessage>
   <af:panelLabelAndMessage id="pt_plam2" label="Password"
     styleClass="NoLabelWrap"
     labelStyle="font-size:small;color:white;">
        <af:inputText id="pt_it2" simple="true"
```

```
            value="#{o_w_s_l_LoginBackingBean.password}"
            columns="15" secret="true"/>
    </af:panelLabelAndMessage>
</af:panelFormLayout>
<af:spacer width="3" height="3" id="pt_s2"/>
<af:panelGroupLayout id="pt_pgl14" layout="horizontal"
            halign="end">
    <af:commandLink id="pt_logincb" text="Login"
        action="#{o_w_s_l_LoginBackingBean.doLogin}"
        inlineStyle="font-size:small;color:white;"/>
        <af:spacer id="pt_s3" width="5px"/>
</af:panelGroupLayout>
</af:subform>
```

The values for the username and password are posted to the **o_w_s_l_LoginBackingBean** bean. This is a bean that can be used for login and logout purposes.

The action of the Login button will trigger the login of the `o_w_s_l_LoginBackingBean` bean. This will validate the user and check if the password is correct.

In the rendered attribute of the subform, we check if the user has been authenticated. If he is, the form will not be shown.

Sometimes, you also want to include the name of the user who has been authenticated to the portal. This can easily be done by using an `outputText`:

```
<af:outputText id="pt_ot1"
    value="Welcome #{securityContext.userName}"
    inlineStyle="color:White; font-size:small;"
    rendered="#{securitycontext.authenticated}"/>
```

The value of the `outputText` is a concatenation of a text with the username from the `securityContext`.

The `rendered` attribute is used so that a public user does not see this message.

You can also use attributes in your template. This allows you to have variables that you can set a default value to in the template definition. When you create a page and use the template, you can overwrite the default value.

This can be used to set the image of the header. Because this is a part of the template, you aren't able to change this when you use the template. When you define an attribute for this, you can overwrite it when you use the template.

You define attributes in the `af:xmlContent` tag in the template definition. You need to put the attributes after the definition of the facets:

```
<attribute>
    <attribute-name>showLogin</attribute-name>
    <attribute-class>java.lang.Boolean</attribute-class>
    <default-value>#{true}</default-value>
</attribute>
```

As you can see, you need to define the name, type, and a default value. This attribute can be used to optionally show a login form as you can see in the rendered attribute of the subform from the first snippet in the *There's more...* section.

You can access the attributes by using the **attrs** collection:

```
<af:panelFormLayout id="pnlLogin"
    rendered="#{attrs.showLogin}">
```

When you want to overwrite an attribute, you need to define the value in the `af:pageTemplate` tag as shown below:

```
<af:pageTemplate viewId="..." id="pt1">
    <f:attribute name="showLogin" value="#{false}"/>
    ...
</af:pageTemplate>
```

Creating a template at runtime

When you create pages at runtime, you can also select a template for those pages. The templates you create in JDeveloper at design time are not available for the pages created at runtime. That's why you also need to create templates in runtime.

When you create a template at runtime, you need to specify an existing template as a reference. This way, you don't need to start with an empty template.

Getting ready

This recipe requires a WebCenter portal application.

Managing the Look and Feel of Your Portal

How to do it...

1. Start your portal and log in as an administrator.
2. From the **Resources** tab, select **Page Templates** in the **structure** section.
3. Press the **Create** button to open the **Create New Page Template** dialog.
4. Specify a **name** for your template.
5. Specify a **description** for the template.
6. Select an existing template that will be used as a starting point for your template.
7. Press the **Create** button.

Your template is now created and you can start editing it:

1. Select the newly created template in the list.
2. From the **Edit** menu, select Edit.

Now you can use all of the Composer's features to edit the template at runtime.

How it works...

All the resources created at runtime will be stored in the MDS and the templates are also stored there.

When you edit the template, the regions that are configured for runtime customizations will be made available in the composer. This means that you can make use of the resource catalog to add resources to the template.

 You can only modify the template sections. This means that the content facet of the template is off limits at runtime editing of the template.

During editing of the template, you can't modify everything in the template, for example, when you define a background image of a `panelGroup`. That image can't be changed. Therefore you need to modify the source code of the template.

The composer is only used to add and arrange resources to the template. For example, if you have a banner that shows the latest news items and you want to add this to the template, this would be an ideal case to use the composer.

There's more...

Some things can only be modified by altering the source code of the template. This can also be done during runtime:

1. Select your page template from the list.
2. From the **Edit** menu, select Edit Source.
3. Modify the source.
4. Press **OK** in order to save.

From this dialog, you can also modify the page definition (bindings, operations, and so on). At the bottom of the Edit source dialog you have two tabs:

- Template: Contains the actual source of the template
- Page Definition: Contains the code of the page definition

Creating a tree navigation

In the first recipe, you have seen how to create a template in JDeveloper. The navigation we created there was horizontal based. In this recipe, we will show you how you can create a vertical navigation that will show up as a tree.

Getting ready

For this recipe, you will need a WebCenter portal application.

How to do it...

We will start by creating a new template in JDeveloper:

1. In JDeveloper press *Ctrl + N* to open the **New Gallery**.
2. In the list on the left, select **JSF** from **the Web Tier**.
3. In the list on the right, select **JSF Page template**.
4. Press **Ok**.
5. Specify a **filename** for your template.
6. Specify the **directory** for the template.

Managing the Look and Feel of Your Portal

7. In the **facet definition**, press the plus sign to add a facet and name it **content**.
8. Press **OK**.

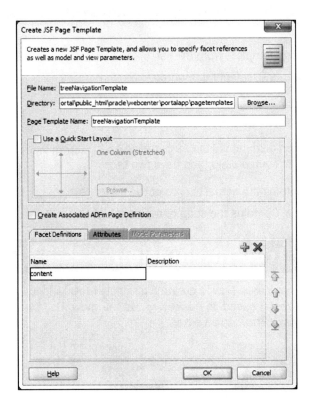

The template will be created and you can start editing it. We will be using a **panelStretchLayout** because this has the facets needed for a nice template. With the `panelStretchLayout`, we can easily add a navigation on the left-hand side of our template.

1. From the **component palette**, drag and drop a **panelStretchLayout** on the page.
2. In the **property inspector**, set the **StartWidth** to 250px.
3. From the **component palette**, drag and drop a **Tree (ADF Faces.common components)** in the start facet.

The **Insert Tree** popup will open where you can specify the properties of the tree. Specify the following values:

1. **id**: Specify an ID for your tree.
2. **value**: `#{applicationScope.navigationContext.currentModel.treeModel['startNode=/, includeStartNode=false']}`.
3. **var**: Node.
4. Press **OK**.

Chapter 5

The tree is now defined, but we still need to add the content of the tree. This needs to be done in the source of the page:

1. Put the following code snippet between the <af:tree> and </af:tree> tags:

```
<f:facet name="nodeStamp">
  <af:goLink id="link" text="#{node.title}"
    destination="#{node.goLinkPrettyUrl}"
    targetFrame="#{node.attributes['Target']}"/>
</f:facet>
```

We also need to add the content facet in order for the template to work properly in a WebCenter portal. This needs to be added in the center facet:

```
<f:facet name="center">
      <af:facetRef facetName="content"/>
</f:facet>
```

You can now use the template for other JSPX pages.

How it works...

The `navigationContext` contains several models for different purposes. In the previous recipes, we have used the `listModel` to show a single level of the navigation. An `<af:tree>` requires a `treeModel` in the value and this is also supported by the `navigationContext`.

The variable we use in the tree is the same as in any other model from the `navigationContext`. We also can make use of the title, `goLinkPrettyUrl` attributes.

A node in the tree is defined by the `nodeStamp` facet. This facet is the actual content of a node. We specify a `goLink` in that facet, but you can specify any component you like. You can add images, outputText, or whatever component you like.

A facet component can only take a single component, so if you want to add multiple components in a facet, you need to group them together with an `<af:group>`.

Managing the Look and Feel of Your Portal

There's more...

In this recipe, I have shown you how you can create a tree navigation in your template. If you want some more control over the layout, then you can also use other components to build the navigation. You can, for example, use an `af:forEach` to iterate the navigation mode. In the following code snippet, you can find an example on how to use the `forEach` to iterate over the navigation mode:

```
<af:panelGroupLayout layout="vertical">
 <af:forEach var="tab" items="${navigationContext.defaultNavigationModel.listModel['startNode=/, includeStartNode=false']}">
   <af:goLink text="#{tab.title}" destination="#{tab.prettyUrl}" id="pt_gl2"/>
 </af:forEach>
</af:panelGroupLayout>
```

In this snippet, we use a `panelGroupLayout` with a vertical layout to show a link for each node in the navigation model. By using the `forEach`, you can do whatever you want to style the navigation model.

Enabling runtime editing of your template

Once your template has been created, you want to make it available in the resource manager of your portal so administrators can edit the template at runtime. This way, you don't need to redeploy the application when you change the template.

In order to enable the template for runtime editing, we need to add some customization components to the template. These components define the regions that can be altered.

In this recipe, we will add some regions to a template that can be used for runtime editing of the template.

Getting ready

For this recipe, you need a WebCenter portal application. We will be using the template that has been created in the first recipe. If you did not follow that recipe, you can find the template in the code accompanied with the book.

How to do it...

First, we will add some regions that can be altered during runtime editing of the template:

1. Open the `corporateTemplate.jspx` from the first recipe or copy it from the code accompanied with the book.

2. Put a `panelCustomizable` around the group with id `pt_g2` so it looks like following code:

```
<cust:panelCustomizable id="pt_pc2" layout="horizontal"
    inlineStyle="border-style:none;">
<af:group id="pt_g2">
<p>
<af:goLink text="Your Company" id="pt_ot4" destination="/"
    inlineStyle="font-size:x-large; color:White;"/>
</p>
</af:group>
</cust:panelCustomizable>
```

3. In the end facet, also surround the `panelGroupLayout` with id `pt_pgl11` with a `panelCustomizable` component.

4. Also surround the `panelGroupLayout` with id `pt_pgl3` with a `panelCustomizable`.

You can also surround an existing component like a `panelGroupLayout` with a `panelCustomizable` by dragging the Panel Customizable component from the component palette on the `panelGroupLayout` in the structure window.

Now that we have created some regions, we need to make the template available for runtime editing:

1. In the Application Navigator, right-click your template.
2. From the context menu, select **Create Portal Resource**.
3. Specify a name for the template.
4. You can optionally select an icon for the template.
5. Specify a description for the template. This will be displayed in the overview of templates in the resource manager.

Managing the Look and Feel of Your Portal

6. Press **OK**:

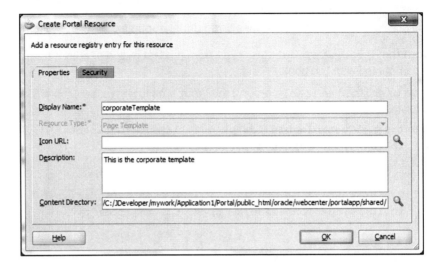

The template is now ready to be managed at runtime.

How it works...

We are first going to show how you can edit the template at runtime:

1. Right-click the **Portal** project and select **Run** from the context menu.
2. Log in in as an administrator.
3. Click on the **Administration** link.
4. In the resource manager, select **Page Templates**.
5. The Corporate template should be available in the list of the templates. Select it.
6. From the **Edit** menu, select **Edit**.

You now can edit the template as shown in the image below:

As you notice, you will get an **Add Content** button for each **panelCustomizable** that we have added to the template. This will bring up the resource catalog so you can add resources to your template.

As you notice, you cannot edit everything from the template like the background or the text, **Your Company**. Therefore you need to edit the template in JDeveloper and redeploy the application.

When you create a portal resource from your template, an entry will be created in the `pagetemplate-metadata.xml` file. You can find this in the `src/META-INF` folder. It looks something like this:

```
<?xml version="1.0" encoding="US-ASCII" ?>
<pageTemplateDefs xmlns="http://xmlns.oracle.com/adf/faces/rich/pagetemplate">
<pagetemplate-jsp-ui-def>/oracle/webcenter/portalapp/pagetemplates/corporateTemplate.jspx</pagetemplate-jsp-ui-def>
   <pagetemplate-jsp-ui-def>/oracle/webcenter/portalapp/pagetemplates/pageTemplate_globe.jspx</pagetemplate-jsp-ui-def>
   <pagetemplate-jsp-ui-def>/oracle/webcenter/portalapp/pagetemplates/pageTemplate_swooshy.jspx</pagetemplate-jsp-ui-def>
</pageTemplateDefs>
```

As you can see, for each template that needs to be available, a **pagetemplate-jsp-ui-def** tag will be added that points to the path of the template.

Creating a new page style

The difference between a page style and page template is that a page style defines how the content will be displayed on your page. While in a page template you define everything except for the content facet, in a page style we will only work with the content facet.

By default WebCenter provides a lot of out-of-the-box page styles. They provide different column views for the content, for example, a single column, three column, narrow column, and so on.

When you want to create your own page style, you can do so in JDeveloper.

Getting ready...

For this recipe, you need a WebCenter portal application.

How to do it...

A WebCenter portal application does not contain a folder for custom page skins. Therefore, we will first create the folder:

1. Right-click the **portalapp** folder in JDeveloper.
2. Select **New** from the context menu.

Managing the Look and Feel of Your Portal

3. Select **General** from the menu on the left.
4. Select **Folder** from the menu on the right.
5. Press **OK**.
6. Specify `pageskins` as a folder name.
7. Press **OK**.
8. Delete the **readme.txt** file.

Now, we will create the actual JSPX page. We will base this upon the corporate template and then do the required modifications so the skin can be used for each template:

1. Right-click on the **pageskins** folder and select **New** from the context menu.
2. Select JSF from the list on the left.
3. Select JSF Page from the list on the right.
4. Press **OK**.
5. Specify **corporateSkin.jspx** as filename/.
6. Select **corporateTemplate** from the **Page Template** drop-down list:

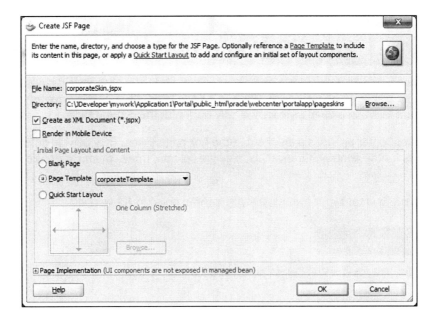

7. Press **OK**.
8. Open the source tab of the page.

9. Modify the `af:pageTemplate` tag and replace it with the following snippet:

   ```
   <af:pageTemplate
     value="#{bindings.pageTemplateBinding.templateModel}"
     id="T">
   ```

10. Use the following code for the content facet:

    ```
    <pe:pageCustomizable id="pcl1">
        <af:panelGroupLayout id="pgl1" layout="scroll">
          <trh:tableLayout id="tl1" width="100%">
            <trh:rowLayout id="rl1">
              <trh:cellFormat id="cf1" width="35%" valign="top">
                <cust:panelCustomizable id="hm_pnc1"/>
              </trh:cellFormat>
              <trh:cellFormat id="cf2" width="65%" valign="top">
                <cust:panelCustomizable id="hm_pnc2"/>
              </trh:cellFormat>
            </trh:rowLayout>
          </trh:tableLayout>
         <trh:tableLayout id="tl2"/>
        </af:panelGroupLayout>
        <f:facet name="editor">
          <pe:pageEditorPanel id="pep1"/>
        </f:facet>
    </pe:pageCustomizable>
    ```

11. Right-click in the page and select **Go to page definition** from the context menu.

12. Press **Yes** if you are prompted to create the page definition.

13. Open the source tab to edit the source of the page definition.

14. Add the following snippet after the variableIterator:

    ```
    <page viewId="#{preferenceBean.defaultPageTemplate}"
      id="pageTemplateBinding" Refresh="ifNeeded"/>
    <taskFlow id="pageeditorpanel"
      taskFlowId="#{pageEditorBean.pageEditorPanel}"
      xmlns="http://xmlns.oracle.com/adf/controller/binding" />
    ```

We also need to make this page style available for runtime managing because otherwise we can't select it when we create a new page:

1. Right-click on the **corporateStyle** file in the Application navigator.
2. Select **Create Portal Resource** from the context menu.
3. Press **OK** in the dialog.
4. Specify a **name** for the page style.
5. Specify an **icon** and description.
6. Press **OK**.

Managing the Look and Feel of Your Portal

When you create a page at runtime, you should be able to see the page style in the list of styles and select it.

How it works...

When you create a page skin, you create a regular JSPX page that is based upon a template. In that page, you will find a reference to the page template. Because we want a generic page style that can be used for each template, we need to create a dynamic reference to the template selected by the user or application.

Therefore we first need to embed the **page definition** of the default template selected by the user. This is done in the page definition of our page style:

```
<page viewId="#{preferenceBean.defaultPageTemplate}"
   id="pageTemplateBinding" Refresh="ifNeeded"/>
```

The most important part is the **viewId**. This is a reference to another page definition being the one from the default page template.

This way we can access the bindings from the default template.

When we have a reference to the default template, we can use this to create a dynamic reference to the template. This is done in the **af:pageTemplate** tag. Normally, you use the `viewId` attribute to select the path of the template, but when we want to create a dynamic reference, we need to use the value attribute:

```
<af:pageTemplate
   value="#{bindings.pageTemplateBinding.templateModel}" id="T">
```

As you can see, we reference the page definition of the default template and we use the `templateModel`. This way, the template that will be selected is dynamic.

After that, we have set a dynamic reference to the template we need to modify the content facet and define how it should look.

The first thing you always need to add is the **pageCustomizable**. This is the necessary component that will allow the usage of the composer component.

In our example, we have built a table with two cells. Each cell has its own **panelCustomizable**. This panel defines a region for your content. Remember that the `panelCustomizable` will show an **Add Content** button, so you can use the resource catalog. So basically the facet content contains a skeleton of the content within each region, a `panelCustomizable`.

We also need to add the `editor` facet and add the **pageEditorPanel** at the end of the `pageCustomizable`:

```
<f:facet name="editor">
   <pe:pageEditorPanel id="pep1"/>
</f:facet>
```

6
Integrating Content with Document Services

In this chapter, you will learn about:

- Preparing UCM for a remote connection
- Creating a connection to a content server
- Creating a content driven navigation model
- Displaying a single content item with the content presenter
- Displaying multiple content items with the content presenter
- Creating a content presenter template for a single item
- Creating a content presenter template for multiple items
- Using the document service taskflows

Introduction

One of the main new features in WebCenter 11g PS3 is the ability to integrate with the content server. This feature has been improved a lot since the last release. In this current release, the emphasis is shifted to content driven portals. This means that you can easily put all your content in the content server and populate the portal with this content. This approach is ideal because you have a loose coupling between the content and your portal. If you decide to use another portal or have another system that also needs to integrate the same content, then this could be easily achieved. You can also make use of the full functionality of the content server. You can, for example, use the workflow to manage the lifecycle of a document, use the content server for version control, and so on.

Integrating Content with Document Services

The way you integrate with the content server has also improved a lot. You can easily drop a folder from the content server to your navigation model or resource catalog.

You also have a lot of support for showing native files in your portal. For example, you can easily show a Microsoft Word document or Microsoft PowerPoint presentation in your portal without needing the file to be downloaded. It blends nicely into your portal.

In this chapter, you will learn different techniques to easily integrate your content from a content server into your portal.

The biggest part of this chapter will teach you how to use the Content Presenter. This taskflow is a very powerful tool to integrate content into your portal.

Preparing UCM for a remote connection

When you install UCM 11g, this will not enable the configuration for allowing a socket connection to the server. This is however needed for creating a connection to the server from JDeveloper or your portal. In this recipe, I will show you how to configure UCM so that it allows remote connections.

This first recipe is not really bound to WebCenter, but is more related to UCM. It is however a prerequisite to be able to connect to your UCM from JDeveloper or from within your portal.

This recipe is only required if you are using UCM 11g. With UCM 10g, this is a setting that is configured during the installation of UCM. Since 11g, this is no longer asked during install and you need to configure this after the installation.

How to do it...

In previous releases of UCM (prior to UCM 11g), you had to make changes in the `config.cfg` file. Because of this, you would need access to the file system of the UCM server. Since UCM 11g, you no longer need access to the file manager because the configuration of UCM can be done in the Enterprise Manager of the WebLogic server:

1. Open the Enterprise Manager of your WebLogic server. If you have installed it on your local host, the address should be `http://localhost:7001/em`.
2. Log in as an administrator.
3. From the left menu, select **Content Management**, **Universal Content Management**, **Content Server** and click on **Oracle Universal Content Management**

4. From the top, click on **UCM** to open the context menu and click on **Configuration**:

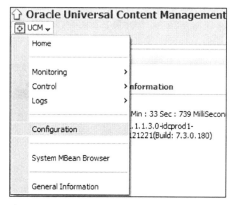

5. Specify a port for the **Intradoc Server port**. This is the port that will be used to create a socket connection.
6. Specify an **IP address filter**. This is used to filter the addresses that are allowed to connect to the server. You can use wildcards in this filter. So for example, we will allow all addresses. For this you need to enter *.*.*.* as the IP filter:

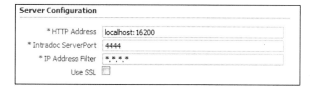

7. Press the **Apply** button in the top-right corner.
8. Restart the UCM managed server.

How it works...

You need to restart the managed server in order for the changes to take effect. This is needed because the intradoc server needs to be booted and should listen to a port. Because we have changed these settings, the server needs to be rebooted.

By enabling the intradoc server to listen on a port, we enable an interface for remote systems. By connecting to the specified port, we can connect to the UCM server and use its features. Now we can use it to create a connection from JDeveloper or from within your portal.

Integrating Content with Document Services

See also

In the next recipe, we will see how we can create a connection to the UCM server by using the settings we have just made.

Creating a connection to a content server

Before we can integrate content into our portal, we need to create a connection to the content server. This needs to be done in JDeveloper.

Getting ready

For this recipe, you need a working instance of a content server and a WebCenter portal application.

How to do it...

1. In the **Application Resources**, right-click **Connections** and select **Content Repository** from the **New Connection** context menu.
2. Specify a connection name.
3. Select **Oracle Content Server** from the **Repository Type**.
4. Check the **Set as primary connection for Documents service** checkbox.
5. Specify **socket** for the **RIDC Socket Type**.
6. Specify **localhost** for the **Server Host Name** (or the hostname where your UCM server is installed).
7. Specify **4444** for the **Content Server Listener Port** (or the port you have specified in the enterprise manager for the intradoc server port).
8. Press the **Test Connection** button.

   You should see a Success message after you have tested the connection, as shown in the image below:

9. Press the **OK** button.

The connection is now created and you can browse your content repository from within JDeveloper. The first time you do this, you will need to provide a username and password:

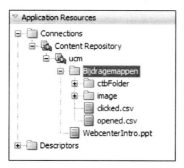

This is an example of the content server on my machine. The content of the connection will be different from your connection. If you used a clean install, you will only see the `Contribution` folder.

Integrating Content with Document Services

How it works...

It is very important to check the **Set as primary connection for Documents service**. This is used in your portal and resource catalog to show the content of a content server. If you don't check this checkbox, you don't have the ability to use out-of-the document services in your portal.

For the Repository Type, you have following options:

- File System: This will create a connection to a file system. This is not recommended for use in your portal. Some features will not even work when using this type of connection.
- Oracle Portal: This will create a connection to the content repository of Oracle Portal.
- Oracle Content Server: This is the type of connection you will be using the most. It creates a connection to an Oracle Content Server.

Each type of repository will have its own **Configuration Parameters**. For the file system, you need to provide the path you want to use and for the Oracle Portal connection, you need to provide a data source that points to the database of the Oracle Portal instance.

As you can see, in the Authentication section, the radio button **Identity Propagation** is checked. This means that if we log in with a specific user into our portal, that user is propagated to the content server. This way, the user will only see the allowed content. There is no further configuration needed to enable this.

There's more...

Besides using a socket connection, you can also use **Web** as a socket type. This will create a connection that uses HTTP to connect to your content server.

If you use this type of connection, you need to provide the URL:

- Content server 11g: http://mycontentserver:4444/_dav/cms/idcplg
- Content server 10g: http://mycontentserver:4444/cs/idcplg

This is not as secure or as fast as a socket connection.

Creating a content driven navigation model

When you have static content in your portal, the best way to store this is in the content server. This way, you can control the workflow for changes, setting a published data, reviewing revisions, and so on. It also enables you to use the same content in different systems.

By using the navigation models, you can easily include several folders from the content server. Each item from those folders will be added to the navigation model. If you add items in the content server to such a folder, it will also be propagated to your portal. This way, you have loose coupling between your content and portal, which is a best practice.

In this recipe, we will be adding a list of jobs to our navigation model. In the content server ,we have a folder called `jobs` which contains several html files. By adding the `jobs` folder to our navigation, each file in the folder will be displayed under the jobs section.

Getting ready

In the code accompanying this book, you will find a folder called `jobs`. You need to upload each file in this folder to your content server. You first need to create the folder `Jobs` and then upload the files.

You also need to have a WebCenter portal application.

How to do it...

1. Open `default-navigation-mode.xml` from the `oracle/webcenter/portalapp/naviagions` folder.
2. Select the **default-navigation-model** root node.
3. Press the Plus sign and select **Content Query** from the context menu.
4. Specify **jobsFolder** for **Id**.
5. Specify ucm for the repository. This must match the name you gave to your connection.
6. Enter the following query:

   ```
   SELECT cmis:name from cmis:document where
      IN_TREE('/ucm/IDC:Folder/988901828852000401')
   ```

7. Replace the long number by the id of your `Jobs` folder. This depends on your system and will definitely be different from mine.
8. Make sure the **Insert Folder Contents** is unchecked.
9. Specify Jobs in the title attribute.
10. Run the portal.

Integrating Content with Document Services

When you run the portal, you should see the Jobs link next to the Home link. When you hover over the Jobs, you will see the three files included in the Jobs folder:

How it works...

The content query is a component that can be added to a navigation model to query the content repository. The most important part of this component is the query. As you might notice, this is not a regular query or a query used in the content server.

The query is a CMIS standard query. CMIS (Content Management Interoperability Service) is a standard that will enable better interoperability of enterprise content management systems.

One of the CMIS specifications is the query language. It is based upon the sql-92 query language used in the database.

For more information about the CMIS standard and the query language, you can look at the Fusion Middleware documentation: `http://download.oracle.com/docs/cd/E17904_01/doc.1111/e15813/toc.htm`.

In the example given in this recipe:

```
SELECT cmis:name from cmis:document where
    IN_TREE('/ucm/IDC:Folder/988901828852000401')
```

We request the names of the documents from a specific folder.

As you can see, this query includes the direct ID of the folder. This is not an ideal query because when you move content from a test environment to a production environment, you are not sure that the id is preserved, so you might have to change the query for each environment.

The checkbox **Insert Folder Content** is also important. When you enable this checkbox, the content of the folder will be shown on the same level instead of items of a subfolder as shown in the image below:

Although this is not hard to use, this is a very important feature, especially if you have a content driven portal. By using this, you have lots of flexibility to include the content into your portal.

Security will be propagated, so this means that when a user logs in who does not have access to see a document, the document will not be added to the navigation model.

There's more...

The CMIS query can be somewhat complex, so that's why I am adding some additional examples that you can use in your navigation model.

With the CMIS query, you can query pretty much everything from the content server. All the metadata is available in the query.

Suppose that you want to add all the files containing a specific part in the name:

```
SELECT * FROM cmis:document WHERE cmis:name LIKE 'Job%'
```

If you want to query custom metadata that is not a part of the CMIS standard, then you will need to use the profile of the document to query the additional metadata. Suppose that you have added a custom metadata field where you can store the product name that applies to your document. When you want to add all those documents to your navigation model, you will use the following query:

```
SELECT * FROM ora:t:IDC:GlobalProfile WHERE ora:p:xProuctID =
  'product'
```

 It is important to know that the query used a case-sensitive search. This means that `xProductID = 'product'` will return different results than when you use `xProductID = 'Product'`

Displaying a single content item with the content presenter

The content presenter is a very powerful tool in WebCenter. It allows you to show content from the content server. There are different templates that allow you to show a single item.

In this recipe, I will show how to use the content presenter to show a single item.

Getting ready

For this recipe, you need to have a WebCenter portal application with a connection to a content server. For this recipe, I will use files accompanying the book. It is the `Jobs` folder. You will find three files in it. You can create a `Jobs` folder in your content server and upload those files in it.

Integrating Content with Document Services

How to do it...

Before we use the content presenter, we will first create a new page:

1. Run your portal project.
2. Log in as an administrator.
3. Go to the **administration** page.
4. From the **Pages**, press the **Create Page** button.
5. Specify **Job** for the **Page Name**:

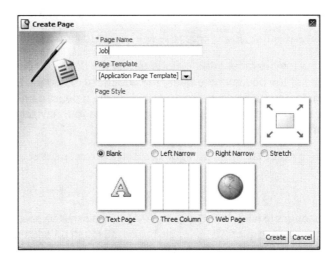

6. Press the **Create** button.
7. Check the **Show Page** checkbox for the Job page in the overview.
8. From the actions menu, select **Edit Page**.
9. Press the **Add Content** button.
10. Open the **Content Management** folder.
11. Press the **Add** button from the **Content Presenter** component:

Chapter 6

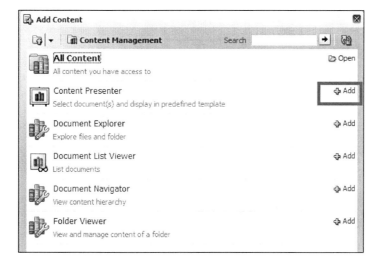

12. Press the **Close** button to close the resource catalog.

The content presenter will now be added to the page. When you close the resource catalog, you will see following message in the content presenter:

Click the first Edit icon to select content and a template.

The content presenter needs to be configured before it can show content:

13. Press the tool icon in the toolbar of the content presenter:

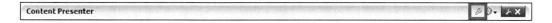

14. Specify **Single Content Item** for the **Content Source** field.
15. Press the **browse** button to select a file from the content server. Browse to the `Jobs` folder and select `dba.txt`.

Integrating Content with Document Services

16. Press **select**:

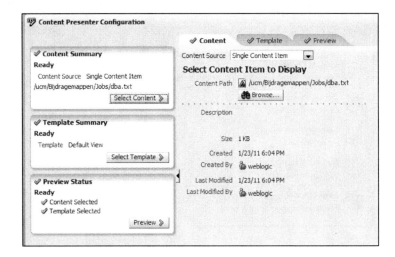

17. Press the **Save** button.

    You should now see the content displayed in the page.

18. Press **Close** in the top-right corner to close the composer and return to the portal.

How it works...

The content presenter is a very powerful tool that you will use a lot if your portal is content driven.

You always need to provide specific properties in order for the content presenter to work. That is why you first get the message when adding the content presenter to your page.

There's more...

In this recipe, we have used the default template. The strength of the content presenter also lies in its templates. The template used in the presenter defines how the content selected will be displayed on the page.

Beside the default view, you have two other templates available:

- Default Document Details view: This template will show all the metadata from the selected item instead of its content. It will also provide a link to the actual item so you can download it.
- Default List Item View: Although this is available for single items, it should be used for multiple items. The template shows an icon and the name of the item as a link.

You can select the template in the **Template** tab in the **Content Presenter Configuration** as shown in the image below:

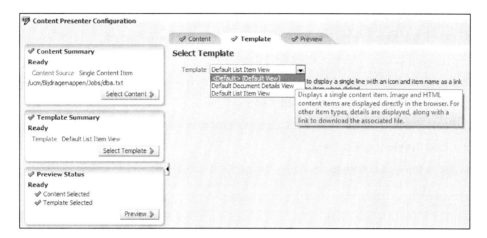

You can also use the **Preview** tab to preview the selected item in the selected template before saving the configuration.

Displaying multiple content items with the content presenter

Often you will want to display all the content from a specific folder or query. This is also possible with the content presenter. There are lots of templates available to choose from.

Getting ready

For this recipe, you need to have a WebCenter portal application with a connection to a content server. For this recipe, I will use files accompanying the book. It is the `Jobs` folder. You will find three files in it. You can create a `Jobs` folder in your content server and upload those files in it.

How to do it...

Before we add the content presenter, we will create a new page:

1. Run your portal project.
2. Log in as an administrator.
3. Go to the **administration** page.
4. From the **Pages**, press the **Create Page** button.

Integrating Content with Document Services

5. Specify Jobs for the **Page Name**.
6. Select **Blank** from **Page Style**.
7. Press the **Create** button.
8. Check the **Show Page** checkbox for the Job page in the overview.
9. From the actions menu, select **Edit Page**.
10. Press the **Add Content** button.
11. Open the **Content Management** folder.
12. Press the **Add** button from the **Content Presenter** component.
13. Close the resource catalog.
14. Press the edit button to configure the content presenter:

15. From the **Content** tab, select **Contents under a folder** from the **Content Source** field.
16. Click on the **Browse** button to select the folder.
17. Browse to the `Jobs` folder, select it, and press the **Select** button.
18. From the **Template** tab, select **Tabbed View** from the template list:

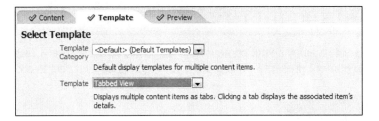

19. Press the Save button.
20. Press the Close button in the top-right corner to close the composer.

You should now see your page with each file as a tab. When you open a tab, it will show the contents of the file:

Chapter 6

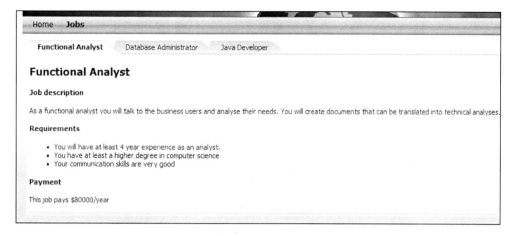

How it works...

The content presenter will retrieve all the items from the selected folder and provide that collection to the template. The template will render the items in the way defined in the template.

There's more...

Besides selecting a folder, you can also select the results of a query as a content source. When you select this, you can define several fields to build the query:

- File name: Specify the name of the file
- Keywords: Keywords that match the contents of the file
- repository (read only)
- Content Type: Specify the content type to filter on
- Limit results: Limit the results to a number of your selection

By pressing the **Preview Results**, you can see the results returned by your query. This way, you can easily check if the parameters you entered matches the results.

You can also add additional fields to your query. When you press the **Add Fields** button, this will open a context menu where you can choose from the following fields:

- Dates: This will add fields so you can filter on the created and last modified dates
- Users: This will add the created and last modified by fields
- Filters: With filters, you can add additional filters
- Sort order: By adding this section, you can specify the sort order of the result

Integrating Content with Document Services

You also have some additional templates to select from:

- Accordion view: Template that will display the items in an accordion. You can only select a single item; the rest will be collapsed.
- Bullet view: All the items will be listed in a bullet list. The name of the file will be shown and is a link to the actual content.
- Bulleted with Folder Label view: This is the same as the bullet view, but the name of the folder will also be shown on top of the bullet list.
- Carousel view: Shows multiple items in a carousel. This is an ideal template if you want to show images. The images are shown and you have a slider to browse through the files.
- Icon view: Displays the content items next to each other with an icon above the filename. When a user hovers over the icon, a popup is shown with the details of the file.
- List with details panel view: This template is something like a master - details view. It will show a list of the files on the left with a details panel on the right. When you select the file, it will show the content in the details panel.
- Sortable table view: Shows the items in a table with sortable columns. The table will have three columns: Document name, Last modified, and Last modified by.

You can of course create your own template. This will be discussed in the following recipes.

Creating a content presenter template for a single item

When the out of the box templates for the content presenter does not meet your requirements, you can create your own templates.

A nice feature in the content presenter templates is that you easily call other templates. This is especially handy when creating a template for multiple items, which I will show in the next recipe.

In this recipe we will create a simple template that will show the details of the selected item. In the next recipe, we will use this template as a reference in a multi-item template.

Getting ready

For this recipe, you will need a Webcenter portal application with a connection to a content server.

How to do it...

1. In JDeveloper, press *Ctrl + N* to open the **New Gallery**.
2. From the list on the left, select **JSF**.
3. From the list on the right, select **JSF Page Fragment**.
4. Press **OK**.
5. Specify a **File name** for the page fragment.
6. Specify the **directory** to put your fragment in. This must be a directory under `oracle/webcenter/portalapp/`.
7. Press **OK**.
8. Copy the following code snippet in the source of the page fragment:

    ```xml
    <?xml version = '1.0'?>
    <jsp:root xmlns:jsp="http://java.sun.com/JSP/Page"
              version="2.1"
              xmlns:af="http://xmlns.oracle.com/adf/faces/rich"
              xmlns:dt="http://xmlns.oracle.com/webcenter/content/templates"
              xmlns:h="http://java.sun.com/jsf/html">
       <dt:contentTemplateDef var="node">
          <h:panelGrid columns="2">
            <af:outputLabel value="Document Title"/>
            <af:outputText value="#{node.propertyMap['dDocTitle'].value}"/>

            <af:outputLabel value="Document Name"/>
            <af:outputText value="#{node.propertyMap['dDocName'].value}"/>

            <af:outputLabel value="Created By"/>
            <af:outputText value="#{node.createdBy}"/>

            <af:outputLabel value="Created on"/>
            <af:outputText value="#{node.createdDate}"/>
          </h:panelGrid>
       </dt:contentTemplateDef>
    </jsp:root>
    ```

9. Save the file.

Integrating Content with Document Services

The template is now created. We only need to make it available to our portal:

1. Right-click the `singleItemTemplate.jsff` in the **Application Navigator**.
2. Select **Create Portlet Resource**.
3. In the popup, specify a **Display Name** for your template.
4. Specify a meaningful **Description** for the template.
5. At the bottom, you also need to specify a **View ID.** This is a unique name for a template:

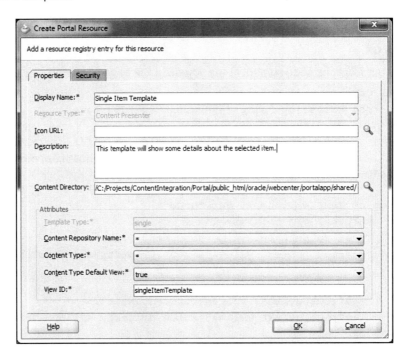

6. Press **OK**.

Your template is now ready to use in your portal. By default the template is hidden, so we first need to make it available for use:

1. Run your portal application.
2. Log in as an administrator.
3. Go to the **Administration** page.
4. Select **Content Presenter** from the resources tab.
5. Select the **Single Item Template** from the list.
6. From the **Edit** menu, select **Show**.

The template will now be available for selection in the content presenter.

When you select the template in a content presenter instance on your page, it should look something like this:

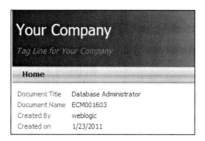

How it works...

When you create a template for the content presenter, you have some additional components you can use. You can find them in JDeveloper in the **Component Palette** in the category **WebCenter Content Display Templates**:

- Content List Template: Calls an existing list template
- Content List Template Def: Defines a template for multiple items
- Content Template: Calls an existing template
- Content Template Def: Defines a template for a single item

In this recipe, we have used the **Content Template Def component**:

```
<dt:contentTemplateDef var="node">
```

The node is a reference to the item we have selected in the content presenter. This way, we can access the properties of the item.

In the following table, you can find some of the properties you can use in the template:

Expression	Description
#{node.propertyMap}	Contains a collection of all the fields available for the item in the content server.
#{node.propertyMap['dDocTitle']}	Returns the title of the document.
#{node.propertyMap['dDocName']}	Returns the name of the document.
#{node.createdBy}	Returns the name of the creator of the document.
#{node.createdDate}	Returns the creation date of the document.
#{node.isFolder}	Returns true if the item is a folder.
#{node.modifiedBy}	Returns the name of the modifier of the document.
#{node.modifiedDate}	Returns the modification date.
#{node.path}	Returns the path of the document.

Creating a content presenter template for multiple items

When you want to show multiple items in the content presenter and the out of the box templates do not meet the requirements, you can always create your own template.

In this recipe, I will show you how you can create a template for multiple items. We will use the template created in the previous recipe as a reference in this template.

Getting ready

For this recipe, you need a WebCenter portal application and a connection to a content server.

We are using the template created in the previous recipe in this recipe. In case you haven't done that recipe, you can find the application in the code accompanying the book.

How to do it...

1. In JDeveloper, press *Ctrl + N* to open the **New Gallery**.
2. From the list on the left, select **JSF**.
3. From the list on the right select **JSF Page Fragment**.
4. Press **OK**.

5. Specify a **File name** for the page fragment.
6. Specify the **directory** to put your fragment in. This must be a directory under `oracle/webcenter/portalapp/`.
7. Press **OK**.
8. Use the following snippet for the code of the fragment:

```xml
<?xml version='1.0' encoding='UTF-8'?>
<jsp:root xmlns:jsp="http://java.sun.com/JSP/Page" version="2.1"
          xmlns:af="http://xmlns.oracle.com/adf/faces/rich"
          xmlns:dt="http://xmlns.oracle.com/webcenter/content/templates">
    <dt:contentListTemplateDef var="nodes">
        <af:panelTabbed id="pnlAcc" styleClass="AFStretchWidth">
            <af:iterator value="#{nodes}" var="node">
            <af:showDetailItem id="pnlDetail" text="#{node.propertyMap['dDocTitle'].value}">
                <dt:contentTemplate node="#{node}"
                    view="singleItemTemplate" nodesHint="#{nodes}" />
            </af:showDetailItem>
            </af:iterator>
        </af:panelTabbed>
    </dt:contentListTemplateDef>
</jsp:root>
```

9. Save the file.

The template is now created. We only need to make it available to our portal:

1. Right-click the `multipleItemTemplate.jsff` in the **Application Navigator**.
2. Select **Create Portlet Resource**.
3. In the popup, specify a **Display Name** for your template.
4. Specify a meaningful **Description** for the template.
5. You can also specify a **Category ID** and **Category Name**, but we are adding our template to the default catalog.
6. Specify a unique **View ID**.

7. Press the **OK** button:

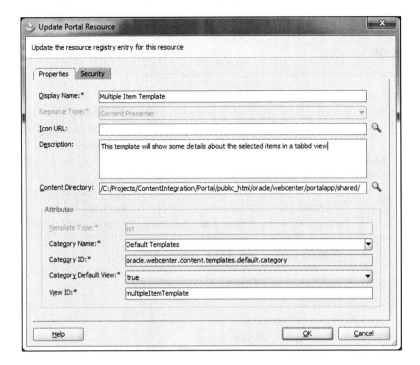

Your template is now ready to use it in your portal. By default the template is hidden so we first need to make it available for use:

1. Run your portal application.
2. Log in as an administrator.
3. Go to the **administration** page.
4. Select **Content Presenter** from the resources tab.
5. Select the **Single Item Template** from the list.
6. From the **Edit** menu, select **Show**.

The template will now be available for selection in the content presenter.

When you select the template in a content presenter instance on your page, it should look something like this:

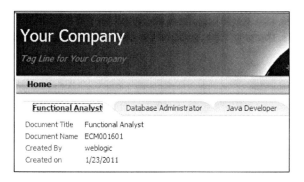

How it works...

For a multiple items template, we use the **Content List Template Def**. This tag defines the template for multiple items:

```
<dt:contentListTemplateDef var="nodes">
```

The nodes is a reference to the items selected in the content presenter. You can use this in an iterator to loop through all the items:

```
<af:iterator value="#{nodes}" var="node">
```

The node is a reference to a single item in the content presenter. This is the same node as described in the previous recipe. For reference and possible properties, please read the previous recipe.

In this template, we reference a template created in the previous recipe. In order to use it, we use the **Content Template** tag:

```
<dt:contentTemplate node="#{node}"
   view="singleItemTemplate" nodesHint="#{nodes}" />
```

The **view** attribute is the most important one. This attribute defines the template we want to include. As a value of this attribute, you need to use the value defined in the **View ID** when you expose the template as a portal resource.

In the **node** attribute, you need to pass the actual node so the template knows which item to use.

Integrating Content with Document Services

Using the document service taskflows

WebCenter suite comes with some taskflows designed for the document services. They allow you to show documents, manage files, explore the content server, and so on.

Getting ready

For this recipe, you will need a WebCenter portal application and a connection to a content server.

How to do it...

1. Run the portal project.
2. Log in as an administrator.
3. Go to the **administration** page.
4. Select the **Home** page.
5. Select **Edit** from the actions menu.
6. Press the **Add Content** button.
7. Open the **Content Management** folder.

In this folder, you will see all the available taskflows related to content:

1. Press the **Add** button from the Document Explorer.

Chapter 6

2. Press the **Edit** button in the toolbar to open the **Component Properties** window:

3. In the **Features off** field, specify **advancedSearch search**.
4. Press **OK**.
5. Press the **Close** button in order to close the composer and return to the home page.
6. Press the expand button on the left to expand the folders:

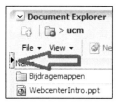

You can now use the Document Explorer to manage your documents. From this taskflow, you can do most of the basic actions like edit content, upload documents, create folders, and so on.

How it works...

The Document Explorer is the taskflow with the most features. There are other taskflows to show or manage documents and they are similar to the document explorer.

The document explorer will use the connection you have defined in JDeveloper and set it as the primary connection. In the component properties window, you can choose another connection if you have a defined multiple connections in JDeveloper.

By specifying a value in the Features Off, we can decide to disable some features. When you focus in the Features Off field, you will get an information box with a list of the values you can use in this field:

> Comma or space delimited list of disabled features. For example: search, advancedSearch, clipboard, dnd, rename, newfolder, upload, newwiki, checkin, checkout, editoffice, edithtml, delete, sidebars, sidebar.history, sidebar.comments, likes, social etc

Integrating Content with Document Services

There's more...

Beside the document explorer, you can use other taskflows in the document services:

- Content Presenter: Displays documents in predefined template. This taskflow is explained earlier on in this chapter.
- Document List Viewer: List: Lists the documents from the content server.
- Document Navigator: Shows the documents in a hierarchy. With this taskflow, you cannot manage the documents, only show them.
- Folder Viewer: This is the same as the document explorer, but it does not have the folder view. It only shows the documents from a specific folder.

Almost all of these taskflows (beside the content presenter) have a similar Component Properties window:

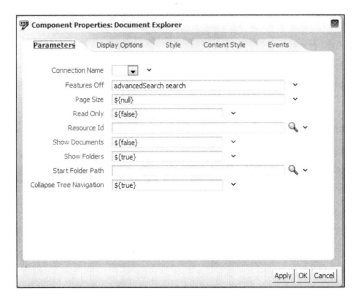

- Connection Name: Specify the connection to be used to populate the taskflow with content. When left blank, the primary connection will be used.
- Features Off: Disable specific features in the taskflow.
- Read Only: Specifies whether or not to disable all write operations. When set to true, you will not be able to upload or modify documents or folders..
- Resource Id: Specifies the selected resource. This can be a folder ID (xCollectionID) or a document Id.
- Show Documents: If set to true, the tree will also include the documents and not only the folders.
- Show Folders: If set to true, folders will also be shown in the display.
- Start Folder Path: Specify a path where the taskflow should start . If left blank, it will start at the root of the content server.
- Collapse Tree Navigation: If set to false, all the nodes of the tree will be expanded.

See also

For more information about the Content Presenter, you can find recipes on how to use the Content Presenter and create your own templates.

7
Discussions and Wiki Services

In this chapter, you will learn about:

- Creating a connection to the discussion service
- Adding discussion forums to your portal
- Creating forums
- Creating topics
- Adding announcements to your portal
- Creating an announcement
- Creating a wiki document
- Editing a wiki document

Introduction

One of the best known Enterprise 2.0 services is the discussion service. It's hard to find a website that does not provide a forum to discuss several things. For an enterprise, it is very important to have discussion forums on their website. It is a good first level of support. People ask for help and other people can help by answering their questions. This can save money by providing a real helpdesk.

Discussions can also be used for collaborative work environments. If you set up an environment for a project, then a discussion forum can be a good place to discuss several topics. This way, different people can elaborate without the need to be in the same place.

Discussions and Wiki Services

With the discussion services, you have the following taskflows:

- Discussion Forums: Taskflow that integrates the basic functionality to allow discussions on a page
- Discussions - Popular topics: Taskflow that shows the popular topics
- Discussions - Quick view: A smaller view to list the topics
- Discussions - Recent topics: Taskflow that shows a list of the recent topics
- Discussions - Watched topics: Taskflow that shows the list of the watched topics from the current user
- Discussions - Watched forums: Taskflow that shows the list of the watched forums from the current user

The discussion services also include the announcement services. With the announcement service, you can create announcements and notify the users about it. Together with the link service (which will be discussed in the next chapter), you can create announcements about events, documents, and so on. When your organization releases a new product, you can easily create an announcement for it on the correct pages. If you have a partner event, you can create an announcement linking to that event so your partners can easily find the new content.

A wiki is another collaboration service that is well known. It allows you to give a collaborative environment to the users. You could, for example, create a wiki to create a knowledge base or documentation for specific products. By allowing other users to edit the wiki, you can delegate the work to the community. This will save time and money for your enterprise. You only need a moderator to check whether or not the content is correct instead of writing the complete work yourself.

Creating a connection to the discussion service

Before you can use the discussion service, you will need to create a connection. By default, the discussion server is installed with the WebCenter Suite. When you create a WebCenter domain, the discussion software will be deployed on the WC_Collaboration managed service. Make sure you have started this managed server before continuing.

 You can test whether or not the discussion service is running by browsing to its URL: `http://localhost:8890/owc_discussions`.

Getting ready

Before you can create a discussion, you need to make sure the WC_Collaboration server is running.

How to do it...

1. In JDeveloper, from the **Application Resources**, right-click **Connection**.
2. Select **New Connection**.
3. Select **Discussion Forum**.
4. Specify a **connection name**.
5. Check the **Set as default connection** checkbox.
6. Press **Next**.
7. Specify the **URL**: http://localhot:8890/owc_discussions. Specify the correct server and port so it matches your environment.
8. Specify the **admin user**. By default this is **weblogic**.
9. Press **Test Connection** to see if everything is working.
10. Press **Next**:

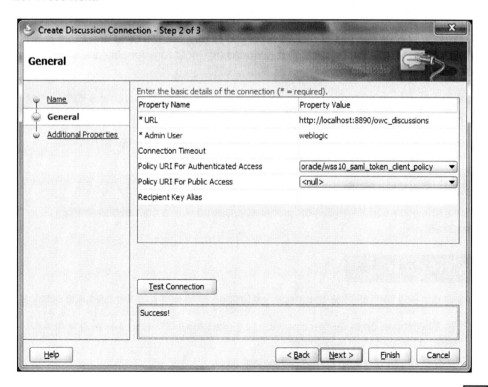

Discussions and Wiki Services

11. We don't need any additional parameters, so just press **Next**.
12. Press **Finish** to create the connection.

When you have created the connection, you can see it in your Application Resources and we can use it in the discussion taskflows.

How it works...

The discussion software we use is the Jive forum software. This is the default forum software installed with the WebCenter Suite. The Jive forum software is also the one used on OTN.

When you create a WebCenter domain, the owc_discussions application will be deployed on the WC_Collaboration managed server by default. During the configuration of the domain, you can deploy it on another managed server if you wish, but it needs to be deployed on at least one managed server. The owc_discussions is a web application, so you can use it as a standalone application for providing forums.

By creating a connection in JDeveloper, we can easily integrate the discussions with our portal. This way, the users do not need to log in again or see another look and feel for the discussions.

Adding discussion forums to your portal

The discussion service has lots of taskflows for you to use, but the most important is the **Discussion Forums**. It is the taskflow that contains the most functionality and allows your users to create and view topics.

This taskflow is not added to the default resource catalog when you create a WebCenter portal, so that's why we will add this first.

As a second task, we will add the Discussion Forums taskflow to a page at runtime.

Getting ready

For this recipe, you need a WebCenter portal application with a connection to the discussion service.

How to do it...

Before you can add the taskflow to a page, we first need to add it to the resource catalog:

1. In JDeveloper, open `default-catalog.xml` from the `oracle/webcenter/portalapp/catalogs` folder.
2. Select the **Social And Communication** node.

Chapter 7

3. Press the Add button and select **Link**:

4. Specify discussionForums as the ID.
5. Specify **Taskflow** as the **Type**.
6. Press the browse button next to the **URL** field.
7. Select **Resource Palette** from the list on the left.
8. Open **My Catalogs**.
9. Open **WebCenter Services Catalog**.
10. Open the **Taskflow** folder.
11. Select **Discussion Forums**:

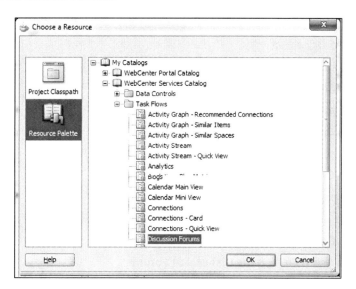

12. Press the **OK** button.
13. Specify Discussion Forums as the **title**.

14. Save the file:

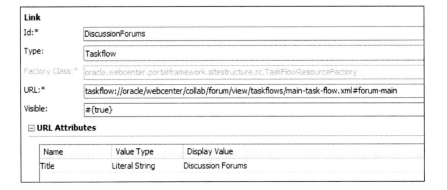

 Instead of adding a link and selecting the taskflow from the browse popup, you can also drag and drop the taskflow from the resource palette to the node in the resource catalog. This will automatically create a link with the needed parameters.

Now that we have added the taskflow to the resource catalog, we can add it to our page at runtime:

1. Run the portal project.
2. Log in as an administrator.
3. Go to the **Administration** page.
4. Select **Pages** from the resource tab.
5. Press the **Create Page** button.
6. Specify Discussions for the **Page Name**.
7. Press the **Create** button.
8. From the page action menu, select **Edit** page.
9. Press the **Add Content** button to open the Resource Catalog.
10. Open the **Social And Communication** folder.
11. Press the **Add** button on the **Discussion Forums**:

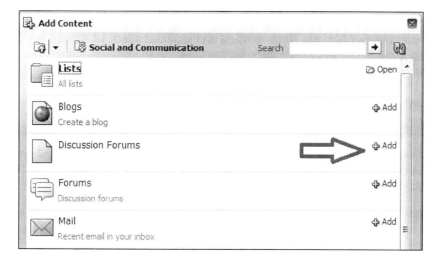

12. Press the **Close** button to close the catalog.
13. Press the **Close** button in the top-right corner to close the Composer.

How it works...

By adding the taskflow to the default resource catalog, you are able to add the discussions at runtime. If you don't add the taskflow to a resource catalog, you can only add the discussion to pages created at design time.

When you add the Discussion taskflow to a page, it will automatically use the default connection. When you have not configured a default connection to the discussion service, the taskflow will give an error.

There's more...

The Discussion Forum taskflow has several parameters that can be used to customize the taskflow:

1. Edit the discussions page.
2. Press the Edit button on the Discussion Forum taskflow.

This will open the **Component Properties: Discussion Forums** popup. In there, you will find the following parameters:

- ▶ Category ID: Contains the ID of the category. This way you can show only the forums from a specific category.
- ▶ Forum ID: Show only the topics from a specific forum.

Discussions and Wiki Services

▶ Show Categories: When enabled, the forums will be grouped by category.

▶ Show recursive Forums: When enabled and you have specified a category ID, this will also show the forums under the subcategories. When disabled, it will only show the forums directly under the specified category.

Creating forums

Managing forums will be a task you have to do a lot in your portal. Finding a good hierarchy for your discussions is vital. When people don't find the correct forum to place their discussion in, they will quickly leave your portal.

In WebCenter, you have only limited functionality to manage the forums. If you want the complete functionality, you need to use the Jive forum software itself. Remember that it is installed and you can use it. Just browse to `http://localhost:8890/owc_discussions/admin` for the administration console of the forum. From there, you can manage everything. You can find the complete documentation of the Jive software and administration console on the site of Jive itself: `http://docs.jivesoftware.com/forums/latest/documentation/index.html`.

In this recipe, I will concentrate on how to manage forums from within your portal.

Getting ready

In the code accompanying the book, you can find a Discussion project that you can use for this recipe. It has a discussion page with the Discussion Forum taskflow on it and a connection to the discussion service on localhost.

If you don't use this application, you will need a WebCenter Portal application with a connection to the discussion service and a page with the Discussion Forum taskflow on it.

How to do it...

1. Start the **Portal** project.
2. Log in as an administrator.
3. Go to the **Discussions** page.
4. Press the **Create Forum** button.
5. Specify a **Forum name**.
6. Specify a Forum Description.
7. Press the Create button.

You now are able to create discussions in the forum.

How it works...

When you add a forum, the Jive API is called from within the taskflow to create the forum.

If you have specified a category ID, the forum will be created under the specified category.

There's more...

You can also modify an existing forum:

1. Run the portal.
2. Log in as an administrator.
3. Go to the **Discussions** page.

If you haven't created a forum yet, create one first:

1. Open a forum by clicking on its name.
2. Press the **Edit Forum** button.

This will open the same popup as when you create a forum, but now the values are preset with the values from the forum. Here you can change the Forum Name and Description.

You can also delete the complete forum:

1. Run the portal.
2. Log in as an administrator.
3. Go to the **Discussions** page.

If you haven't created a forum yet, create one first:

1. Open a forum by clicking on its name.
2. Press the **Delete Forum** button.

You will see a confirmation dialog. When you press the Delete button, the forum and all the topics in the forum will be removed. Notice that you can not reverse the delete. Once a forum has been deleted, you can not bring back the discussions created in that forum!

Discussions and Wiki Services

Creating topics

Creating topics is quite trivial in WebCenter. If you are used to participating in other forums, you can easily use the forums in WebCenter.

Getting ready

For this recipe, you need a WebCenter Portal Application with a connection to the discussion services.

In the code accompanying the book, you will find a WebCenter Portal with a connection to the discussion service on your localhost and with a page set up for the discussions.

How to do it...

1. Run the Portal project.
2. Log in as an administrator.
3. Go to the Discussions page.
4. Open a forum by clicking on the name of a forum.
5. Press the Create Topic button.
6. Specify a Subject.
7. Write the discussion.
8. Press the Create button:

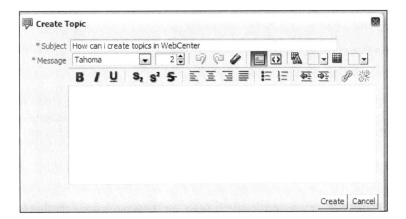

How it works...

When you add topics, the taskflow will call the Jive API to create the topic in the forum.

There's more...

When you created a topic, you can also edit it:

1. Run the portal.
2. Log in as an administrator.
3. Go to the **Discussions** page.
4. Open a forum by clicking on its name.
5. Open the topic you want to edit.
6. Press the **Edit Topic** button.

You will see the same popup as when you create a topic, but the Subject and topic field are already filled in. From there, you can edit the topic.

When you want to remove the topic, you just need to press the **Delete Topic** button.

Adding announcements to your portal

By adding announcements to your portal, you can let the user know about something special like the release of a new product or an event he might be interested in.

Announcements are very powerful in combination with the link service. It allows you to link an announcement to another resource like a document or an event. This will be discussed in the next chapter when we talk about Organizing and finding content.

Because the announcements are stored in the Jive software (which is the software used for the discussions), you need a connection to the discussion services for working with announcements. Read the first recipe on how to create a connection to the discussion services.

In this recipe, we will add a page that will show the announcement. We will just add the announcement taskflow to a page. In the next recipe, I will show how to manage the announcement.

Getting ready

For this recipe, you need a WebCenter Portal application with a working connection to the discussion services.

Discussions and Wiki Services

How to do it...

1. Run the Portal project.
2. Log in as an administrator.
3. Go to the **Administration** page.
4. Select **Pages** from the **Resource** tab.
5. Press the **Create Page** button.
6. Specify Announcements for the **Page Name**.
7. Press the **Create** button.
8. Check the **Show Page** checkbox in the pages overview.
9. Select **Edit Page** from the action menu on the **Announcements** page.
10. Press the Add Content button to open the Resource Catalog.
11. Open the Alerts and Updates folder.
12. Press the Add button on the Announcements component:

13. Press the Close button in the Resource Catalog.
14. Press the Close button in the top-right corner to close the Composer.

You will see the announcements taskflow on your page, but there are currently no announcements, so the message **No announcements were found** is displayed:

There's more...

The announcement taskflow has lots of properties for you to customize the taskflow.

When you edit the announcements page or any page with the announcement taskflow, you can press the **Edit** button on the announcement taskflow. This opens the **Component Properties: Announcements** popup:

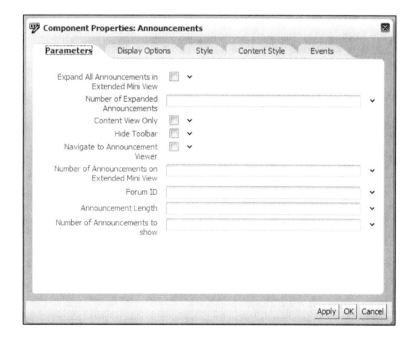

In this popup, you can specify the number of announcements, the length of an announcement before it breaks, and forum ID to which the announcements are linked.

You can also specify whether or not to display the toolbar and other parameters.

Discussions and Wiki Services

Creating an announcement

With the Jive software, you can add announcements in the Jive software itself or in the announcement taskflow. In this recipe, I will show how you can add announcements by using the announcement taskflow. You don't need a special taskflow for it, just the one added in the last recipe.

Getting ready

For this recipe, you will need a WebCenter Portal application with a connection to the discussion services and a page that has the announcements taskflow on it. You can also follow the previous recipe to achieve this.

How to do it...

1. Run the **Portal** project.
2. Log in as an administrator.
3. Go to the page were you have put the announcement taskflow.
4. Press the Open Announcement Manager button:

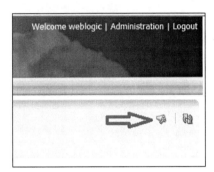

5. Press the **Create** button.
6. Specify a **subject** for your announcement.
7. Enter the announcement body in the text area.
8. Specify an activation date when applicable.
9. Specify an expiration date when applicable.
10. Press the **Create** button.

Your announcement is now created and the user will see it.

How it works...

When you create an announcement, the taskflow will call the Jive API to create the announcement in the Jive software. If you haven't specified a forum ID, the announcement will be created under the ROOT, else it will be created under the specified forum ID.

There's more...

When you specify an activation date, the announcement will only be set to public when the date is reached. This way you can create announcements a while before they need to be published.

The same can be done for the expiration date. You can specify a date or an amount of days that the announcement needs to be online. When the specified date is reached, the announcement will automatically be removed.

Creating a wiki document

With the latest release of WebCenter, the complete wiki integration has been revamped. In the previous release, there was a separate wiki server allowing you to create standalone wiki's and integrate them in WebCenter. These days, Oracle has changed the idea of wikis. A wiki is nothing more than a document stored in the content server. This means that if you want to have a wiki on your portal, you need a content server instead of a wiki server.

For more information about the document services and how to create a connection, you can read the previous chapter.

Getting ready

For this recipe, you need a WebCenter Portal application with a connection to a Content Server. If you don't how to create a connection, you can read the first two recipes of the previous chapter.

How to do it...

1. Run the Portal project.
2. Log in as an administrator.
3. Go to the Administration page.
4. Select Content from the Services tab.
5. Select the folder you want to create a wiki document in.
6. Press the **Create Wiki Document** button.

7. Specify a **Title**.
8. Write the body of the page.
9. Press the **Create** button next to the **Title** field.

How it works...

When you create a wiki document, you create an `htm` file in the Content Server. A check in will be done in the background.

Some other metadata will be set like the content type. This will be set to **Application** because the file is owned by an external application which is WebCenter.

The security will also be set to Public by default.

Editing a wiki document

Editing a wiki is always a special feature. You have special abilities for editing a wiki in WebCenter. It allows you to easily link to an existing wiki document or create a link to a new wiki document so you can edit it later.

In this recipe, we will create a new wiki document, edit it, and create a link to a new wiki document.

Getting ready

For this recipe, you need a WebCenter Portal application with a connection to a Content Server. If you don't how to create a connection, you can read the first two recipes of the previous chapter.

How to do it...

1. Run the Portal project.
2. Log in as an administrator.
3. Go to the Administration page.
4. Select Content from the Services tab.
5. Select the folder you want to create a wiki document in.
6. Press the **Create Wiki Document** button.
7. Specify Knowledge Base as the **Title**.
8. Specify a text in the body.

9. Press the **Create** button next to the **Title** field.
10. Click on **Knowledge Base** to view the content.
11. Press the **Edit** button.
12. Select a word from the body.
13. Press the **New Resource** button:
14. Select **Wiki document** from the list.
15. Specify a **title** for the new document.
16. Press **OK**.
17. Press **Save and Close**.

You now have to create a link to a new wiki document. When you click on the newly created link, you will be linked to the new wiki document. Now you can edit this document.

This is how you can create a full wiki in WebCenter.

How it works...

For each wiki document you create, no matter how you create it, a new check in will be done on the content server. It will create an `htm` file with the content of the body you entered.

When you create a new wiki document from the new resource button, it will create the document in the same folder as the document you are editing.

There's more...

Besides creating a new document, you have some other tools to create links:

From left to right:

- Link: Create a link to an external URL or anchor. This way you can also create a link to an e-mail address.
- Unlink: When the cursor is placed in a link, you can remove the link with the unlink button.
- Select resource: This button will open a popup that allows you to browse the content server and select a document. This can be a wiki document or any other content checked into the content server.

Discussions and Wiki Services

- ▶ New resource: This button allows you to create a new resource.
- ▶ Embed image: With this button, you can select an existing image from the content server or upload a new document into the content server.

Another way to edit a wiki document is by using the shortcut. When you view a wiki document in your portal, you can press *Ctrl + Shift + C*, which opens the editor for editing the wiki document. This way, you don't need to go to the administration console and browse to your wiki document in the document library.

8
Organizing and Finding Content

In this chapter you will learn about:

- Creating a connection for the link and tagging services
- Enabling tagging functionality to pages
- Showing related content
- Showing a tag cloud
- Linking content
- Linking to a document
- Linking to a discussion

Introduction

When you create a portal, it will often contain different types of content shattered over the complete portal.

Users come to your portal for a reason. One of the reasons could be finding content. If they don't easily find the content they are looking for, they will leave your portal. For this reason, it is very important to provide different ways to allow your users to organize the content and let them find what they are looking for.

Organizing and Finding Content

There are three major techniques that we will discuss in this chapter that will allow you to help users organize and find content:

- **Link service**: with the link service, you allow users to create links between content. This way you can easily add documents to events or link announcements to content you create.
- **Tags service**: when editors create pages, you can allow them to add tags to the page or content. This way the content can easily be found during a search. You can also allow regular users to tag the content they want so they can create a personal tag set that help them find the content they want.
- **Search service**: the search service allows you to let the users find content.

There is a fourth technique that will help users organize and find content, which is the **Activity Graph Service**. This one is discussed in *Chapter 14, Using WebCenter Analytics* in the book. This service will give the user a truly personalized user experience based upon previous activities.

It is really important to grasp the concept of the services described in the earlier sections. It is often forgotten how important it is to implement a good search service. A helpdesk often gets questions which are answered in documents published on a portal but people just don't find those documents. This can be because of bad tagging or no tagging at all, no proper index on the documents, bad search service, and so on.

When you use the link, tag, and search service in a proper way, your users will easily find what they are looking for.

Creating a connection for the link and tagging services

Both the link and tag services use the WebCenter schema. That's why we first need to create a connection to the WebCenter schema from within JDeveloper.

It is mandatory that you name the connection WebCenter.

Getting ready

Before you can create a connection to the WebCenter repository, you first need to create the repository. Normally, this is a mandatory step when you install WebCenter suite. The WebCenter schema gets created by running the **Repository Creation Utility** (**RCU**).

How to do it

1. In the **Application Navigator** right click the Connection folder.
2. Select **New Connection** and select Database from the **context** menu.
3. Specify **WebCenter** for the connection name. It is important that you actually call the connection **WebCenter**. If you give it another name, it will not work!
4. **Connection Type: Oracle (JDBC)**.
5. **Username**: the username you specified during the RCU.
6. **Password**: Password for the WebCenter schema. You also specified this in the RCU.
7. **Driver: thin**.
8. **Host name**: The hostname of the database server were the WebCenter schema has been created.
9. **SID**: Service name for the database.
10. Press the **Test Connection** button to see if the parameters are correct.

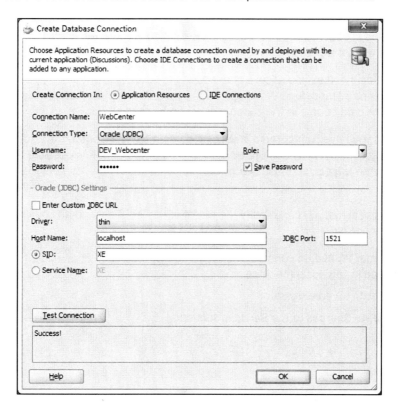

Organizing and Finding Content

11. Press the **OK** button to create the connection.
12. Select **WebCenterDS** in the **Associate to Data Source** popup window:

13. Press the **OK** button to close the popup and save your selection.

The connection is now created and you should be able to use the tag and link services.

There's more

Both the link and tag service require a data source called WebCenter. If you don't have it, those services will not work.

By creating the connection, you allow a connection in JDeveloper, but when you deploy to a managed server or a standalone WebLogic server, you still need to create the data source. You can create a data source in the console of your managed server.

Normally, when you have configured a WebLogic domain for WebCenter, the data sources will be created for you and you don't need to create them yourself. It is possible that you need to modify the targets, because the WebCenter data source only targets the WebCenter Spaces server.

With the following steps, you can modify the target of the WebCenter data source in a standalone WebLogic server:

1. Go to your **WebLogic** console `http://localhost:7001/console` if you have installed in your local machine.
2. Log in with an administrator
3. Click **Data Sources** in the Services section:

Chapter 8

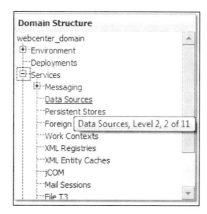

4. Click on **WebCenterDS**. This is the data source used by the link and tagging service.
5. Open the second tab: **Targets**.
6. Check the checkboxes for each server you want to use the data source on.
7. Press **save**:

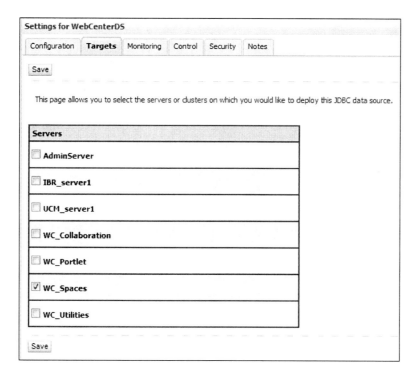

Organizing and Finding Content

Enabling tagging functionality to pages

By enabling tagging, you allow the user to add meaningful keywords to your content. When multiple users tag the same content, it will contribute to the search service. This way people can easily find the content they are looking for.

Tagging also allows the user to organize tags. In the tagging centre you are able to see the relations between the tags and the tagged content.

In this recipe, we will see how you can add the tagging button which allows the users to add tags to your pages. Because we want to enable tagging to all the pages, it is a good idea to add the tagging button to the template. This way we only need to edit a single file.

Getting ready

For this recipe, you need a WebCenter Portal application with a connection to the WebCenter schema's which is described in the first recipe.

How to do it

1. In JDeveloper open the `pageTemplate_globe.jspx` file from the `oracle/webcenter/portalapp/templates` folder.
2. From the **Component Palette**, select **WebCenter Tags Service** from the dropdown list.
3. Drag the **Tagging Button** to the template after the commandLink with ID `pt_glnk4`.

4. Specify **#{facesContext.viewRoot.viewId}** for the **ResourceId**.
5. Specify **#{facesContext.viewRoot.viewId}** for the **ResourceName**.

6. Specify **oracle.webcenter.page** for the **ServiceId**:

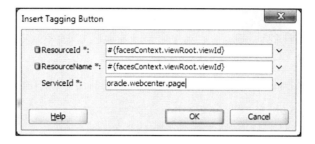

7. In the **Component Palette** select **Tagging** from the dropdown list.
8. Drag and drop the **Tagging Dialog** after the tagging button.
9. From the **create** context menu select **Region**.

You are now ready to test the page. When you run the portal and login with a user you should be able to see the tagging button as shown in the following screenshot:

How it works

When you press the tagging icon or link you will see a popup which allows you to tag the page. This dialog is the taskflow we added after the button. Without the Tagging Dialog taskflow, the tagging button will not work. It is important that you always add the Tagging Dialog taskflow and the tagging button, because one cannot work without the other.

In the popup you see the path to the page and you have a Tags input field that allows you to add the tags.

When a user adds tags, he can decide to share those tags or to keep them private by using the Shared checkbox:

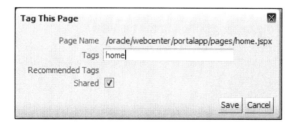

Organizing and Finding Content

A tagging button shows up in your code as a `<tag:taggingButton>` tag as shown in following snippet:

```
<tag:taggingButton          resourceId="#{facesContext.viewRoot.viewId}"
   showLabel="false"                        resourceName="#{facesContext.viewRoot.viewId}"
      serviceId="oracle.webcenter.page"
      id="pt_tb1"/>
```

The following attributes are mandatory for the tagging button:

- `resourceId`: They specify the ID of the resource you want to tag. In case you want to tag a page you need to use the `#facesContext.viewRoot.viewId}` expression. This will return a unique id of the page.
- `resourceName`: They specify the name of the resource you want to tag. In case, you want to tag a page you need to specify the same value as the `resourceId`.
- `serviceId`: They specify an application wide ID. For tagging spaces you need to provide oracle.webcenter.page as the value.

When you drop the **Tagging** Dialog taskflow on your page, it will create a region and bind the taskflow to that region:

```
<af:region value="#{bindings.tagginglaunchdialog1.regionModel}"
   id="pt_r2"/>
```

The code cannot be copied or just typed on your page because you also need the bindings. That's why the best way to add taskflows is by dragging and dropping them on your page.

In the page binding, you will find the link to the taskflow:

```
<taskFlow id="tagginglaunchdialog1"
            taskFlowId="/oracle/webcenter/tagging/controller/taskflows/launch-dialog.xml#tagging-launch-dialog"
            activation="deferred"
            xmlns="http://xmlns.oracle.com/adf/controller/binding"/>
```

As you can see, the value of the region is bound to the ID of the taskflow in the bindings.

You do not need to bind the tagging button to the taskflow.

Showing related content

The idea of tagging your content is not only to organize the content but also to enable you to find related content tagged by other users. Therefore, we have the Related Links taskflow. Although the name says 'links' but it has nothing to do with the link services. The taskflow will read the tags of the current page and look if there are other pages with similar tags and show them in the taskflow.

In this recipe I will show how you can use this taskflow.

Getting ready

For this recipe you need a WebCenter portal application with a configured connection to the WebCenter schema as described in the first recipe.

How to do it

Before you can add the Related Links taskflow to your pages, you first need to add it to the resource catalog:

1. In JDeveloper open `default-catalog.xml` in the `oracle/webcenter/portalapp/catalogs` folder.
2. Select the **Tagging and Searching** folder.
3. Press the **add button** and select link from the **context** menu.
4. Specify **relatedLinks** for the id.
5. Specify **Taskflow** for the type.
6. Click the **browse** button next to the URL field to open the browse window.
7. Select **Resource Palette** from the list on your left.
8. Select **Tagging | Related Links** from the `My Catalogs/WebCenter Services Catalog/Task Flows` folder.

Organizing and Finding Content

9. Press **OK**:

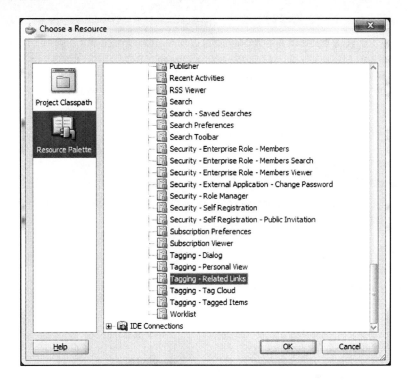

10. Specify **Related Links** as the title:

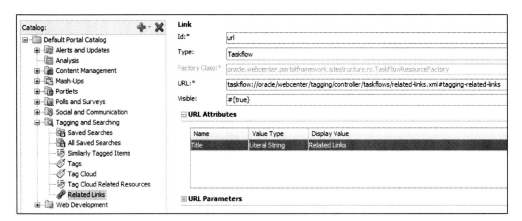

Now that we have added the Related Links taskflow to the resource catalog, we can add it to our pages:

1. Run the portal project.
2. Log in with an administrator.
3. Go to the **administration** page.
4. From the **action** menu of the Home page select **Edit**.
5. Press the **Add Content** button to open the **resource** catalog.
6. Open the **Tagging and Searching** folder.
7. Click the **Add** button on the **Related Links** component:

That's it. You should now see the taskflow with the related links. When you add tags to the page and add the same tags to other pages you should be able to see the other page's link in the Related Links taskflow.

How it works

The Related Links taskflow will search the tags for all the content on the current page. It will look for other content with similar tags and display them in the taskflow.

There's more

Suppose that you have multiple content types on a page like a discussion forum and a list of documents and you want to use the related links to only display related forums and not documents. By default, the taskflow will look for both tags in the forums and documents.

By configuring the parameters of the taskflow, you can choose which resources need to be used to look for related content:

1. Go to edit mode.
2. Press the **Edit** button of the taskflow to bring up the **Component Properties** popup.

Organizing and Finding Content

In the first tab, you can specify both the resource ID and the service ID so you can select which content has to be used for looking for related resources.

Showing a tag cloud

A tag cloud is a good indication on what the weight of each tag is. A tag cloud shows a visual representation on what are the popular tags.

The Tag Cloud taskflow will show each tag with a size showing how popular the tag is. This means that tags which aren't popular will be shown with a small font size while popular tags will have a larger font size.

In this recipe I will show how to use the tag cloud.

Getting ready

For this recipe, you need a WebCenter Portal application with a connection to the WebCenter schema as described in the first recipe.

How to do it

Before you can add the taskflow to the pages you first need to add it to the resource catalog.

1. In JDeveloper open `default-catalog.xml` in the `oracle/webcenter/portalapp/catalogs` folder.
2. Select the **Tagging and Searching** folder.
3. Press the **add** button and select link from the context menu.
4. specify relatedLinks for the id.
5. Specify Taskflow for the type.
6. Click the **browse** button next to the URL field to open the browse window.
7. Select **Resource Palette** from the list on your left.
8. Select **Tagging | Tag Cloud** from the `My Catalogs/WebCenter Services Catalog/Task Flows` folder.
9. Press OK.

10. Specify Tag Cloud for the title:

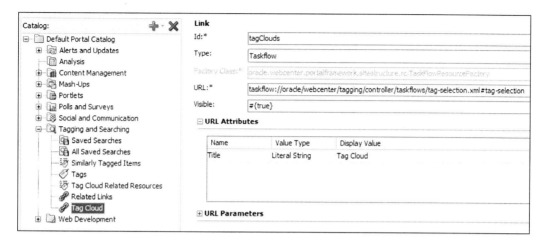

11. Run the portal project.
12. Log in with an administrator.
13. Go to the **administration** page.
14. From the **action** menu of the Home page select **Edit**.
15. Press the **Add Content** button to open the resource catalog.
16. Open the **Tagging and Searching** folder.
17. Click the **Add** button on the **Tag Cloud** component:

18. Close the Composer by pressing the **Close** button in the top right corner.

You now can see the tag cloud on your page with the different font sizes for the tags depending on the popularity:

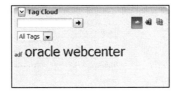

How it works

The Tag Cloud taskflow will look for all the tags in the database and calculate the font size accordingly. The taskflow cannot be configured to select specific resources or services. It always shows all the tags from the database.

There's more

The Tag Cloud taskflow gives some additional functionality.

In the top left corner of the taskflow you have a search field which allows you to search for tags containing the string you enter. The tag cloud will then be generated based upon your search.

You can also filter the tag cloud so it only shows the tags you have created. This is useful so you can see what tags you have used the most in the portal.

In the right corner you have some icons:

- **Cloud / list view**: with this button you can switch from cloud to list view and vice versa. By default the cloud view is selected. When you switch to list view, all the tags will have the same size but the most popular will be at the top
- **Sort options**: You can sort the tags on the name, date or popularity. By default it will be sorted on the name. The functionality of this field depends on the view. When you are in cloud view, it will sort the tags depending on the selected field but the size will be calculated depending on the popularity. When you switch to list view, the default sort field is popularity. When you change it to name, the tags are sorted by name and you don't see which one is the most popular.
- **Refresh button**: Refreshes the cloud or list.

Linking content

By enabling the linking service, you let the user create connections between content. For example you can create a page about a new product and link it to a PDF uploaded to the content server. You also can create a link to a discussion about the new product. This way you can easily organize the content of your portal if it is shattered over different places.

- You can link from the following resources:
    - Announcements
    - Discussions
    - Documents
    - Events
    - Lists
    - Pages
- You can link to the following existing resources:
    - Announcements
    - Discussions
    - Documents
    - Events
- You can create the following resources when creating a new link:
    - Discussions
    - Documents
    - Events
    - Notes
    - URLs

In this recipe, I will show you can add the linking service to your pages. We will add the Link button to the template so it is available for all the pages.

Getting ready

For this recipe, you need a WebCenter Portal Application with a connection to the WebCenter schema as discussed in the first recipe.

Organizing and Finding Content

In this recipe, you will find screenshots for linking documents and discussions to your pages. It is not mandatory to create a connection to a content server or discussion server. If you want to create that connection, please read the chapters about Integrating Content and the chapter about Wiki and Discussion services.

How to do it

1. In JDeveloper open the `pageTemplate_globe.jspx` file from the `oracle/webcenter/portalapp/templates` folder.
2. From the **Component Palette**, select **WebCenter** Link Service from the dropdown list.
3. Drag the **Links Detail** button after the **commandButton** with id `pt_glnk4`.
4. Specify an **ObjectDescription**: This is a description of the link icon.
5. Specify an **ObjectId**: This is the id attribute of the **linkButton**.
6. Specify an **ObjectName**: This will be the name of the button.
7. specify a **ServiceId**: This is an application wide ID.

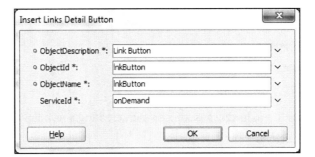

8. Press the **OK** button.
9. In the **Component Pallet** select **Links** from the dropdown list.
10. Drag the **Links** Dialog taskflow after the link button.
11. Run the Portal project.
12. Log in with a user.

You should be able to see the link button. When you click it, it will open the link detail taskflow. In this taskflow you can add links to existing resources or create new resources:

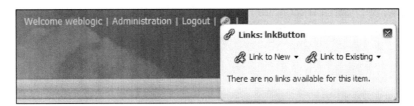

How it works

1. When clicking on the **Link** button the **Links** Dialog taskflow allows you to manage the links for the current page.
2. The **context** menu for the **Link to New** and **Link to Existing** will depend on the services that are enabled in your portal. If you create a connection to a content server then you will see **Document** in the context menu of those buttons.

   In the following example, I have enabled both the document and discussions service

   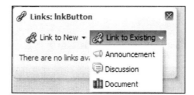

3. Each service will have its own popup. In case you select **Document**, you will see a popup to browse the content server and select an item.
4. In case you select **Discussion** you are able to select a forum and topic. Each service has its own implementation of a popup window for the link service.

Linking to a document

Linking documents is quiet useful in a lot of cases. By linking documents, the users will have a better overview of the content. No need for linking documents in the content itself, just create a link to an existing document. This also allows you to keep the content and document separated.

Getting ready

For this recipe you need a WebCenter Portal application with a connection to a content server. You can find the recipe on how to create a connection to a content server in *Chapter 6, Integrating content with document services*.

You will also need a connection to the WebCenter schemas, which is described in the first recipe of this chapter.

Organizing and Finding Content

How to do it

You first need to add the Link Button to your template or page. Read the previous recipe on how to do it.

1. Run your portal project.
2. Log in with an administrator.
3. Go to the **administration** page.
4. Click on the **Create Page** button.
5. Specify a name for your page.
6. Select the template containing the **Link Button**:

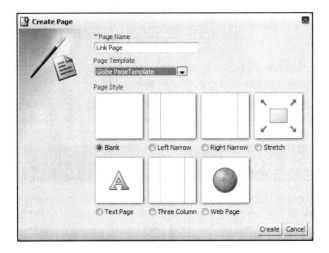

7. Press the **Create** button.
8. Click on your newly created page to browse to it.
9. Press the **link** button to open the **Create Link** dialog.
10. Open the **Link to Existing** menu and select **Document**.

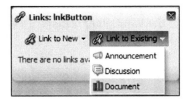

11. Browse to your document and select it.

12. Press the **Select** button to select the document:

Your document is now linked to the page and it should appear in the links dialog:

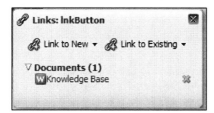

How it works

1. When you create a connection to the content server and set it is as a primary connection, you automatically enable the document service for your portal.
2. The link service will check the available service to see which he can use to link resources.
3. When you select **Document** from the **Link to Existing** menu, you will see a popup that allows you to browse the folders of your content server.
4. When you add different services to your portal or to a single page, then you will be able to link items between services. Suppose that you have added the discussion service and document service to your portal. With the linking service, you can link an existing discussion with a document.

There's more

You can also create a new document while creating a link instead of linking to an existing document.

When you select **Document** from the **Link** to new menu, you will get a popup that allows you to upload a document.

Organizing and Finding Content

In this popup, you can browse to select a folder. When you press the **Upload** button, the document will be added to your content server and a link will be created to that document:

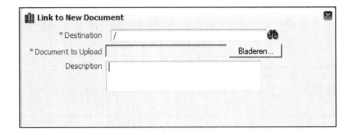

Linking to a discussion

A lot of websites or portals have a separate section for discussions. This is a good idea, but often you want to link a specific page of your portal to a discussion. For example: a page about a specific product. When you link to the part of the forum where people can discuss the product, it will not only help improve the user experience, but it will also help the search engine optimization.

Getting ready

For this recipe you will need a WebCenter Portal application with a connection to a discussion server. In order to create a connection to a discussion server, you can refer to Creating a connection to the discussion service recipe of *Chapter 7, Discussions and Wiki Services.*

You will also need a connection to the WebCenter schema which is described in the first recipe of this chapter.

How to do it...

You first need to add the Link Button to your template or page. Refer to the *Linking content* recipe on how to do this:

1. Run your portal project.
2. Log in with an administrator.
3. Go to the **administration** page.
4. Click on the **Create Page** button.
5. Specify a name for your page.
6. Select the template containing the **Link Button**.
7. Press the **Create** button.

8. Click on your newly created page to browse to it.
9. Press the **link** button to open the **Create Link** dialog.
10. Open the **Link to Existing** menu and select Discussion:

11. In the popup you can select a forum and topic:

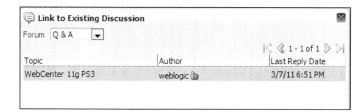

12. Select the topic and press the **link** button.

You should now see the discussion linked in the link dialog:

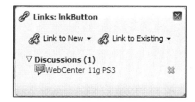

How it works

1. When you create a connection to the discussion server and set it as a primary connection, you automatically enable the discussion service for your portal.
2. The link service will check the available service to see which he can use to link resources.
3. When you select **Discussion** from the **Link to Existing** menu, you will see a popup that allows you to browse the folders of your content server.

Organizing and Finding Content

There's more

You can also link to an existing announcement. Instead of selecting **Discussion**, you will need to select **Announcement** from the **Link to Existing** menu. In the popup, you will see a list of all the existing announcements. Just select one and press the **ok** button.

You can also create a new discussion instead of linking to an existing discussion. Therefore, you need to open the **Link to New** menu in the link dialog taskflow. This will open a popup where you can select the forum, specify the subject, and enter the message of the forum. When you create the discussion, a link will also be created:

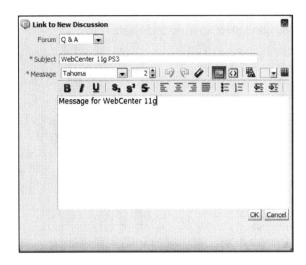

9
Using Polls and Surveys

In this chapter you will learn about:

- ▶ Creating a connection for the poll service
- ▶ Creating a poll
- ▶ Adding a poll to a page
- ▶ Managing sections
- ▶ Managing questions
- ▶ Scheduling a poll
- ▶ Analyzing results
- ▶ Creating a poll template
- ▶ Appling a template to a poll

Introduction

The poll and survey service allows you to create your own polls or surveys. With polls or surveys you can ask your users for their opinion on specific items. For example, you could create a poll asking about the use of a product or how your users like the new portal.

Polls can be as complex as you like. You can create sections, with each containing different questions.

When a poll has been published, you can view the result and analyze the answers of the users. WebCenter shows the different answers in a nice graphical way with bar charts and so on where you can easily analyze the responses.

Creating a connection for the poll services

The poll services use the WebCenter schema. That's why, we first need to create a connection to the WebCenter schema from within JDeveloper.

It is mandatory that you name the connection **WebCenter**.

Getting ready

Before you can create a connection to the WebCenter repository, you first need to create the repository. Normally, this is a mandatory step when you install WebCenter suite. The WebCenter schema gets created by running the RCU (Repository Creation Utility).

How to do it

1. In the Application Navigator right click the **Connection** folder.
2. Select **New Connection** and select **Database** from the context menu.
3. Specify WebCenter for the connection name. It is important you actually call the connection WebCenter. If you give it another name, it will not work!
4. **Connection Type**: Oracle (JDBC).
5. **Username**: The username you specified during the RCU.
6. **Password**: Password for the webcenter schema. You also specified this in the RCU.
7. **Driver**: Thin.
8. **Host name**: The hostname of the database server where the WebCenter schema has been created.
9. **SID**: Service name for the database.
10. Press the **Test Connection** button to see if the parameters are correct:

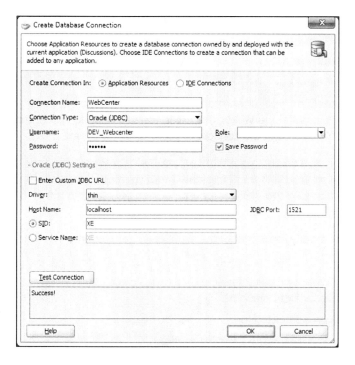

11. Press the **OK** button to create the connection.
12. Select **WebCenterDS** in the Associate Data Source popup window:

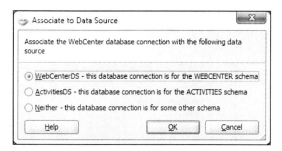

13. Press the **OK** button to close the popup and save your selection.

The connection is now created and you should be able to use the tag and link services.

Using Polls and Surveys

There's more

The poll services require a data source called WebCenter. If you don't have it, those services will not work.

By creating the connection, you allow a connection in JDeveloper, but when you deploy to a managed server or a standalone WebLogic server, you still need to create the data source. You can create a data source in the console of your managed server.

Normally, when you have configured a WebLogic domain for WebCenter, the data sources will be created for you and you don't need to create them yourself. It is possible that you need to modify the targets because the WebCenter data source only targets the WebCenter Spaces server.

This is how you can modify the target of the WebCenter data source in a standalone WebLogic server:

1. Go to your WebLogic console: `http://localhost:7001/console` if you have installed in your local machine.
2. Log in with an administrator.
3. Click **Data Sources** in the Services section:

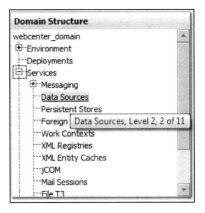

4. Click on **WebCenterDS**. This is the data source used by the link and tagging service.
5. Open the second tab and select **Targets**.
6. Check the checkboxes for each server you want to use the data source on.
7. Press **save**.

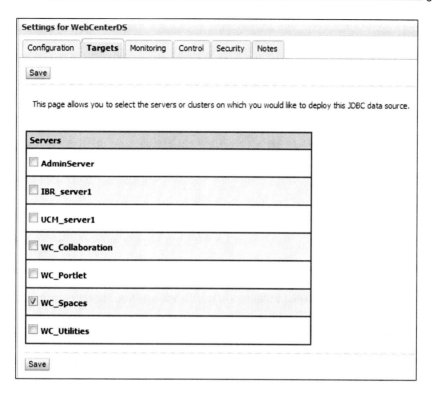

Creating a poll

In this recipe, you will learn how you can create a poll in WebCenter. The poll we create in this recipe will only have a single question. In the next recipe, I will discuss the different types of questions.

Getting ready

For this recipe, you need a WebCenter Portal Application with a connection to the WebCenter schema which is described in the first recipe of this chapter.

How to do it

1. Run the portal project.
2. Log in with an administrator.
3. Go to the administration page.
4. Open the **Services** tab.

Using Polls and Surveys

5. Click on **Polls** from the list on the left.
6. Press the **Create Poll** button.
7. Specify a **Name**.
8. Specify a **Description**.

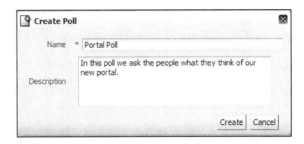

9. Press the **Create** button.
10. When you have pressed the **Create** button, the design mode of the poll will automatically be opened. In this mode you can create your sections and questions.
11. Press the **Add** button in the top right corner.
12. Select **Add question** from the context menu.
13. Select **Multiple Choice (Only one Answer)** from the **Question Type**.
14. Specify a **Question**.
15. Specify the answers. Each row will be a single answer.
16. Enable the **Require Answer to Question checkbox**, so this question will be mandatory:

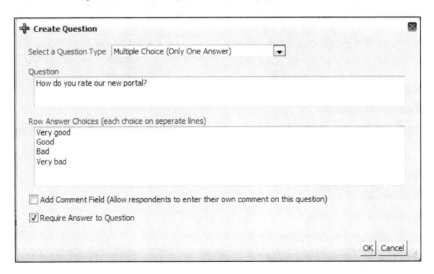

17. Press the **OK** button.

You will now see a preview of the question in design mode:

1. Press the **Save** button and select **Save** from the context menu.
2. Press the **Close** button to close the design mode and return to the poll overview.
3. From the actions menu of the created poll select **Publish** so we can use the poll on our pages:

The poll is now created and published which means that we can use it on our pages. In the next recipe I will show how you can add this poll to a page.

How does it work

A poll exists of sections and questions. Each section can have several questions. As you notice, we didn't define sections so the question we created does not belong to a specific section.

A poll does not get published by default, because you first need to design it. That is why we need to explicitly publish the poll from the overview.

See Also

You can read more about sections in the *Managing Sections* recipe in this chapter.

Adding a poll to a page

When you have published a poll, you want to expose the poll to your users. This can be done by using the Poll taskflow.

In this recipe, I will show how you can add and configure the Poll taskflow.

Getting ready

For this recipe, you will need a WebCenter Portal application with a connection to the WebCenter schema which is described in the first recipe.

How to do it

1. Run the portal project.
2. Log in with an administrator.
3. Go to the administration page.
4. From the **Resource** tab select **Pages**.
5. Press the **Create page** button.
6. Specify **Polls** for the **Page Name**.
7. Don't change the Page Template.
8. Select **Right Narrow** for the **Page Style**:

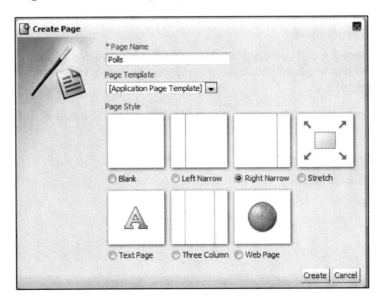

9. Press the **Create** button.
10. Check the **Show Page** checkbox in the overview of the pages.
11. Select **Edit Page** from the actions menu of the Polls page.
12. Press the **Add Content** button in the right column.
13. Open the **Polls and Surveys** folder.
14. Press the **Add** button from the **Take Polls** component:

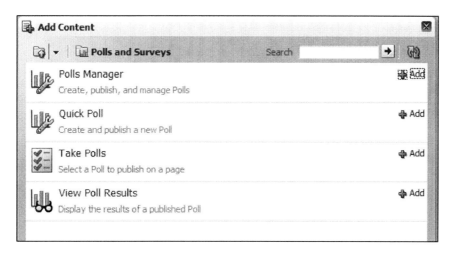

15. Press the **Close** button in the Resource Catalog to close the catalog.
16. Press the **Close** button in the top right corner of the composer to close the edit mode.

You should now see a poll on your page. If you have done the previous recipe than your page might look something like this:

Using Polls and Surveys

How does it work

The Take Poll taskflow will render the poll on your page. It will automatically select the most recent poll.

There's more

Besides showing the most recent poll, you can also select the poll you want to show on the page. This can be done in the configuration of the taskflow:

1. Go to edit mode of a page were you have placed the Take Poll taskflow.
2. Press the **Edit** icon on the **Take Poll** taskflow. This will open the **Component properties** popup.
3. Select the poll you want from the Poll Id dropdown list:

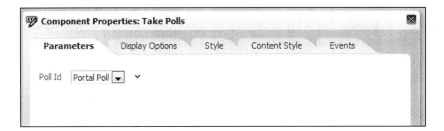

4. Press the **OK** button to close the Component Properties popup.
5. Press the **Close** button to go back to view mode.

Managing sections

When you want to create complex surveys with lots of questions, you may want to divide the survey into sections. A section contains questions that have a common subject. For example if you want to create a survey about a product than you might want to create a section with questions about the use of the product and another section with questions about the service they get related to the product.

In this recipe, I will show you how you can add and manage sections for your survey.

Getting ready

For this recipe, you will need a WebCenter Portal application with a connection to the WebCenter schema configured which is described in the first recipe.

Chapter 9

How to do it

We first need to create a new poll before we can add sections:

1. Run the Portal project.
2. Log in with an administrator.
3. Go to the administration page.
4. From the **Services** tab select **Polls**.
5. Press the **Create Poll service**.
6. Specify a **Name**.
7. Specify a **Description**:

8. Press the **Create** button. When the poll has been created, you will be in design mode so you can design the poll.
9. Press the **Add** button and select **Add Section**.
10. Specify the header of the section in the **Create Section** popup:

Using Polls and Surveys

11. Press the **OK** button.

> The section has its own Add button so you can add questions to that section. We will now add another section to add questions about our service.

12. Select **Add Section** from the Add menu on the **Product Survey**.
13. Specify a body for this section.
14. Press the **OK** button.
15. Press the **Save** button and select **Save** from the context menu.

Your survey should look something like this:

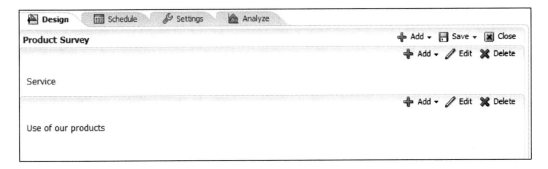

In the next recipe, I will show how you manage questions so you can complete the survey.

Managing questions

Questions are the most important part of your survey. You can't have a poll or survey without a question.

This recipe will show you how you can manage the questions in your survey or poll. We will create a poll and add a question of each type so you can see the difference between the question types.

In the current build of WebCenter, the types of questions are rather limited compared to other survey tools, but in most cases it will be enough.

Getting ready

For this recipe, you need a WebCenter Portal application with a connection to the WebCenter schema configures as described in the first recipe.

Chapter 9

How to do it

1. Run the Portal project.
2. Log in with an administrator.
3. Go to the administration page.
4. From the **Services** tab select Polls.
5. Press the **Create Poll** button.
6. Give the poll a **Name**.
7. Give the poll a **Description**:

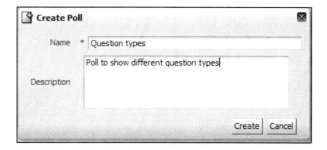

8. Press the **Create** button.
9. Press the **Add** button and select **Add Question** from the context menu.
10. Specify **Multiple Choices (Only One Answer)** for the **Question Type**.
11. Specify a **Question** that only requires a single item.
12. Specify the possible answers in the **Row Answer Choices**:

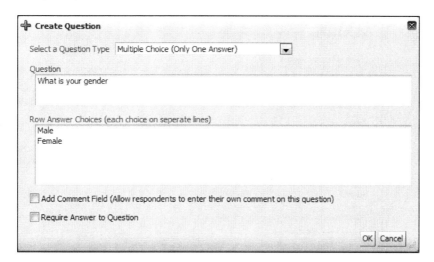

Using Polls and Surveys

13. Press the **OK** button to create the question.
14. Press the **Add button** and select **Add Question** from the context menu.
15. Specify **Multiple Choice (Multiple Answers)** as the question type.
16. Specify a question that can have multiple answers.
17. Specify the possible answers in the **Row Answers Choices**:

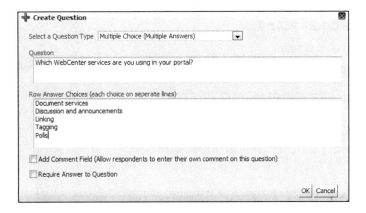

18. Press the **OK** button to create the question.
19. Press the **Add button** and select **Add Question** from the context menu.
20. Specify **Matrix of choices (Only one Answer per row)**.
21. Specify a Question.
22. Specify the values for the row of the matrix in the first text area.
23. Specify the values for the column of the matrix in the second text area:

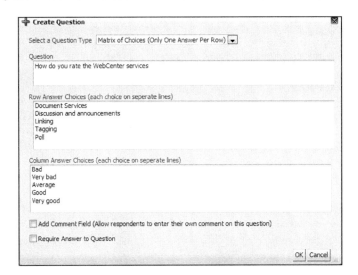

24. Press the **OK** button to create the question.
25. Press the **Add button** and select **Add Question** from the context menu.
26. Specify **Matrix of choices (Multiple Answers per row)** for the **Question type**.
27. Specify the values for the row of the matrix in the first text area.
28. Specify the values for the column of the matrix in the second text area:

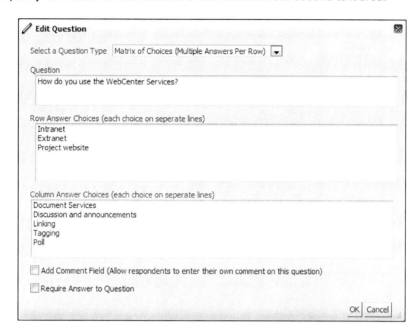

29. Press the **OK** button to create the button.
30. Press the **Save** button on the poll so the questions are saved.
31. Open the **Schedule** tab.
32. Select the **Publish Now** radio button.
33. Press **Save**.

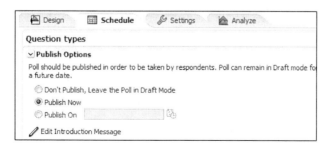

Using Polls and Surveys

We have now created a poll with all the different question types. If you have done the **Add a poll to a page** recipe, you only need to open the page and the newly created poll will be displayed because it always shows the most recent poll:

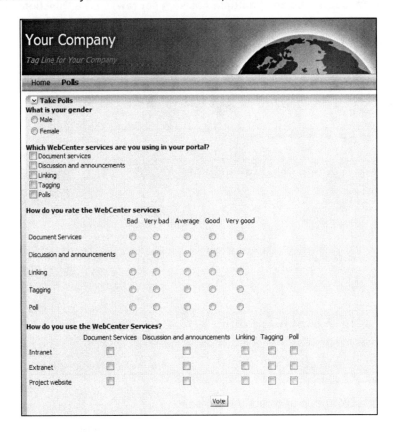

How it works

Each question type has its own characteristics. Based upon the type, the answers will be rendered so it matches the type.

These are the following types:

- **Multiple Choice (Only One Answer)**: Each possible answer will be rendered as a radio button so you can only select a single answer.
- **Multiple Choice (Multiple answers)**: Each possible answer will be rendered as a checkbox, so you can select multiple answers in the question.
- **Matrix of choices (Only one answer per row)**: Allows you to create a matrix of multiple choice questions were you can only select a single question per row. You need to specify the values for the rows and the column.

▶ **Matrix of choices (Multiple answers)**: Allows you to create a matrix of multiple choice questions were you can select multiple answers per row. You need to specify the values for the rows and the columns.

There's more

When you created a question, you cannot change the order in the poll so you need to know the correct order in the poll in advance. When you want to add a question later on, you don't need to remove the questions that already existed before. You can easily add the question between the existing questions.

You notice that each question has an Add button. This determines the order of the question. So if you have four questions and you press the Add button on the second question, then your new question will be added after the second question, before the third.

Scheduling a poll

With the poll service you have different options for publishing a poll. You can just publish a poll without any time constraint. You can also specify a date range when publishing a poll.

In this recipe, we will show you how you can publish a poll with a date constraint.

Getting ready

For this recipe, you will need a Webcenter Portal application with a connection to the WebCenter schema as described in the first recipe of this chapter.

You will also need a poll. If you don't already have polls in your portal, you can refer to the *Creating a poll* recipe.

How to do it

1. Run the portal project.
2. Log in with an administrator.
3. Go to the administration page.
4. From the **Services** tab select Polls.
5. From the action menu of a poll select **Design**.
6. Open the **Schedule** tab.
7. Specify a date in the **Publish On field**.
8. Specify a date in the **Close on Specific date and time**.

9. Press the **Save** button to save your changes.

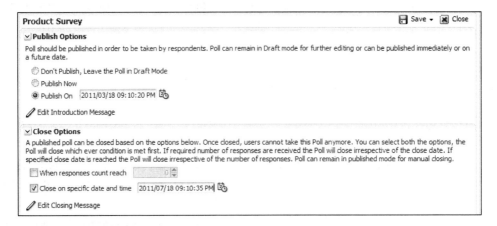

How does it work

By specifying publish and closing date, your poll will only be published within those dates. This allows you to create the polls in advance and schedule them.

There's more

There are other constraints you can put on the poll for closing.

You can also specify the number of responses. In the schedule tab in the Close options you can check the When responses count reach checkbox and specify a value. When you have done this, the poll will close when it has reached the responses provided in the input field:

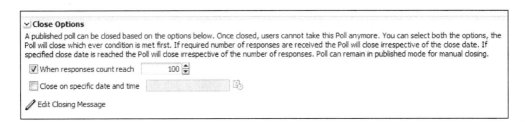

When you have selected both the When responses count reach and the Close on specific date and time, then the poll will close when the first constraint is reached.

In the schedule tab, you also have a Edit Introduction Message link that allows you to specify an introduction message. With this message you can give the user some information about the survey.

You also have a Edit Closing Message which will be displayed when a user has taken the poll.

Analyzing the results

Polls and surveys wouldn't be helpful if you couldn't look at the results and analyze them.

This recipe will show you how you can take a look at the results.

Getting ready

For this recipe you need a WebCenter Portal application with a connection to the WebCenter schema which is described in the first recipe.

You also need a poll with some results. If you don't have such a poll, you can create one as described in the *Creating a poll* recipe. You can take the poll a few times in order to populate the results.

For this recipe, I have taken the poll created in the Managing questions recipe.

How to do it.

1. Run the portal project.
2. Log in with an administrator.
3. Go to the administration page.
4. From the **Services** tab select **Polls**.
5. Select the poll for which you want to view the result.
6. From the actions menu select **Analyze**:

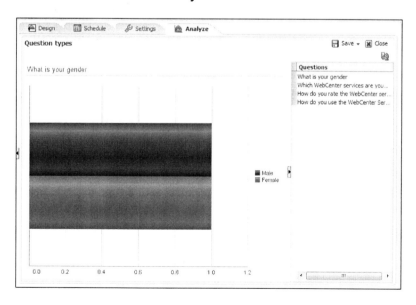

Using Polls and Surveys

On the left hand side you see the result of a question. On the right hand side you can select a specific question and view the results.

How does it work

The analyze tab will generate a graph for each question in the poll. When the question type is a matrix you will see the row values on the x-axis and the values specified in the column of the matrix will be mapped to different colors.

There's more

Instead of a regular 2D graph, you can choose to display the graph in 3D. This can be done in the settings tab of the poll by specifying 3D Graph:

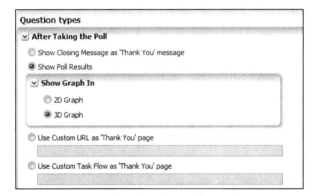

Creating a poll template

You can also create a template from your poll. The advantage of this is that you can build your poll and reuse it later on. Suppose that you are a software company and want to create a poll for each release of your product. Those polls will always have the same questions. Instead of always recreating the same poll, you can create a poll template and apply it when you release new software.

Getting ready

For this recipe you need a WebCenter Portal application with a connection to the WebCenter schema which is described in the first recipe.

How to do it

1. Run the portal project.
2. Log in with an administrator.
3. Go to the administrator page.
4. From the **Service** tab select **Polls**.
5. Press the **Create Poll** button.
6. Specify a **Name** and **Description**:

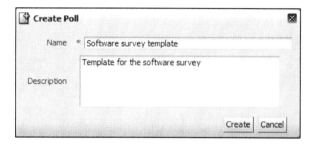

7. Press the **Create** button.
8. Press the **Add** button and select **Add Question**.
9. Specify a **Question Type**.
10. Specify the **Question**.
11. Specify the **Answers**:

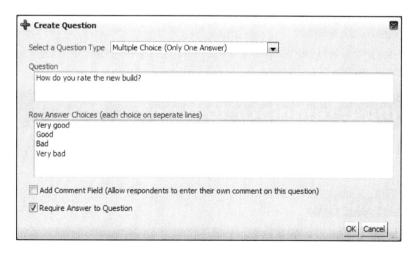

12. Press the **OK** button in order to create the question.

Using Polls and Surveys

13. From the **Save** menu select **Save as template**.

14. Press the **Close** button to go back to the overview of template.
15. As you can see, the poll we just created does not show up in the list of existing polls. This is because it is a template. In order to show the template, we need to select Templates from the Show dropdown list:

How does it work

By saving the poll as a template, the poll will not get published and will not appear in the list of available polls. This way the poll will also never show up for the users.

The template allows you to create new polls based upon the template without needing to create the same questions over and over again.

See also

Previous recipes in this chapter tell you how you can manage sections and questions so you can create complex polls or templates.

Applying a template to a poll

In the previous recipe I showed how you can create a template for a poll. In this recipe you will see how to use that template and apply it to a new poll.

Getting ready

For this recipe you will need a WebCenter Portal application with a connection to the WebCenter schema which is described in the first recipe of this chapter.

Chapter 9

For this recipe you will also need a poll template. If you don't have a template, you can follow the previous recipe which shows how to create a template.

How to do it

1. Run the Portal project.
2. Log in with an administrator.
3. Go to the administration page.
4. From the **Services** tab select **Polls**.
5. Press the **Create Poll** button.
6. Specify a **Name** and **Description**:

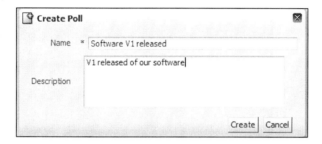

7. Press the **Create** button.
8. From the **Add** menu select **Apply Template**.
9. Select your template from the **Choose From Template** popup:

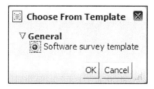

10. Press the **OK** button.
11. From the **Save** menu select **Save** to save the poll.
12. Press the **Close** button to return to the overview.

You now have applied the template to your poll and you should see the questions in your poll.

Using Polls and Surveys

How does it work

When you select the template and apply it to your poll, all the questions and sections that are defined in the template will be added to your poll.

 You have to know that when you apply a template, all the questions you have created in the poll will be replaced with the questions from the template so if you want to add additional questions, you first need to apply the template and add questions after that the template has been applied!

10
Integrating External Content and Applications

In this chapter you will learn how to:

- Register an external application in JDeveloper
- Register an external application at runtime
- Adding an external application to your portal
- Register the WebClipping portlet
- Integrate external content with the WebClipping portlet
- Register the Omniportlet
- Integrate external content with the Omniportlet

Introduction

When you want to build a rich portal for your users where you want to integrate as much content and applications as possible. You want to provide the users with a single user interface to do all their work. Often this will require you to integrate external content or applications. External content often has a different look and feel and not every site offers the possibility to integrate their content with another portal. Some sites offer RSS feeds or expose web services so you can easily integrate them.

Integrating External Content and Applications

In WebCenter, we have lots of features to integrate external content in any way you want. You can also register external applications which mimic SSO capabilities, so the login will be transparent for the users. You can use the WebClipping portlet that allows you to select regions from other websites and include them in your own pages. You can also use Data Controls based upon web services and layout the results as you wish.

All these techniques will be explained in this chapter with a detailed example.

Registering an external application in JDeveloper

An external application is an application not managed by the server you control. This means that you cannot easily setup single sign on with that application. WebCenter provides a technique to automatically post the credentials from your users to these applications so they have the idea that it is SSO-enabled.

This way you can easily integrate other web applications into your portal and your users don't need to navigate away from the portal.

In this recipe, we will register Google groups as an external application so we can integrate the Google groups functionality in our portal.

Getting ready

For this recipe, you need a WebCenter Portal application.

How to do it

1. In JDeveloper right click the **Connections** folder in the **Application Resources**.
2. Select **New Connection** and **External Application** from the context menu.
3. Specify the **Application Name**.
4. Specify the **Application Display Name**.

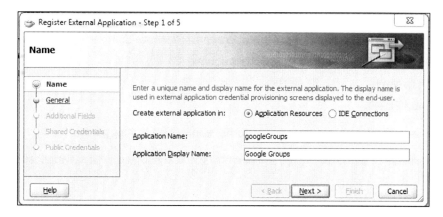

5. Press **Next**.
6. Specify the login URL. This is the URL where you can find the login form. For Google Groups I use the following URL: **https://www.google.com/accounts/ServiceLog in?service=groups2&passive=1209600&continue=http://groups.google.com/ &followup=http://groups.google.com/**
7. Specify the **User Name/ID Field Name** of the HTML input text in the login form. For Google Groups this is Email.
8. Specify the **Password field Name**. For Google Groups this is **Passwd**:

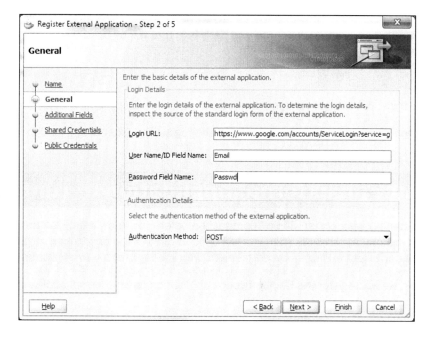

Integrating External Content and Applications

9. Press **Next**.
10. Press **Next** in the **Additional Fields** screen because we do not need additional fields.
11. Press **Next** in the **Shared Credentials** screen.
12. Press **Next**.
13. Press **Finish**.

You have now successfully registered an external application to your portal.

In the third recipe of this chapter, you will see how you can use this external application in your portal.

How it works

In order to integrate an external application, you first need to know the correct login URL and the HTML field for both the username and password. This is used because WebCenter will mimic the login by posting the username and password to these fields.

There's more

In this recipe I have skipped the public and shared credentials. These can be used if you don't want your users to login with their own account but instead use a shared login that will be used by everybody.

The public credentials are the username and password that will be used for anonymous users.

See also

In the next recipe, you will see how you can register an external application at runtime.

In the third recipe, you will see how you can use the registered external application in your portal.

Register an external application at runtime

More often than not your portal will be in production before you know it and you have to integrate an external application. Then you will need to register the application at runtime because you don't want to deploy the portal each time you register a new application.

In this recipe, we will register the Google Groups application as an external application.

Getting ready

For this recipe you will need a WebCenter Portal application.

How to do it

1. Run the portal project.
2. Log in with an administrator.
3. Go to the **administration** page.
4. Open the **Services** tab.
5. Select **External Applications** from the menu on the left.
6. Press the **Register** button.
7. Specify an **Application Name**.
8. Specify a **Display Name**.
9. Check the **Enable Automatic Login** checkbox.
10. Specify the login URL. For Google Groups this is: **https://www.google.com/accounts/ServiceLogin?service=groups2&passive=1209600&continue=http://groups.google.com/&followup=http://groups.google.com/**
11. Specify the **HTML USER ID Field Name**, which represents the HTML field for the username on the login form.
12. Specify the **HTML User Password Field Name**, which represents the password on the login form.

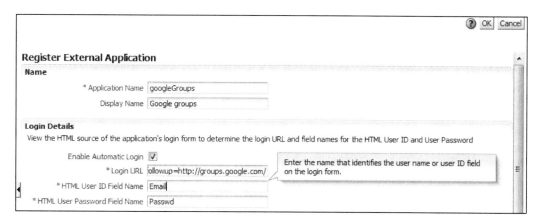

13. Press the **OK** button in the top right corner.

The application is now registered and you can use it in your portal. This will be shown in the next recipe.

Integrating External Content and Applications

How it work

In order to integrate an external application you first need to know the correct login URL and the HTML field for both the username and password. These fields are used because WebCenter will mimic the login by posting the username and password to these fields.

There's more

Below the **Login Details** section, you have a few more sections:

- **Authentication details**: These details allow you to specify what method is used to post the values from the form. These are the default form action values like POST and GET.
- **Additional Login fields**: In this section you can specify additional fields. When you have hidden input fields on the login form, you should add these fields in this section. These will also be posted when you log in to the external application.
- **Shared Credentials**: When you enable the shared credentials, all authenticated users will use the same username and password combination to log in to the external application.
- **Public Credentials**: When the public credentials are enabled, you specify the username and password that will be posted when an anonymous user tries to access the external application.

See also

In the next recipe, you will see how you can use a registered external application in your portal.

Adding an external application to your portal

Once you have registered an external application, you want to make it available for all your users. This can be done by adding the external application as a link to your navigation model.

When the users open the external application for the first time, they will need to enter their personal username and password. They also will have the option to store their credentials so the next time they open the application; they no longer need to provide their credentials.

In this recipe, we will add the external application that we registered at runtime.

Getting ready

For this recipe you need a WebCenter Portal application with a registered external application.

Chapter 10

If you don't have an external application, you can follow the previous recipe. This will show you how to add an external application in JDeveloper, so you can use it in this recipe.

How to do it

1. In JDeveloper open the `default-navigation-model.xml` from the `oracle/webcenter/portalapp/navigations` directory.
2. Select the **default-navigation-model** node.
3. Press the **Add** button and select **Link** from the context menu.
4. Specify an **ID** for your link.
5. Specify **External Application** as the type.
6. Click the **browse** button next to the URL field and select the external application:

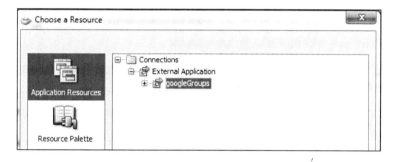

7. Press the **OK** button in the **Choose a Resource popup**.
8. Specify a **Title** for the link that will be shown in the navigation:

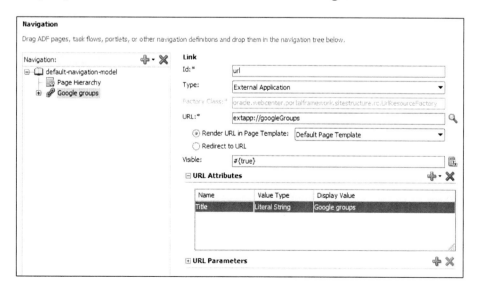

Integrating External Content and Applications

9. Save the navigation model.
10. Run the Portal project.
11. Log in with a user.

You now should see the link to the Google Groups application:

How it work

An external application needs to be linked in the navigation model. You cannot add it to a resource catalog; it can only be a navigation resource.

When you open the link to the application, you will first see the login page for external applications by Webcenter:

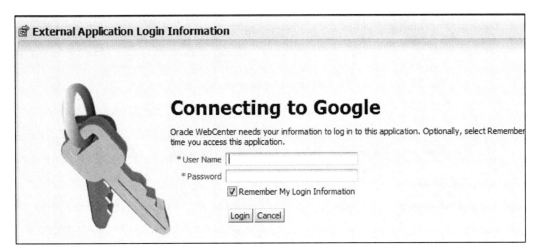

This is the screen where users enter their credentials for the external application.

When they check the **Remember My Login Information**, the next time they open the external application, the username and password will be automatically posted to the external application so they no longer need to provide their credentials.

Chapter 10

Register the WebClipping portlet

The WebClipping allows you to integrate content from other sites that you don't control. It allows you to select a specific region based upon a URL and the portlet will include the content of that region into the portlet.

Getting ready

For this recipe, you will need a WebCenter Portal application.

The `WC_Portlet` managed server from a WebCenter domain must also be running.

How to do it

1. Open a browser and browse to `http://<host>:<port>/portalTools/webClipping`. When you have installed a WebCenter domain on your localhost, the URL will be: `http://localhost:8889/portalTools/webClipping`.

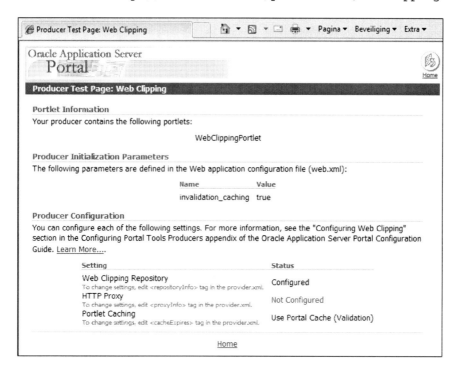

2. Copy the URL to your clipboard.
3. Open JDeveloper with your WebCenter Portal application.
4. Run the portal project.

225

Integrating External Content and Applications

5. Log in with an administrator.
6. Go to the **administration** page.
7. Open the **Services** tab.
8. Select **Portlet Producers** from the menu on the left.
9. Click on the **Register** button.
10. Specify a name for the producer.
11. Select **Oracle PDK-Java Producer** as the **Producer Type**.
12. Paste the URL from step 2 in the URL **Endpoint** field.
13. Press the **Test** button to test the producer.

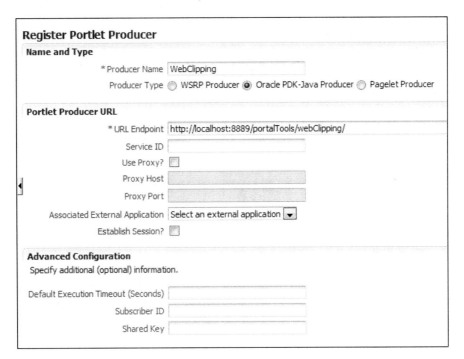

14. Press the **Ok** button.

You now have successfully registered the WebClipping portlet. In the next recipe, you will learn how to use it.

How it work

The WebClipping portlet is a portlet that comes from the Oracle Portal world. It is a rather old portlet that has been used a lot. For WebCenter they have made some changes so it is compatible with WebCenter.

It isn't a JSR168 portlet producer but a producer created with the Oracle PDK framework. That's why we don't need to register it as a WSRP producer.

The portlet is also part of the portal tools that are deployed by default on the portlet server that comes with a WebCenter domain. That's why we need the portlet server to be up and running.

Integrating external content with the WebClipping portlet

By using the WebClipping portlet, you are able to integrate external content from sites you do not control. For example you want to integrate a page from Amazon that shows some products. You only want to show the list, not all the menus or left and right sidebars, so an iframe is just not possible.

This is where the WebClipping comes into play. It allows you to clip specific regions from a webpage so you can integrate it in your portal.

Getting ready

For this recipe, you need a WebCenter Portal application where you have registered the WebClipping portlet. The recipe on how to register the WebClipping portlet can be found in the previous recipe.

How to do it

We first will add a page where we will be adding the WebClipping portlet:

1. In JDeveloper run the Portal project.
2. Log in with an administrator.
3. Go to the **Administration** page.
4. In the **Resource** tab select Pages from the menu on the left.
5. Press the **Create Page** button.
6. Specify **Amazon** as the Page Name.

Integrating External Content and Applications

7. Press the **Create** button.

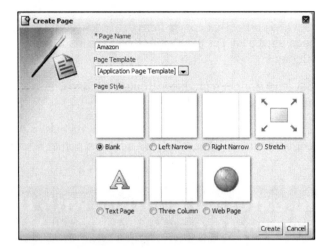

8. Check the **Show Page** checkbox in the overview for the Amazon page so that the page is available in the navigation.
9. Select **Edit** Page from the **Page Actions** menu.
10. Press the **Add Content** button.
11. Open the **Portlets** folder.
12. Open the **WebClipping** folder.
13. Press the **Add** button on the **WebClipping Portlet**:

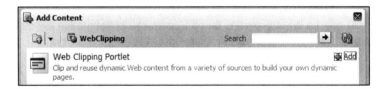

14. Press the **Customize** button:

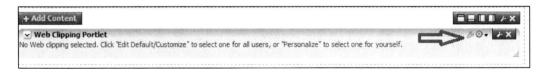

15. Specify the URL of the external page that you want to integrate. For this recipe we use a search on WebCenter books on Amazon. The URL for this is the following: `http://www.amazon.com/s/ref=nb_sb_noss?url=search-alias%3Daps&field-keywords=webcenter`. Paste that URL in the URL Location field.

16. Press the **Start** button.
17. Press the **Section** button in the top right corner:

18. Click the **Choose link** on the section with the results:

19. Press the **Select** button in the top right on the page to finalize the selection.
20. Specify a title for the WebClipping portlet.
21. Specify a description.

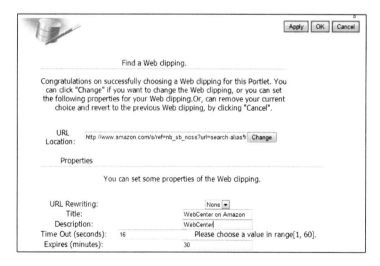

22. Press the **OK** button in the top right corner to close the customization.
23. Close the Composer by clicking on the **Close** button in the top right corner of the page.

Integrating External Content and Applications

The integration is now done and when you visit the page it should look something like this:

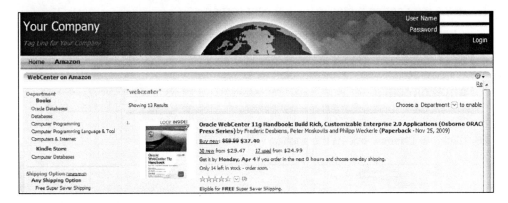

How it work

When you enter the URL of the external page and press the Start button, the WebClipping portlet will parse the HTML of that page and tries to identify different sections. This can be based upon tables, divs or other containers in HTML.

When you select a specific section, the WebClipping portlet will only show the HTML from the container you have selected.

This means that you cannot select whatever you want. You are still dependent on how the developers of the external page have designed their pages.

Registering the Omniportlet

The Omniportlet is a portlet like the WebClipping portlet. It was created for Oracle Portal so it is a PDK portlet. With the Omniportlet you can integrate external resources like CSV's, web services, database queries and so on. It also allows you to layout the output so it fits right into your portal.

Before you can use the Omniportlet, you will need to register it. This is a similar process to registering the WebClipping portlet.

Getting ready

For this recipe you will need a WebCenter Portal application.

The `WC_Portlet` managed server from a WebCenter domain must also be running.

Chapter 10

How to do it

1. Open a browser and browse to `http://<host>:<port>/portalTools/omniPortlet`. When you have installed a WebCenter domain on your localhost, the URL will be: `http://localhost:8889/portalTools/omniPortlet`.

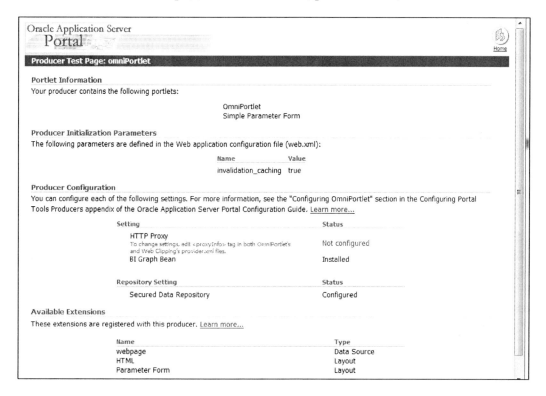

2. Copy the URL to your clipboard.
3. Open JDeveloper with your WebCenter Portal application.
4. Run the portal project.
5. Login with an administrator.
6. Go to the **administration** page.
7. Open the **Services** tab.
8. Select **Portlet Producers** from the menu on the left.
9. Click on the **Register** button.
10. Specify a name for the producer.
11. Select **Oracle PDK-Java Producer** as the **Producer Type**.
12. Paste the URL from step 2 in the **URL Endpoint** field.

13. Press the **Test** button to test the producer.

14. Press the **OK** button.

You have now successfully registered the Omniportlet. In the next recipe, you will learn how to use it.

How it work

The Omniportlet is a portlet that comes from the Oracle Portal world. It is a rather old portlet that has been used a lot. For WebCenter they have made some changes so it isn't a JSR168 portlet producer but a producer created with the Oracle PDK framework. That's why we don't need to register it as a WSRP producer.

The portlet is also part of the portal tools that are deployed by default on the portlet server that comes with a WebCenter domain. That's why we need the portlet server to be up and running.

Integrating external content with the Omniportlet

With the Omniportlet you can integrate pretty much everything you want. It is a powerful portlet.

In this recipe, I will use the Omniportlet to generate a table to compare the stock values of Oracle, Microsoft, IBM, and Apple.

Getting ready

For this recipe you need a WebCenter Portal application.

Chapter 10

You also need the Omniportlet for this recipe. The previous recipe shows how you can register the Omniportlet to your application.

How to do it

Before we can use the Omniportlet, you first need the URL of the CSV. The base for the Yahoo stock server is: `http://download.finance.yahoo.com/d/quotes.csv`. You can add all the list of quotes you want. If we want Oracle, Microsoft, IBM, and Apple the URL will be: `http://download.finance.yahoo.com/d/quotes.csv?s=ORCL+MSFT+IBM+AAPL&f=snl1d1t1ohgdr`

This is what we will be using in the Omniportlet:

1. In JDeveloper run the Portal project.
2. Log in with an administrator.
3. Go to the **Administration** page.
4. In the **Resource** tab select **Pages** from the menu on the left.
5. Press the **Create Page** button.
6. Specify **Stock** as the **Page Name**.
7. Press the **Create** button:

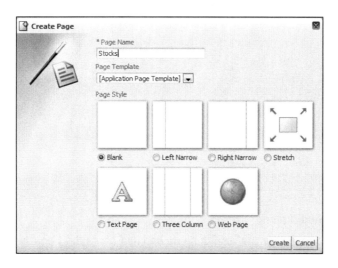

8. Press the **Create** button.
9. Check the **Show Page** checkbox so the page will be shown in the navigation.
10. Select **Edit** Page from the page actions.
11. Press the **Add Content** button to open the **Resource Catalog**.

12. Open the **Portlet** folder.
13. Open the **Omniportlet** folder.
14. Press the **Add** button on the Omniportlet.
15. Close the Resource Catalog.
16. Press the **Customize** button on the Omniportlet.

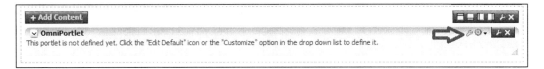

17. Select **Spreadsheet** and press the **Next** button.
18. Enter `http://download.finance.yahoo.com/d/quotes.csv?s=ORCL+MSFT+IBM+AAPL&f=snl1d1t1ohgdr` as the CSV URL
19. Uncheck the **Use first row of spreadsheet for column names** checkbox because the Yahoo stock service does not provide column names:

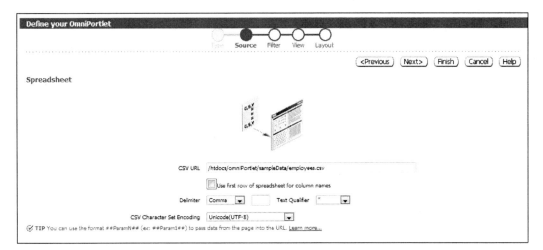

20. Press the **Next** button.
21. We don't need to filter the results so we can just press **Next** on the filter screen.
22. Specify **Stocks** as the title.
23. Uncheck the **Show Header text** and **Show Footer text**.
24. Specify **HTML** as the **Layout Style**:

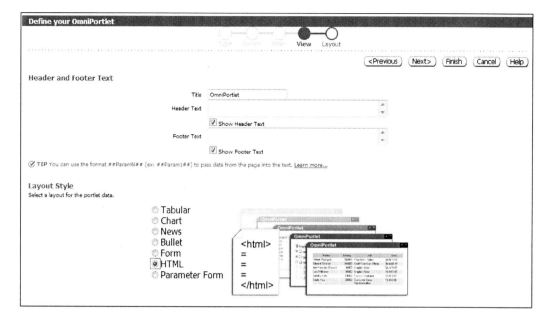

25. Press the **Next** button.
26. Specify the following HTML code for the Non-Repeating Heading Section:
    ```
    <TABLE BORDER='0' WIDTH="100%">
      <TR CLASS='PortletSubHeaderColor'>
        <TH CLASS='PortletHeading1'>Stock</TH>
        <TH CLASS='PortletHeading1'>Corporation</TH>
        <TH CLASS='PortletHeading1'>Value</TH>
      </TR>
    ```
27. Specify the following HTML code for the Repeating Section:
    ```
    <TR CLASS='PortletText1'>
      <TD>##column1##</TD>
      <TD>##column2##</TD>
      <TD>##column3##</TD>
    </TR>
    ```
28. Specify following HTML code for the Non-Repeating Footer Section </TABLE>
29. Press the **Finish** button.
30. Close the composer by clicking the **Close** button in the top right corner of the page.

Integrating External Content and Applications

You have now successfully integrated the stock values on your page. It should look something like this:

How it work

The Omniportlet is a complex portlet that allows you to integrate all sorts of content.

In the first step we need to decide the type of content:

- **Spreadsheet (CSV)**: It allows you to provide the portlet with a URL to a CSV that can be used as input for the data of the portlet.
- **SQL**: Provide an SQL statement as the input of your portlet. You can also define the connection to the database for the SQL.
- **XML**: Provide the URL to an XML file that will be used as input for the data of the portlet.
- **Web Service**: Provide a WSDL for a web service. You also will need to provide which method you want to execute that will return some data for the Omniportlet.
- **Web Page**: Here you can provide a URL to an external web page, which provide similar functionality as the WebClipping portlet.

In the next step, the Source step, you need to define the specification of your source. This step depends on what type of data you have selected in the first step. In our case, we have selected a CSV so we need to provide the URL to a CSV. This can be an external URL but it can also be the location to a path on the server.

In the Filter step, we can filter out data. With the user interface you can easily build conditions.

It is also possible to specify an order by clause. Suppose that we would like to order our stock quotes based upon the current value than we would need to specify column-3 as the first order by column.

A last configuration we can do in the filter tab is to limit our results. This can be useful when the source gives lots of rows and you only want to show the top ten.

In the next screen we need to define how the data will be shown on the portlet:

- **Tabular**: Show the data in a table
- **Chart**: Create a chart based upon the data
- **News**: Each item will have a title and small detail
- **Bullet**: Show the data as a list
- **Form**: Create input fields for each column that can be used to execute web service
- **HTML**: With the HTML view, you can specify your own HTML, so you can customize the output as you like
- **Parameter form**: Can be used to execute web services or enter the values for bind variables in your query

The Layout screen also depends on what you have chosen in the View screen.

In this recipe we have selected HTML so we can provide the portlet with our own HTML. When you select HTML you can provide a non repeating header. This will be outputted only once. The next text area is the one that will be outputted for each row in our result, and the last is the footer that will be outputted when all the rows are iterated.

11
WebCenter Spaces

In this chapter, you will learn about:

- Creating a discussion and announcement service connection
- Creating a document service connection
- Registering external applications
- Registering a portlet producer
- Creating a group space
- Enabling additional pages
- Creating subspaces
- Creating lists
- Creating a space template
- Exporting group spaces
- Importing group spaces

Introduction

WebCenter Spaces is designed to provide a collaborative environment. It integrates all the necessary services such as documents, discussions, events, linking, tagging, and so on.

In WebCenter Spaces, you build group spaces. Each space is a separate mini-portal with its own configuration, look and feel, security model, and services. Spaces can be created as a child of another space.

WebCenter Spaces is ideal to build intranets where you have to collaborate a lot with your colleagues. Let's take a software developer as an example. Each project can have their own space, so you could set up a wiki, document library, discussions, and so on. All these resources will be the same. Or suppose you are a software vendor. Each product can have their own space, so you can group documents, support, and discussions that are related to one product. If a product is part of a division, you could create parent group spaces for each division with each product as a child space.

WebCenter Spaces also has a rich set of features for social networking. It has Facebook-like features: you can invite other people to your network, write on their wall, and so on.

In this chapter, you will learn how to configure and use WebCenter Spaces so you can get the most out of it.

In the first part of this chapter, we will manage the connections to the different services.

With WebCenter Spaces, you have a very powerful tool in your hands. It allows you to build collaborative intranets without needing to develop a lot. The problem you will be having with WebCenter Spaces is that it is not as easily customizable as a regular WebCenter Portal application. Therefore, you can combine the best of both worlds. When you need a high level of customization or you need to extend the site with your custom functionality, then you should create a WebCenter Portal application. When you need a collaborative environment where customization or added functionality is not as important as the collaborative services, then go for WebCenter Spaces.

Creating a discussion and announcement service connection

A collaborative environment is nothing without a place to discuss. Before you can use discussions and announcements in your WebCenter Spaces environment, we first need to configure the connection in the Enterprise Manager.

Getting ready

For this recipe, you need a working WebCenter domain with at least the AdminServer, WebCenter Spaces server, and WebCenter Collaboration server running.

How to do it...

1. Go to the Enterprise Manager (`http://localhost:7001/em`).
2. Log in as the administrator.
3. On the left, open the **WebCenter** folder.
4. Open the **WebCenter Spaces** node.

5. Select the **webcenter** node:

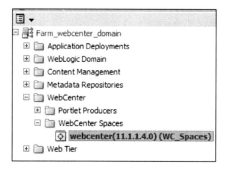

6. On top, select **WebCenter**.
7. Select **Settings | Service Configuration** from the context menu:

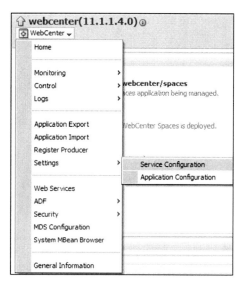

8. Select **Discussions and Announcement** from the list on the left.
9. Press the **Add** button to create a new connection.
10. Specify a **Name** for the connection.
11. Check the **Active Connection**.
12. Specify the **URL** of the discussion server.
13. Specify the **Administrator User Name**.
14. Press **test** to test the connection.

WebCenter Spaces

15. Press **OK** to save the connection:

You will notice that when you press the **test** button, you will get a message that you will need to restart the Spaces server before the connection will take effect. This is because connections are initialized during the startup of the server.

How it works...

Although you can have multiple connections to different discussion servers, there must be at least one that has been set as the active server. This connection will be used by default. If you don't have an active connection, you always have to provide the name of the connection in the configuration of the discussion and announcement taskflows.

The URL of the discussion server is of the format `http://<host>:<port>/<context root>`. When you have a default installation, the URL will be `http://localhost:8890/owc_discussions`.

See also

For more information about the discussion and announcement service, you can read the recipes in *Chapter 7*. They will tell you how to use the different taskflows. The same taskflows are used in WebCenter Spaces.

Creating a document service connection

The document service is a popular service in WebCenter Spaces. It allows you to share documents and provide comments on documents. In combination with other services, you can tag documents or link documents with discussions, and so on.

Before you can use the discussion services, you first will need to create a connection in the enterprise manager.

Getting ready

For this recipe, you need a working WebCenter domain with at least the AdminServer, WebCenter Spaces server and UCM server running.

How to do it...

1. Go to the Enterprise Manager (`http://localhost:7001/em`).
2. Log in as the administrator.
3. On the left, open the **WebCenter** folder.
4. Open the **WebCenter Spaces** node.
5. Select the **webcenter** node.
6. On top, select **WebCenter**.
7. Select **Settings | Service Configuration** from the context menu.
8. Select **Content Repository** from the list of services.
9. Press the **Add** button to create a new connection.
10. Specify a **name** for the connection.
11. Select the **type** of content repository.
12. Check the **Active Connection** if you want to make this the primary connection.
13. Specify the **Content Administrator**.
14. Specify a **root folder** for the documents.
15. Enter an **Application Name**. This is used to identify the documents that are uploaded by WebCenter Spaces.
16. Specify **Socket** as the **RIDC Socket Type**.
17. Specify the **server Host**: localhost.
18. Specify the **Server Post**: 4444.
19. Specify the **Administrator User Name**.
20. Press **test** to test the connection.

WebCenter Spaces

21. Press **OK** to save the connection:

How it works...

When you select the **Active Connection** checkbox, you will get the WebCenter Spaces Content Repository section. In this section, you need to specify additional parameters so that the connection can be used as the primary connection for WebCenter Spaces.

If you select the Socket type connection, you also need to configure UCM so the socket connection will be enabled. In a default installation, the socket connection is disabled. That's why you need to enable it. For this, you can read the first recipe of *Chapter 6*. This explains how to prepare UCM for a remote connection.

There's more...

When you have installed and configured a web tier on your middleware and you have configured the Oracle HTTP server for both WebCenter Spaces and UCM, then you can enable more integration features between UCM and WebCenter. For this, you also need to provide the **Web Server Context Root** in the connection setting. When both WebCenter Spaces and UCM are configured to the same host and port via the OHS, then you will also be able to use check-in profiles and more Site Studio features in WebCenter Spaces.

The configuration for the OHS can be found in the WebCenter Administration guide: http://download.oracle.com/docs/cd/E17904_01/webcenter.1111/e12405/wcadm_app_http.htm#BABHIGHC.

Chapter 11

See also

Chapter 6 explains the different taskflows and how to use them. You will be able to use most of these recipes in WebCenter Spaces.

Registering external Applications

When you use a collaborative environment, you also want your users to be able to use external applications. When you register external applications, you allow WebCenter Spaces to mimic the single sign on process. This way, the applications looks integrated into your portal.

Getting ready

For this recipe, you need a working WebCenter domain with at least the AdminServer and WebCenter Spaces server.

How to do it...

1. Go to the Enterprise Manager (http://localhost:7001/em).
2. Log in as the administrator.
3. On the left, open the **WebCenter** folder.
4. Open the **WebCenter Spaces** node.
5. Select the **webcenter** node.
6. On top, select **WebCenter**.
7. Select **Settings | Service Configuration** from the context menu.
8. Select **External Application** from the list of services.
9. Specify an **Application Name**.
10. Specify a **Display Name**.
11. Check the **Enable Automatic Login** checkbox.
12. Specify the **Login URL**.
13. Specify the **HTML USER ID Field name** which represents the HTML field for the username on the login form.

WebCenter Spaces

14. Specify the **HTML User Password Field Name**, which represents the password on the login form:

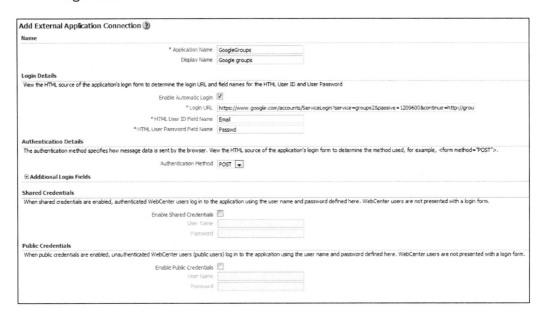

15. Press the **OK** button to create the connection.

How it works...

In order to integrate an external application, you first need to know the correct login URL and the HTML field for both the username and password. This is used because WebCenter will mimic the login by posting the username and password to these fields.

There's more...

Below the **Login Details** section, you have a few more sections:

- **Authentication Details**: This allows you to specify what method is used to post the values from the form. These are the default form action values like POST and GET.

- **Additional Login Fields**: In this section, you can specify additional fields. When you have hidden input fields on the login form, you should add these fields in this section. These will also be posted when you log in to the external application.

- **Shared Credentials**: when you enable the shared credentials, all authenticated users will use the same username and password combination to log in to the external application.

- **Public Credentials**: When the public credentials are enabled, you specify the username and password that will be posted when an anonymous user tries to access the external application.

See also

In *Chapter 10*, you can find more information about the connection to external applications and how to use them in your portal.

Registering a portlet producer

One of the things that you will need to do a lot is register a portlet producer. Portlets allow you to extend the portal. Each provider can have multiple portlets. WebCenter Spaces uses Web Service for Remote Portlets (WSRP) to register portlets. This allows you to deploy portlets on a different server than the portal itself. This is especially useful for scalability.

Getting ready

For this recipe, you need a working WebCenter domain with at least the AdminServer and WebCenter Spaces server.

How to do it...

1. Go to the Enterprise Manager (`http://localhost:7001/em`).
2. Log in as the administrator.
3. On the left, open the **WebCenter** folder.
4. Open the **WebCenter Spaces** node.
5. Select the **webcenter** node
6. On top, select **WebCenter**.
7. Select **Settings | Service Configuration** from the context menu.
8. Select **Portlet Producers** from the list of services.
9. Press the **Add** button to create a new connection.
10. Specify the **type** of producer.
11. Specify a name for the producer.
12. Specify the **WSDL URL** in case you have selected WSRP Producer as the type.
13. Specify a **proxy** in case the WSRP is behind a proxy.
14. Press the **test** button to test the connection.

WebCenter Spaces

15. Press the **OK** button to save the connection:

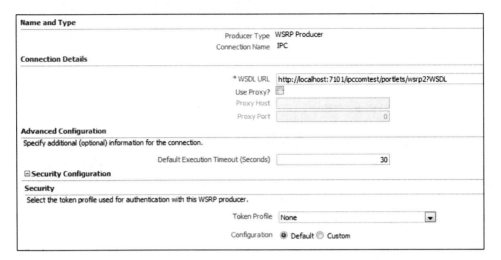

How it works...

There are different portlet producers that you can register in WebCenter:

- **WSRP producer**: Register a portlet producer by entering a WSDL URL.
- **Oracle PDK Producer**: Producer created by the Portlet Development Kit for Java by Oracle. This is an SDK for portlets that dates back from Oracle Portal.
- **Pagelet Producer**: A WebCenter-specific producer.

When you have registered a producer, the content will automatically be added to the resource catalog so you can begin to add the portlets to your pages.

See also

You can read *Chapter 2* on how to consume portlets. This chapter will show you how you can add and use portlets on your pages.

Creating a group space

When you build a collaborative portal, you will divide the portal into different groups. Each group can be seen as a micro portal. It can have its own set of users, services, security model, and so on.

Suppose you have a company with multiple divisions, then it seems like a good idea to provide each division with their own group space. Each division will have their own section on the portal to store documents, discuss with people, build a wiki, and so on.

In this recipe, I will show you how to create a group space.

Getting ready

For this recipe, you need a working WebCenter Spaces environment.

How to do it...

1. Open WebCenter Spaces: `http://localhost:8888/webcenter`.
2. Log in as an administrator.
3. Press the **Spaces** link in the top menu.
4. Select **Create a Space** from the context menu.
5. Specify a **name** for the Space.
6. Specify a **description**.
7. Specify **keywords** that describe the space:

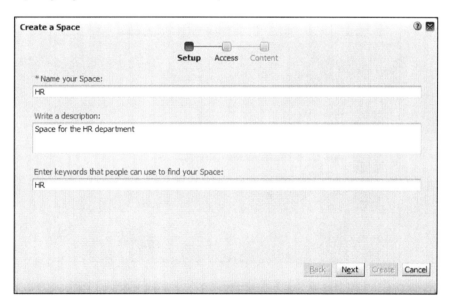

8. Press the **Next** button.
9. Specify the **URL** that will be used for this space.

10. Specify the **access level** for your space:

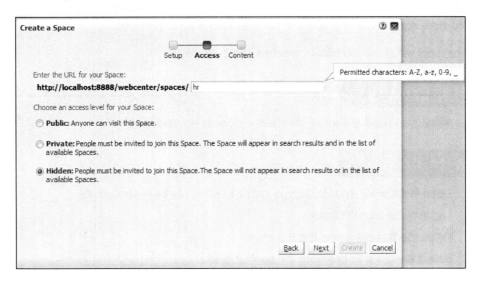

11. Press the **Next** button.
12. Select a template .
13. Press the **create** button:

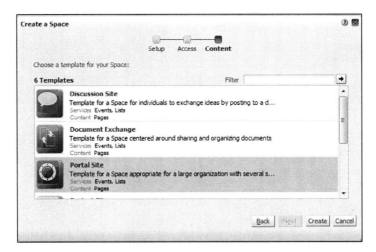

When you have created the space, you will be redirected to the home page of the space. From now on, you can start building the space by adding pages and services.

How it works...

In the first step, you need to specify the name and description of your space. The keywords can be used in combination with the search service. This way, people can find the space if they are looking for specific keywords.

In the second step, you need to provide the URL of your space. This is used so you can have a clean URL instead of an URL with a large GUID in it.

You also need to provide the access level:

- Public: Everybody can access the space without needing to ask approval.
- Private: People cannot access this space unless they are invited by a moderator. This space will also appear in the search list and list of all spaces.
- Hidden: This is the same as the private access level, but this type of space does not appear in the search list or list of available spaces.

As a last step, you can elect to build your space based upon some predefined templates. These templates configure the space in such a way that you can easily start building it without needing to configure lots of other things.

These are the available templates:

- Discussion Site: Enables the discussion and announcement service. This requires an active connection to the discussion and announcement service as described in the first recipe of this chapter.
- Document Exchange: Template that can be used to exchange documents. It will need an active connection to a content repository as described in the second recipe of this chapter.
- Portal Site: This is a template ideal for departments of sites.
- Project Site: Template that can be used to manage a project. It will enable a calendar and service to share information like documents and wiki. This template also requires a content repository connection.
- Team Site: Template ideal for building spaces for a team.
- Blogger: Creates a space that is build for blogging. Blog articles are also stored in the content server, so this template also requires an active connection to the content server.

WebCenter Spaces

See also

In order to manage pages, resource catalogs, and navigation models, you can read *Chapters 1*, *3*, and *4*. The techniques described there can also be used in WebCenter Spaces. All the recipes describing how to do things at runtime are the exact same in Spaces. You can access the resource manager in the Resource tab of the settings of a group space. This resource manager is the exact same as when you create a WebCenter Portal, so all the recipes apply here as well.

Enabling additional pages

When you create a group space based upon a template, it will create some extra pages. By default, they aren't visible in the navigation model.

In this recipe, I will show how you can make those pages available in the navigation model.

Getting ready

For this recipe, you need a WebCenter Spaces environment with an existing group space.

How to do it...

1. Open WebCenter Spaces: http://localhost:8888/webcenter.
2. Log in as an administrator.
3. Press the **Spaces** link in the top menu.
4. Open an existing group space.
5. Open the actions menu.
6. Select **Manage | Pages** from the context menu:

7. Check the checkbox in the **Show Page** column for each page you want to include in the navigation model.

When you have selected the Show Page column, you will directly see the link appear in the navigation model.

How it works...

This behaviour is default navigation model behaviour. All these pages are included in the navigation model, but they have the visible property set to false. By checking the **Show Page**, you set the visible property to true and the link will be shown in the navigation.

It does not mean that the pages are not available when the checkbox is not set. You can access them if you know the correct URL.

Creating subspaces

From WebCenter PS3, you can create a hierarchy of spaces. Each space can have multiple child spaces and each child space can also have multiple child spaces.

Suppose you have an international company, you could create spaces for each country the company is working in. In each space, you can create a subspace for a division that operates in that country.

Getting ready

For this recipe, you need a WebCenter Space environment.

How to do it...

1. Open WebCenter Spaces: `http://localhost:8888/webcenter`.
2. Log in as an administrator.
3. Press the **Spaces** link in the top menu.
4. Open an existing group space.
5. Open the actions menu.
6. Select **Create | Subspace** from the context menu:

7. Specify a **name** for your space.
8. Specify a **description** for your space.

9. Specify **keywords** for the space.
10. Press the **Next** button.
11. Specify the **URL** for your subspace. Notice that you cannot use the hierarchy in the URL.
12. Press the **Next** button.
13. Specify the **template** for your subspace.
14. Press **Create** to create the subspace.

How it works...

When you create a subspace, the space will be created in the hierarchy of the parent page. The steps for creating a subspace are identical to creating a regular space except for the URL and access level.

As for the URL, you might expect that the subspace will have the path of the parent space in the URL but this is not true. The subspace, no mater how deep in the hierarchy, will have the same level in the URL as the parent spaces.

Creating lists

In WebCenter spaces, you can create lists. Lists can be all sorts of things. You can compare them to a spreadsheet, but you don't have the calculate functionalities.

For example, you can create a list with all the issues for a specific product, a list of milestones, to-do's, and so on.

By default, you have some templates available, but you can also create an empty list and add your own columns.

Getting ready

For this recipe, you need a WebCenter Spaces environment.

How to do it...

1. From the action menu of the space, select **Manage | Lists** from the context menu.
2. Press the add button to create a new list:

3. Specify a **Name** for your list.
4. Specify a **Description**.
5. Select the **Custom List** from the **Template**.
6. Press the **OK** button to create the list:

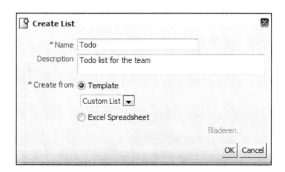

Now we have a list but it does not have any columns yet:

1. Select the list from the list of lists on the left.
2. Press the **Edit list** button.
3. Press the **Create button** in the **Columns** section.
4. Specify a **Name** for the column.
5. Specify the **Data Type** of the column.
6. Select the **Required** checkbox if the column needs to be mandatory.
7. Press the **OK** button to create the column:

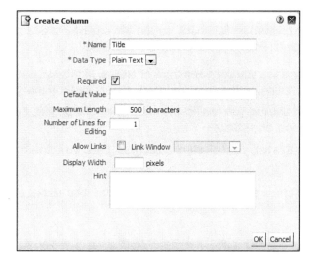

WebCenter Spaces

Our to-do list will also need a due date, so we will add another column:

1. Press the **Create** button on the columns section.
2. Specify the **name** of the column.
3. Select **DateTime** as the **Data Type** of the column.
4. Specify **Date** as the **Format**.
5. Press the **OK** button to create the column:

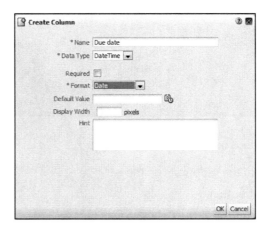

6. Press the **Close** button to go back to the view mode of the list.

You now have created the list and can start adding rows.

How it works...

In this recipe, we have created a custom list, so you can see how to add custom columns. You can also select a template. Following templates are available:

- Issue list: In this list, you can keep track of issues. In this list, each issue has a number, description, target date, assigned, status, and comments field.
- Milestones: In this list, you can list the milestones of a project. Each milestone has a date, description, and status.
- Objectives: In this list, you can store objectives. Each objective has a title and description.

Even if you create a list from a template, you can customize it by adding or removing columns.

When you add columns, following data types are available:

- Plain text: Just regular text, everything is possible.
- Rich Text: Text with format. When you add this to a list, you will get a rich text editor to specify the text.
- Number: Only numbers will be allowed in this text field. You can specify the format of the number as number, currency, or percent. You can also specify the minimum and maximum value.
- DateTime: With a DateTime field, you can use a date picker to select a date. You can specify the format of the date by selecting Date, Time, or Date and Time.
- Boolean: This will add a checkbox to your list.
- Picture: You can also add pictures to the list.
- Person: This will add a field with a browse button where you can search for existing users. You can specify whether or not to only be able to select space users or all the users from the identity store.

There's more...

Besides creating a list based upon a template and columns, you can also import a spreadsheet. This way, you don't need to specify all the columns.

Creating a space template

When you create a group space, you are able to select the template. If those templates do not fit your needs, you can always create your own templates.

Suppose each division in your company can have their own space, but they all need to have the same structure and services. This is an ideal situation to create a space template. When you create a new space for a division, you just need to select the division template and that's it. This way you don't need to create all the pages over and over again.

A template is always created based upon an existing group space, so you first need to create a space that will be the source for your template.

Getting ready

For this recipe, you need a WebCenter Space environment.

How to do it...

1. Open WebCenter Spaces: `http://localhost:8888/webcenter`.
2. Log in as an administrator.
3. Click the **Administration** link.
4. Open the **Spaces** tab.
5. Select **Space Template** from the sub navigation.
6. Press the **Create a Space Template** button.
7. Specify a **name** for the template.
8. Specify a **description** for the template:

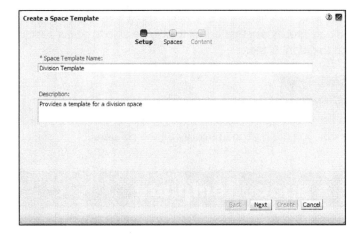

9. Press the **Next** button.
10. Select the group space that you will use as the template:

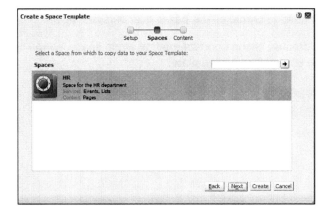

11. Press the **Next** button.
12. Select the **resources** that you want to embed in the template:

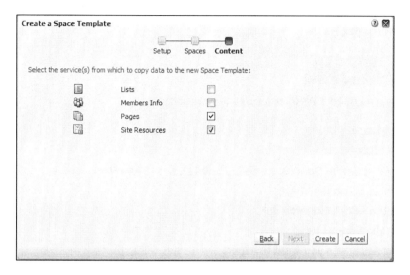

13. Press the **Create** button.

Now that we have created the template, we have to make it available for use:

1. Select the newly created template.
2. Select **Make Public** from the **Edit** menu.

How it works...

When you select the space that will be used for the template, all the selected resources will be embedded in the template. When you create a new space based upon your template, all these resources will already be created. This way, you don't need to create the resource again.

By default, a new template is private, which means that other people cannot use it when they want to create a new space.

By setting the default templates to Private, you disable them for other users, so they can only use their own custom templates.

Exporting group spaces

When you have a development, test, and production environment, you don't want to recreate your spaces on each different environment. That's why you can easily export and import spaces from one environment to another.

WebCenter Spaces

You can also use the export functionality to back up your space, just in case something went wrong.

In this recipe, I will show you how to create an export archive, so you can later import this in another environment.

Getting ready

For this recipe, you need a WebCenter Space environment.

How to do it...

1. Open WebCenter Spaces: `http://localhost:8888/webcenter`.
2. Log in as an administrator.
3. Click the **Administration** link.
4. Open the **Spaces** tab.
5. Select the space you want to export.
6. Press the **Export** button.

You will see the list of the spaces you want to export on the right:

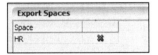

On the bottom you can specify the archive name:

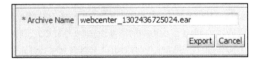

1. Specify the archive name.
2. Press the **Export** button.

You will see a popup with a progression bar, so you can monitor the export. Once the export has finished, the **Download and Save to Server** button will be enabled and you can download the `ear` file.

How it works...

When you export a group space, all the resources will be created in an `ear` file. You will export the pages, navigation models, resource catalogs, and so on.

Importing group spaces

When you have exported a group space, you can easily import this into another spaces environment.

Getting ready

For this recipe, you need a WebCenter Spaces environment and an `ear` file from an exported group space. You can export an existing group space by following the previous recipe.

How to do it...

1. Open WebCenter Spaces: `http://localhost:8888/webcenter`.
2. Log in as an administrator.
3. Click the **Administration** link.
4. Open the Spaces tab.
5. Press the import button.
6. Specify the `ear` file that contains the space.
7. Press the **Browse archive** button:

8. Select the space you want to import.
9. Press the **import** button.

How it works...

When you select the `ear` file, WebCenter will read the contents of the file and show the available spaces. When you select a space, you can import it and the space will be available in your environment.

12
Securing Your WebCenter Portal

In this chapter, you will learn about:

- Securing pages with the page hierarchy
- Securing pages at runtime
- Using the Oracle Identity Directory as an identity store
- Enabling SSL for a WebCenter portal application
- Securing taskflows

Introduction

One of the most important aspects of an application or portal is securing the content. You don't want regular people to be able to modify pages or add content.

Security in the fusion stack of Oracle is divided into two separate parts. First of all, you have the authentication. This is all about who can access the application. In WebCenter, this has been delegated to the WebLogic server. In WebLogic, you have an embedded LDAP server which acts as the repository for users. You also have the possibility to add providers so you can use Oracle SSO or OAM.

It is important to know that you cannot add or delete users from within your WebCenter portal application. This is because this task has been delegated to the WebLogic console.

The second part is the authorization. This part is all about what a user can do and see. Authorization is configured in your portal and can be configured both at design and runtime. In WebCenter, you can authorize users to see pages, use taskflows, and so on.

Securing pages with the page hierarchy

One of the first things you want to do when dealing with security in your portal is to make sure that people only see the pages they are allowed to see. Suppose you have some pages with internal applications on them or internal content—you don't want public users or customers to see those pages.

This kind of security is configured in the page hierarchy of your portal. The security model of WebCenter is based upon the ADF security model. The security we will set in the page hierarchy is an addition to the ADF security model.

With the page hierarchy, you can define hierarchies of pages, which means that each node can have different child nodes. This also applies to the security of the pages. Each child node can inherit the security of the parent node, but you can also choose to deviate from it and specify a custom security for a specific child.

Getting ready

For this recipe, you need a WebCenter Portal application.

I have prepared an application for this recipe which you can find in the code accompanying the book. It's called `SecuringPages`. In this application, I have created a page called `internal.jspx`, a user: `internalUser`, and a role: `internal`, which we will use to secure the page. You can use that application to follow this recipe.

How to do it...

1. In JDeveloper, open the `pages.xml` from the `oracle/webcenter/portalapp/pagehierarchy` folder
2. Drag the `internal.jspx` from the `pages` folder on top of the **Root** node:

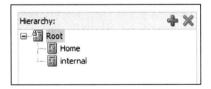

3. Select the **Internal** node.
4. Select the **Delegate Security** radio button in the **Security** section.

5. Press the add button and select **internal** from the context menu:

6. Uncheck all the checkboxes in the **authenticated-role** row.
7. Uncheck all the checkboxes in the **anonymous-role** row.
8. Check the **Personalize** and **View** checkboxes for the **internal** row:

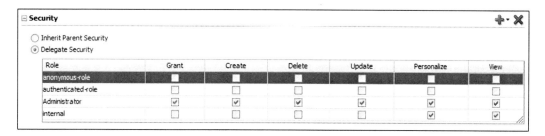

Now we have set the security for the internal page and you can test this. Just run the portal application. By default, you aren't logged in, so you will see the pages that have the view rights for the anonymous-role set:

When you log in with the `internalUser` I have created with the project (the password is `internal123`), you will see that the internal page has been added to the navigation:

Securing Your WebCenter Portal

How it works...

All the security settings are stored in the `jazn-data.xml` file. This can be found in the `META-INFO` folders from the **Descriptors** in the **Application Resources**. In this file, you will find all the additional users and roles. It also contains the authorization settings.

When we add permissions for a specific role or user, an entry will be added in `jazn-data.xml`. When we launch the application, the portal will read the `jazn-data.xml` file and look for the permissions for the current user. If there is no entry for the user for a specific page, then the page will not be added to the navigation.

A page has different types of permissions which we can use in our portal:

- Grant: When you give the grant permission to a role, you allow the user with that acquired role to also grant permissions to other roles or users.
- Create: The create permission allows users to create subpages for the specific page.
- Delete: The delete permission allows users to delete subpages for the specific page.
- Update: The update permission allows users to update subpages for the specific page.
- Personalize: With the personalize permission, you allow users to personalize the page. This is used when you have portlets or taskflows with personalization features. When you check this permission, the view permission will automatically be selected.
- View: This permission allows the user to view the page.

Securing pages at runtime

In the previous recipe, you have seen how you can secure pages by using the page hierarchy. In that case, you need to redeploy the application before changes take effect. In some cases, you don't want to do this, for example, when you create pages at runtime. These pages are not available in JDeveloper, so you also need to set the security at runtime.

In this recipe, we will do the same thing as in the previous recipe. We will secure the `internal.jspx` page, so only the internal role has access to the page.

Getting ready

For this recipe, you need a WebCenter Portal application.

I have prepared an application for this recipe which you can find in the code accompanying the book. It's called `SecuringPages`. In this application, I have created a page called `internal.jspx`, a user: `internalUser` and a role: `internal` which we will use to secure the page. You can use that application to follow this recipe.

Chapter 12

How to do it...

1. Run the portal project.
2. Log in as an administrator.
3. Go to the **Administration** page.
4. From the **Resources** tab, select **Pages** on the left.
5. Press the **Create Page** button.
6. Specify Internal for the **Page Name**.
7. Press the **Create** button to create the page:

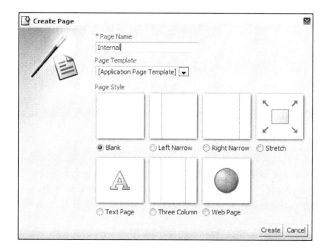

8. Check the **Show Page** checkbox on the **Internal** page so the page will be included in the navigation.
9. Select **Set Access** from the page actions menu of the **Internal** page.
10. Select the **Delegate Security** radio button.
11. Press the **Add Roles** button.
12. Specify internal for the **Search Application Role** field and press the **Go** button.
13. Select **internal** and press the **OK** button:

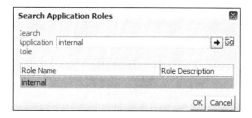

267

Securing Your WebCenter Portal

14. Uncheck all the checkboxes in the **authenticated-role** row.
15. Uncheck all the checkboxes in the **anonymous-role** row.
16. Check the **Personalize** and **View** checkboxes for the **internal** row:

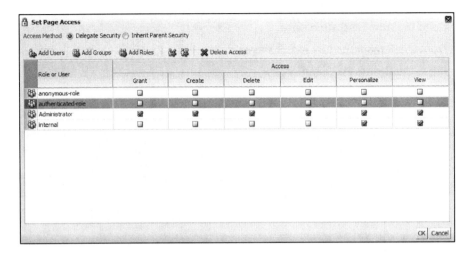

17. Press the **OK** button to close the popup.

You have now set up the security for the internal page. When you log out, the internal page will not be available. When you log in with an Administrator account or with an account which has the internal role assigned, you will see the internal page.

There's more...

At runtime, you can also use groups or users to specify security, which is not possible when you configure the security at design time.

The Add Users and Add Groups button works in a similar way as the Add Roles button. You get a popup with a search field and you can select the users or groups you want.

The reason why you have these additional buttons at runtime is because JDeveloper does not know which WebLogic you are using for deploying the portal. When you have deployed the portal, the security is bound to the security realm of the WebLogic server, so from then on, the portal can query the application server for users, groups, or roles.

Chapter 12

Using Oracle Identity Directory as an identity store

By default, when you install WebCenter on a WebLogic domain, it will use the embedded LDAP of the WebLogic server as an identity store. You will most likely have an existing LDAP server, OAM, OID, or AD, and you will want to use that identity store in your portal.

In WebLogic, you can create authentication providers, which can be any type of LDAP. For some identity stores, Oracle has specific providers for OID and Microsoft Active Directory.

In this recipe, I will show you how you can configure an existing OID as the identity store.

Getting Ready

For this recipe, you only need a running WebLogic server.

How to do it...

1. Go to the WebLogic console: `http://localhost:7001/console`.
2. Log in as an administrator.
3. Click on the **Security Realms** link in the **Domain structure** pane:

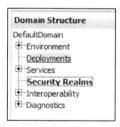

4. Click on **myrealm** to open the default security realm.
5. Open the **Providers** tab.
6. Click **New** to create a new provider.
7. Specify a name for the provider.

8. Specify **OracleInternetDirectoryAuthenticator** as the provider:

9. Press the **OK** button to create the provider.
10. Click on the provider you just created to open the properties.
11. Set the Control Flag to **SUFFICIENT**.
12. Open the **Provider Specific** tab.
13. Specify the **hostname** of your OID.
14. Specify the **port** of your OID.
15. Specify the user **principal** of a user that will be used to connect to the OID. Use the full DN.
16. Specify the **credential** for the user specified in the principal field to log in to the OID.
17. Confirm the credential.
18. Specify the **User Base DN**.
19. Specify the **All Users Filter**.
20. Specify the **User Name Attribute**.
21. Specify the **User Object Class**.
22. Specify the **Group Base DN**.
23. Specify the **Groups filter**.

24. Press **Save** to save the setting:

Connection	
Host:	localhost
Port:	389
Principal:	cn=orcladmin
Credential:	••••••••
Confirm Credential:	••••••••
SSLEnabled	
Users	
User Base DN:	ou=people, o=example.co
All Users Filter:	(&(cn=*)(objectclass=pers
User From Name Filter:	(&(cn=%u)(objectclass=pe
User Search Scope:	subtree
User Name Attribute:	cn
User Object Class:	person
Use Retrieved User Name as Principal	

25. Restart the WebLogic server so the changes will be active.

You now have configured the provider OID as your provider. Normally, you should be able to log in with the users that are defined in the OID.

How it works...

A WebCenter Portal application uses the WebLogic security realm to authenticate the users. By default, the WLS has an integrated LDAP server. When you add a provider, the users and groups of the integrated LDAP will still be available, but you will also be able to use the users from the configured identity store.

Most of the identity stores are kind of based upon the LDAP standard. So is the OID and Microsoft AD. Because of this, the configuration of the vendor-specific provider will be similar.

It is important to know that when you add a provider, you should look for the vendor-specific provider and not use the default LDAP provider. Only use the default provider when you don't find a specific provider for it.

There's more...

You can add more than one provider. In fact, you can add as many providers as you want. Because of this, you will need a way to tell the server what the order of the providers is.

In order to reorder the providers, go to the Providers tab of the security realm and press the reorder button on the overview of the providers.

Select the provider you want and use the button next to the list to reorder it:

When you add a provider, you can specify the Control Flag for the provider. The control flag defines the level for your authenticator. Based upon that flag, you can tell WebLogic that the user should always authenticate to that provider or that the authenticator is an optional one. The following values are possible for the control flag:

- REQUIRED: This authenticator is required. Even if the user has a successful login with other authenticators, the complete login process will fail if this authenticator fails.
- REQUISITE: This is the same as REQUIRED with the only difference that when you have other authenticators defined, these will not be executed if this one fails.
- SUFFICIENT: Failing of this login module does not block the application. When this authenticator succeeds, it will not execute the other authenticators.
- OPTIONAL: This authenticator does not need to succeed. Whatever the outcome of this authenticator is, it will execute the other authenticators.

Enabling SSL for a WebCenter portal application

When you want to enable a secure connection to your portal application, you want to use the secure socket layer protocol. This way, all the traffic from and to your portal will be encrypted, so sniffers cannot read the content when they sniff the network.

Using SSL is a very common practice to provide a secure connection to your portal.

In this recipe, I will show you how you can configure SSL for a custom WebCenter portal application.

Getting ready

For this recipe, you need a deployed WebCenter portal application on a WebLogic server and an installed JDK.

How to do it...

A first thing we need to do before enabling a SSL connection is to create a custom keystore to store the identity for encrypting the data:

1. Open a command prompt.
2. Browse to `<jdk_home>/bin`.
3. Execute the following command to create the keystore:

    ```
    keytool -genkeypair -keyalg RSA -dname "cn=weblogic" -alias webcenter_portal -keypass welcome1 -keystore webcenter_portal.jks -storepass welcome1 -validity 720
    ```

4. Execute the following command to export the keystore:

    ```
    keytool -exportcert -v -alias webcenter_portal -keystore webcenter_portal.jks -storepass welcome1 -rfc -file webcenter_portal.cer
    ```

5. Open the WebLogic console (`http://localhost:7001/console`).
6. In the **Domain Structure**, open the **Environment** node.

Securing Your WebCenter Portal

7. Click on the **Servers** link:

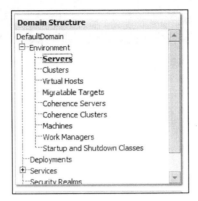

8. Click on the managed server where your WebCenter Portal application has been deployed.
9. Open the **Keystores** tab from the **Configuration** tab.
10. Copy the `webcenter_portal.cer` we created in step 4 to the directory specified in the **Jave Standard Trust Keystore** location:

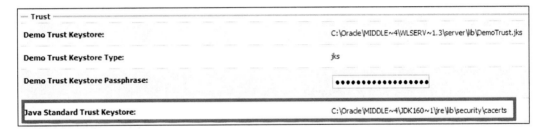

11. Open a command prompt and browse to the directory of the Java Standard trust Keystore.
12. Execute the following command:

    ```
    keytool -importcert -trustcacerts -alias webcenter_portal -file
    webcenter_portal.cer -keystore cacerts -storepass welcome1
    ```

13. When prompted to trust the certificate, specify yes.

Chapter 12

You should now see the message that the certification has been added as a trusted one:

1. Open the WebLogic console again.
2. Click on the **Servers** link from the **Environment** node in the **Domain Structure**.
3. Click on the managed server where your WebCenter portal application has been deployed.
4. Open the **Keystores** tab from the **Configuration** tab.
5. Click on the Change button in the Keystores field.
6. Select **Custom Identity and Java Standard Trust**:

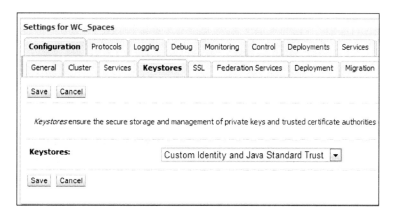

7. Press the **Save** button.
8. Specify the path to the custom keystore from step 3 in the **Custom Identity Keystore** field.
9. Specify **JKS** as the Custom **Identity Keystore Type**.
10. Specify the password you provided in step 3 for the keystore in the **Custom Identity Keystore Passphrase** field.
11. Confirm the password.
12. Specify the password for the **Java Standard Trust Keystore** as specified in step 12.
13. Confirm the password.

14. Press the **Save** button:

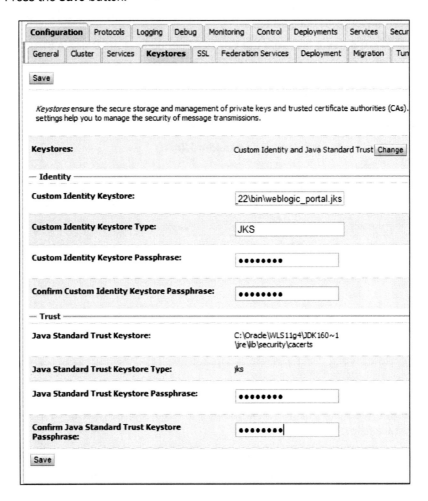

15. Open the **SSL** tab.
16. Specify the alias specified in step 3 for the **Private Key Alias** (webcenter_portal).
17. Specify the password for the keystore in the **Private Key Passphrase**.
18. Confirm the password.
19. Click **Save**.
20. Open the **General** tab.
21. Check the **SSL Listen Port Enabled**.
22. Specify the **port** to listen for the SSL connection.
23. Press the **Save** button.

Restart the managed server. You should now be able to connect to your WebCenter Portal application deployed on that managed server by using SSL (https) on the port specified in step 35.

How it works...

Before configuring the managed server, we need to create the keystore. This is done with the keytool of a JDK.

The command we use is the following:

```
keytool -genkeypair -keyalg RSA -dname "cn=weblogic" -alias webcenter_portal -keypass welcome1 -keystore webcenter_portal.jks -storepass welcome1 -validity 720
```

The keytool takes the following parameters:

- genkeypair: This parameter tells the keytool to create a key pair.
- keyalg: This parameter tells the keytool which algorithm to use to encrypt the data. For our SSL connection, it is important to use RSA!
- dname: Contains the username for the keystore. This needs to be a full DN.
- alias: This is an alias for the keystore so we can use it in other commands to refer to the generated keystore.
- keypass: This is the password for the keystore. We need this later on to configure WLS when specifying the keystore.
- keystore: This is the file where the keystore will be saved.
- storepass: Password to secure the keystore.
- validity: The number of days that the keystore will be valid. When this period has been exceeded, you will need to create a new one.

Once the keystore has been created, we need to create a certificate out of it because the WebLogic server will create SSL based upon trusted certificates.

We also use the keytool to export the keystore into a certificate:

```
keytool -exportcert -v -alias webcenter_portal -keystore webcenter_portal.jks -storepass welcome1 -rfc -file webcenter_portal.cer
```

We use the following parameters for the export:

- exportcert: This tells the keytool to export a keystore into a certificate.
- alias: This is the alias of the keystore which we provided in the previous command.
- keystore: This is the file generated by the previous command.

Securing Your WebCenter Portal

- storepass: This needs to match the password provided in the previous command.
- file: This will be the resulting file containing the actual certificate.

Once we have the certificate, we need to import it into the trusted certificate of our WebLogic server:

```
keytool -importcert -trustcacerts -alias webcenter_portal -file
webcenter_portal.cer -keystore cacerts -storepass changeit
```

The keytool uses the following parameters to import the certificate:

- importcert: Tells the keytool to import an existing certificate into a trusted store.
- alias: The alias of the keystore from the certificate. This must match the alias specified in the first command.
- file: Specifies the actual certification file generated by the second command.
- keystore: The keystore of our WebLogic server which you can see in the Keystore tab.
- storepass: Specifies the password of the keystore of the WebLogic server. By default, this is changeit.

Once the keystore and certificate has been generated and imported in the WebLogic server, we can tell the managed server to use that specific keystore by providing its alias and password.

Securing taskflows

Your portal will not contain only out-of-the-box features. Often, you will need to build your own taskflows. You also want those taskflows to be secure, meaning that only people with specific grants can see those taskflows. This can be configured in the `jazn-data.xml` of your portal.

For each taskflow, you can specify who can view it. When people don't have sufficient rights to see the taskflow, the taskflow will not render on the page. They will not see an error message, so it is an ideal technique to secure the taskflow.

In this recipe, we will learn how you can secure a taskflow.

Getting ready

For this recipe, you need a WebCenter Portal application with at least one taskflow.

In the code accompanying the book, you will find an application called `TaskflowSecurity`. This project contains a WebCenter Portal application with a simple taskflow created in the `WEB-INF` folder. We will secure that taskflow in this recipe.

Chapter 12

How to do it...

1. In JDeveloper, open the **jazn-data.xml** file from the **Descriptors | META-INF** folder in the **Application Resources**:

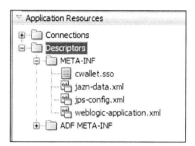

2. Select **Resource Grants** from the list on the left.
3. Select **Task Flow** as **Resource Type**.
4. Select the taskflow you want to secure.
5. Press the add button and select **Application Role** from the context menu.
6. Select the role you want to grant access to the taskflow:

7. Press the **OK** button to close the popup.

Securing Your WebCenter Portal

8. Select the actions you want to grant the role rights to:

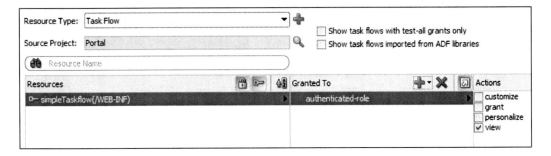

9. Save the `jazn-data.xml`.

You now have secured the taskflow. When you add the taskflow to a page and the user does not have access to the taskflow, he will not see it. When the user is granted the role you have added to the taskflow, he will see it.

How it works...

The `jazn-data.xml` file is the file where all the security related data is stored. Each resource type can have an entry in the `jazn-data.xml`.

By default, a taskflow or a page will not have an entry in the `jazn-data.xml`. This means that there is no specific configuration for the item, and everybody can use the item. Once you specify a single role for the taskflow, only that role will have access to the taskflow.

You can, of course, add multiple roles or users to the same taskflow in the `jazn-data.xml`.

There's more...

You can also use this technique to secure existing, out-of-the-box taskflows. When you open the `jazn-data.xml` and select **Task Flow** as the **Resource Type**, you only see the taskflows you have created in the current project.

By selecting **Show task flows imported from ADF libraries**, you can see all the taskflows from the WebCenter libraries or other taskflows you have imported:

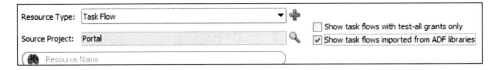

13
Managing WebCenter Portal Applications

In this chapter you will learn how to:

- Creating a connection to an application server
- Deploying a WebCenter Portal Application
- Undeploying an application
- Managing connections in the Enterprise Manager
- Propagating changes from staging environment to production
- Viewing log messages in the Enterprise Manager
- Monitoring the performance of an application

Introduction

Managing WebCenter Applications will be one of your most important tasks. You will be responsible for moving the application from one environment to another without losing the metadata. Once the application is in production, you will need to monitor its performance and find leaks.

This chapter will show you different recipes on how you can achieve all these tasks.

Creating a connection to an application server

In JDeveloper you can deploy applications directly to an application server. Before you can do this, you first need to create a connection to the application server.

In this recipe, I will show how you can create a connection to an application server.

Getting ready

For this recipe you need a running standalone WebLogic server.

How to do it

1. In JDeveloper open the **File** menu and select **New**.
2. Select **Connection** from the **General** section in the left list.
3. Select **Application Server Connection** from the list on the right.
4. Press **OK**.
5. Specify a **Name** for your connection.
6. Press **Next**.
7. Specify the **Username** and **Password** for the administrator in the server.
8. Press **Next**.
9. Specify the **Hostname** of your remote server.
10. Specify the **Port**.
11. Specify the domain (**Weblogic Domain**) that you want to use in the WebLogic server:

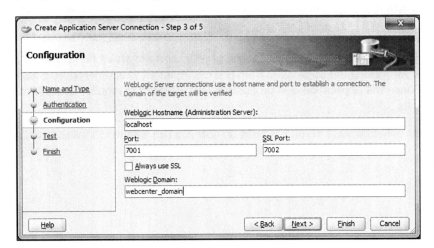

12. Press the **Next** button.
13. Press the **Test Connection** button so you can test if the connection is working.
14. Press **Finish**.

How it works

The connection you just made is an IDE connection which means that it will be available for all of your application you create in JDeveloper. You do not need to recreate the connection when you develop another application or portal.

The domain you specify in the connection must match the domain that has been created on the server.

By using the **Test Connection** button, you can test if all the parameters are correct.

Deploying a WebCenter Portal Application

Deploying a WebCenter Portal application is quiet easy because we can make use of JDeveloper. From within JDeveloper, you can create a connection to your WebLogic server and deploy the application directly to it.

It is even better to deploy the application from within JDeveloper than deploying it by using the WebLogic console. As a WebCenter Portal application not only contains an EAR file as you expect, but it also contains some MAR (metadata archive) files. When you deploy from JDeveloper these MAR files are also deployed to the application server. When you deploy manually by using the console, you will also have to deploy the MAR files manually.

Getting ready

For this recipe, you need to have a WebCenter Portal application and a running standalone WebLogic server.

How to do it

1. Right click the Portal project and select **Deploy** from the context menu.
2. Select the deployment profile that is there by default.
3. Select **Deploy to Application Server**.
4. Press **Next**.
5. Select your application server where you want to deploy the application.
6. Press **Next**.

7. Select **Deploy to selected instances in the domain**.
8. Specify the instance where you want to deploy to and press **Next**.
9. Press **Finish**.
10. The deployment will now start and you can see the progress in the deployment messages.
11. You also should see a popup asking for the MDS.
12. Specify the **Repository Name** for your MDS repository that will be used for your portal application.

 Make sure you do not select the **mds-SpacesDS** if it is available because this should only be used for WebCenter Spaces!

13. Specify the **Partition Name** for your application:

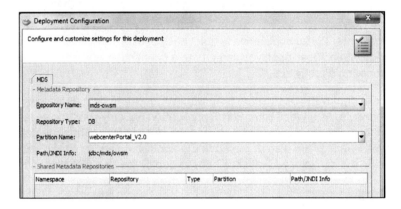

14. Press the **Deploy** button.

The deployment process will continue. When the deployment has finished you should see a message in the deployment log that looks something like this:

```
[08:57:26 PM] Deploying Application...
[08:57:36 PM] [Deployer:149192]Operation 'deploy' on application
'webcenterPortal [Version=V2.0]' is in progress on 'AdminServer'
[08:57:49 PM] [Deployer:149194]Operation 'deploy' on application
'webcenterPortal [Version=V2.0]' has succeeded on 'AdminServer'
[08:57:49 PM] Application Deployed Successfully.
[08:57:49 PM] Elapsed time for deployment:  3 minutes, 26 seconds
[08:57:49 PM] ----  Deployment finished.  ----
[08:57:49 PM] Elapsed time for deployment:  3 minutes, 26 seconds
[08:57:49 PM] ----  Deployment finished.  ----
```

How it works

When you create a WebCenter Portal application, the application will contain a default deployment profile that has all the parameters set for your portal. When you take a closer look at this profile, you will notice that a lot of the resources are not included in the deployment:

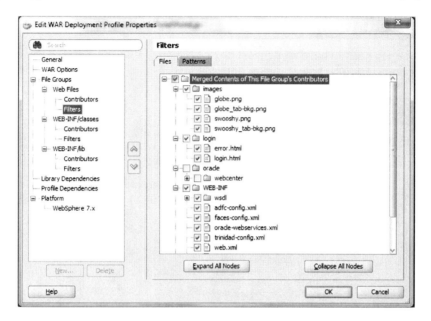

As you can see, all the important filters are not included in the deployment. The complete `Oracle` folder is not included when you deploy.

When you deploy the application, you will notice in the deployment log that JDeveloper creates an additional MAR file:

```
[09:04:56 PM] Exporting portlet metadata and customizations.
[09:04:56 PM] Wrote MAR file to C:\Projects\Deploy\deploy\
AutoGeneratedMar.mar
```

This MAR file contains all the files that are not included in the original EAR file. A MAR file is a special archive that will not be deployed to the application server. Instead, it will add its files to the metadata. That's why we need to specify the MDS repository. The MAR file will be uploaded to that repository.

 It is very important that you never select the 'mds-SpacesDS', because this is reserved for your WebCenter Spaces environment. If you deploy your MAR file to the spaces MDS than you have a good chance to corrupt the complete WebCenter spaces environment!

Managing WebCenter Portal Applications

Undeploying an application

When you have an application that is no longer needed, you want to remove it from the server, because otherwise they will consume unneeded memory and resources.

Getting ready

For this recipe you need to have an application deployed to a WebLogic server. You can also read the previous recipe on how to deploy applications.

How to do it

1. Go to the console of your WebLogic server.
2. Log in with an administrator.
3. Click on **Deployments** in the tree in the **Domain Structure**:

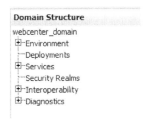

4. Check the checkbox next to the application you wish to undeploy.
5. Press the **Delete** button located above the table.

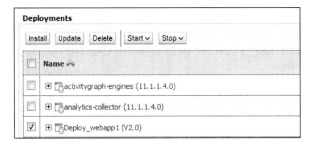

That's it. The application has been undeployed.

How it works

When you undeploy an application, the EAR and WAR file will be removed from the server as well as all the metadata that has been stored in the MDS repository.

Managing connections in the Enterprise Manager

When you develop a WebCenter Portal application, you often need to create connections to several services. For example you will need to create a connection to a content repository or to a discussion server. When you deploy the portal to a staging or production environment, you need to modify these connection parameters. You can do this by either modifying the connection itself in JDeveloper, or you can just modify the connection in the Enterprise Manager.

By using the Enterprise Manager, you do not need to redeploy the portal when you want to modify parameters of the connection. Say that one of the servers has moved to another host, than you can modify the hostname in the Enterprise Manager without needing to redeploy the application.

Getting ready

For this recipe, you need to have a standalone WebLogic server with a WebCenter Portal application deployed to it. For instructions on how to deploy a WebCenter portal application, you can read the previous recipe.

How to do it

1. Open the Enterprise Manager (http://localhost:7001/em).
2. Log in as an administrator.
3. Open the **Farm** node of your domain.
4. Open the **Application Deployment** node.
5. Select the application were you want to modify a connection:

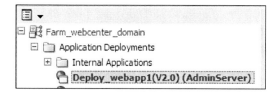

Managing WebCenter Portal Applications

6. Select **Application Deployment** on the top.
7. Select **ADF** from the context menu.
8. Select **Configure ADF Connections** from the popup menu:

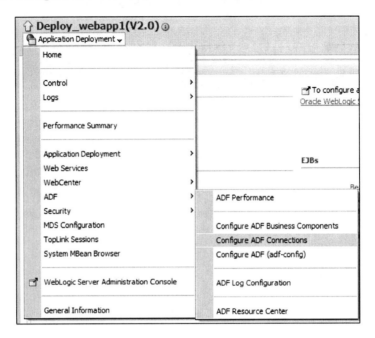

9. Select the connection you want to edit.
10. Press the **Edit** button.
11. Modify the parameters.
12. Press **OK** to save the connection.

How it works

Depending on the type of connection you select, you will get another popup. The popup will match the parameters from what you normally get when you create the connection in JDeveloper.

Currently, the Enterprise Manager does not support editing of all the types of connections we can create in JDeveloper. The following connections are currently supported for editing in the EM:

- ADF Business Component Service
- BAM
- Discussions and Announcements

- File System
- Mail Server
- Secure Enterprise Search
- Url
- Web Service
- Enterprise Scheduling Service

All other connection types cannot be modified in the EM.

When you have applied the changes, you do not need to restart the instance.

There's more

Besides editing connections, you can also create new connections for your portal in the enterprise manager.

Apart from the list of available connections, you have a form where you can specify the **Connection Type** and **Connection Name**:

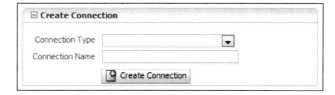

When you press the **Create Connection** button you will see an extended form containing the parameters for the **connection type** you have specified.

Propagating changes from a staging environment to a production environment

Modern portals have the capabilities to manage resources at runtime. This is a good thing, as you can provide business users the functionality to manage their own section of the portal. A problem with this technique is that it is not always easy to move changes from a staging area to the real production environment.

WebCenter provide a special **Propagation** tab in the resource manager where you can propagate the latest changes. This tab is not visible by default. In order to see the tab, you should create a link to the production environment.

In this recipe, I will show you how to enable the propagation tab and propagate the changes to your production environment.

Managing WebCenter Portal Applications

Getting ready

For this recipe, you need to have a WebCenter application deployed on two different standalone WebLogic servers.

How to do it

A first thing we need to do is to enable the **Propagation** tab in our resource manager. This is done by creating a connection of the type URL with a specific name:

1. Open the **Enterprise Manager** of the staging server.
2. Log in as an administrator.
3. Open the **Farm** node.
4. Open the **Application Deployments** node.
5. Select the application where you want to enable the propagation tool:

6. Open the **Application Deployment** menu on the top.
7. Select **ADF** and **Configure ADF Connections** from the context menu.
8. Specify **Url** for **Connection Type**.
9. Specify **ProductionURLConnection** as the **Connection Name**:

10. Press the **Create Connection** button.

Chapter 13

The connection is now created, but we still need to modify its parameters:

1. select the newly created connection and press the **Edit** button.
2. Specify the URL of your production server for example **http://productionServer:7001**.
3. Specify the administration **User Name** and **Password**.
4. Specify the **Authentication Realm**.
5. Press the **OK** button to save the changes:

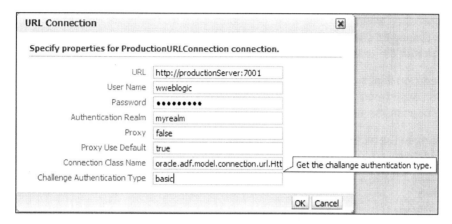

6. Press the **Apply** button in the top right corner of the **Enterprise Manager**.

Now that we have created the required connection for the propagation tool, we can start using it:

1. Browse to the application were we have created the URL for.
2. Log in with an administrator.
3. Go to the **administration** page.
4. You will notice an additional tab:

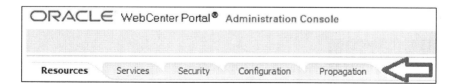

5. Open the **Propagation** tab.
6. Press the **Propagate** button on the left hand side of the screen.
7. Press **Propagate** in the confirmation popup.

Your changes are now propagated to your production server (or whatever server you have configured in the URL connection).

How it work

Creating the connection is very important. It is also very important that the connection has the name **ProductionURLConnection**. This name is required for the **Propagation** tool. Without a URL that has a name like that, the **propagation** tab will not appear.

The URL of that connection points to the WebLogic server that contains the same application as the application where you create the URL connection in. This is also important, because when you propagate changes from one server to another, the tool will try to find the application with the exact same name.

The propagation itself is based upon labels. By default, you will have a single label that got its name upon deployment. The last label is a label without name. This contains all the changes that have been made since the last propagation.

When you open the label, you will see all the files that have been changed since the last propagation:

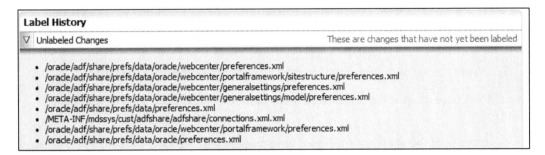

When you propagate these changes, it gets a label appointed by the propagation tool. When you make new modifications, these will be stored in an unnamed label.

The propagation tool is based upon a single transaction. This means that if there is a single error in the transport, all changes will be rolled back.

There's more

In this recipe, I showed you how you can define the connection for the propagation tool in the Enterprise Manager. If you know in advance that you will need to propagate changes, you can create the URL in JDeveloper:

1. In the **Application Resources** of your Portal application right click on the **connections** folder.

2. Select **New Connection** and **URL** from the context menu.
3. Specify the name of the connection: **ProductionURLConnection**.
4. Specify the **URL Endpoint**.
5. Specify the **Username** and **Password**.
6. Specify the security **Realm**.
7. Press **OK**:

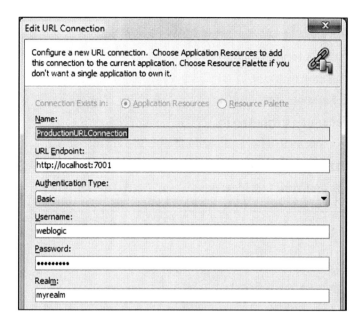

When you deploy the application with the connection URL, the propagation tool will automatically be visible. If you want to make changes to the connection at runtime, you can do this by reading the previous recipe of this chapter.

Viewing log messages in the Enterprise Manager

Everything that happens in your WebLogic server gets written in several log files. From a basic trace or notification to a complete stacktrace of an error, you can trace the message back to their module.

In the Enterprise Manager, you can also search for specific messages or filter based upon a timestamp. This is ideal when you get requests from people asking you to investigate a specific event at a specific moment.

Managing WebCenter Portal Applications

In this recipe, I will show you how you can investigate the log files for WebCenter Spaces, but the technique also applies to any other application deployed to your WebLogic server.

Getting ready

For this recipe, you need a standalone WebLogic server with an Enterprise Manager and an application deployed to the WebLogic server.

How to do it

1. Browse to the **Enterprise Manager**.
2. Log in as an administrator.
3. Select the **Farm** node.
4. Select **Application Deployments**.
5. Select the application where you want to view the log messages.
6. Click on the **Application Deployment** on top of the page.
7. Select **Logs** and **View Log Messages**:

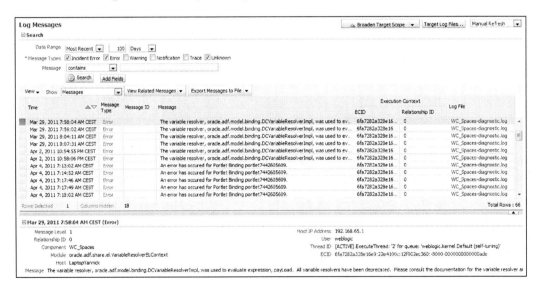

8. Click on a specific message to view the details.

How it works

Every log message is stored in a specific log file. You can see what log file contains the message. This is the last field of the table. The log file is a link. When you click on that link, you drilldown to the specific file and you can see all the messages from that specific file.

The table also contains the following fields:

- **Time**: Complete timestamp that the message was written into the log.
- **Message Type**: The type of message. This can be Incident Error, Error, Warning, Notification, Trace, or Unknown.
- **Message ID**: When the message can be identified by a standard message ID, this field contains the exact number. It is easy to lookup the meaning of the error on the internet or to provide a feedback to Oracle support.
- **Message**: A short explanation of the message itself.
- **ECID**: A unique identifier for the message. Messages can be related to each other based upon the ECID. When you view the details of a message, the ECID is a link where you can drilldown to all messages linked to that ECID.
- **Relationship ID**: ID containing the relationship of messages.
- **Log File**: Specifies the actual log file where the message has been written to.

When you select a message from the table, you can see the same fields as in the table in addition to the complete message. If the message is an error, the message will contain the complete stacktrace, so you can see on what line of which java class the error occurred, which will help you to give feedback to the developers.

There's more

In the top section of the **Log Messages** screen, you can use the search and filter functionality:

Managing WebCenter Portal Applications

In this field you can specify following filters:

- **Date Range**: Specify the data range. You can choose between Most Recent messages and messages between a time interval.
- **Message Types**: Specify which messages you want to view—Incident Error, Error, Warning, Notification, Trace, and Unknown.
- **Filter on Message**: You can specify an operator and a value to search the contents of the message itself.

With the **Add Fields** button, you can also add fields to filter on. The following are some fields that you might want to use:

- **Host**: By filtering on the hostname, you can view the messages of a specific instance in a clustered environment
- **User**: Filter on the user who triggered the message
- **Message level**: Filter a specific level of messages
- **component**: Filter the messages of a specific component
- **module**: Filter the messages of a specific module of your application
- **instance**: Filter the messages based upon the instance the application it is running on

Monitoring the performance of an application

When an application is slow, you want to know where the bottleneck is. Therefore you can monitor the performance of your application in real time. You can view different parameters and metrics.

Getting ready

For this recipe, you need a WebLogic server with an Enterprise Manager and a deployed application on it.

How to do it

1. Browse to the **Enterprise Manager**.
2. Log in as an administrator.
3. Select the **Farm** node.
4. Select **Application Deployments**.

Chapter 13

5. Select the application where you want to monitor the performance.
6. Click on the **Application Deployment** on top of the page.
7. Select **Performance Summary**.

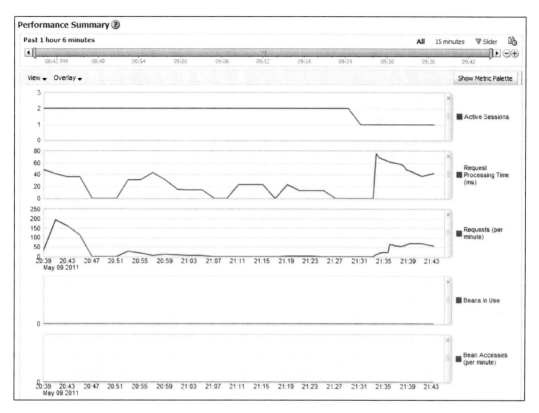

How it works

When you view the performance you will see five charts showing the different parameters:

- **Active sessions**: It shows a graph of the number of active sessions. This way you can monitor how many people currently are using the application.
- **Request Processing** Time: It shows an overview of the processing time in milliseconds. This way you can see if there are any special peaks that aren't normal.
- **Request per minute**: It shows an overview of the number of requests per minute. This graph combined with the previous graph can contain a lot of powerful information. When you have only a few requests per minute, but if the average request time is high, then something is wrong.

Managing WebCenter Portal Applications

- **Beans in use**: It shows an overview of the beans that are currently in use. This combined with the active sessions can tell you how many beans are used per session. If there are a lot of beans used and just a few sessions active than it means that each session is using a lot of beans and the developers should do some refactoring.

- **Bean Accesses per minute**: It gives an overview on how many beans are accessed per minute. This graph compared by the beans in use can tell you how long the lifecycle of the beans is. If it's a big difference you might reconsider the scope of your beans.

There's more

This time there is a lot more. The Enterprise Manager can present a lot of metrics to add to the performance summary. You can monitor almost everything you can imagine. Just press the **Show Metric Palette**:

Some of these folders are empty, but most of them contain items that you can monitor. I will give a brief overview of some useful parameters to monitor:

1. From the **ADFC Taskflow Metrics** folder:
    - **Active taskflows per minute**: It shows how many taskflows are active per minute.
    - **Entered taskflows per minute**: It shows a graph of how many taskflows are entered per minute.

- **Taskflow Invoke time**: This graph shows the average invoke time of a taskflow. This graph compared with some other graphs can help you identify the bottleneck of the problem. When the average invocation time is high you know that there are issues with taskflows, but when they are low, you can rule out all the taskflows.

2. From the **ADFC Taskflow request processing time** folder:

   - **Average Request Processing Time**: This graph can be used when you know that taskflows are slow. This will show you what the times are for the taskflows.
   - When your application uses data sources you can add some metrics about those data sources. This way you can check if the data sources are causing the bottleneck.
   - The `MDS metrics` folder contains some metrics about the MDS. You can add graphs that show the number of updates, average write time to the MDS, and so on.

3. The **Overview Metrics** folder contains some general metrics:

   - **Bean access failures per minute**: It shows a graph of the number of failures while accessing beans.
   - **Bean destroyers per minute**: It shows how many times per minute the destroy method of a bean has been called. This can be used to check whether or not the garbage collection is working properly.
   - **Cached beans**: The cached beans graph can show you how much of the beans are cached. It can give a nice overview of how much the Java Object Cache (JOC) is used.

4. The **Servlet/JSP Metrics** folder contains all the servlets specified in the application. You can monitor each servlet separately. For each servlet you can view the request time. This is a very good way to see which servlet is slow.

5. In the **WebCenter** folder, you can view metrics of each Webcenter service. You can view the average processing time, number of invocations, and successful invocations. This is a good way to check which services are used a lot. It can also help you find out which service is causing problems.

6. In the **Web Service Endpoint Metrics**, you can monitor the web service calls. If you use web services, a lot in your application you can check these metrics to see which web service is slow and how many web service calls you do.

14
WebCenter Analytics and Activity Graph

In this chapter you will learn about:

- Registering a WebCenter Portal application to the Analytics collector
- Manually run the Gathering Engine
- Schedule the Gathering Engine
- Creating a connection to the activities schema in JDeveloper
- Using the WebCenter Analytics taskflows
- Creating your own analytics report
- Showing an activity stream on your portal

Introduction

When you create a portal, you create it with a reason. For example, you want people to discover new products, find documents they want, and so on. You also want to know if the people are doing exactly what you want in your portal. If you put a new section of your portal online, you want to know if people are using it. With WebCenter Analytics you can view all of these parameters of your portal. You can drill down to specific pages or portlets to see how popular they are.

When different people are showing the same behavior in your portal, you want them to provide a list with resources they may like. Before you can do this, you need a service that gathers data about the user experience. This is done by the Activity Graph in WebCenter. After the data has been gathered, you can do propositions to the user, so they can easily discover the content they are looking for.

WebCenter Analytics and Activity Graph

In WebCenter Spaces, you can even use the Activity Graph in combination with the people connection. This way you can recommend connections to people.

You can also use the data from the Activity Graph in a personalization scenario. This way you can provide the user with a truly unique and personalized user experience.

Registering a WebCenter Portal application to the Analytics collector

By default, no data from your application gets collected. In order to use WebCenter Analytics, you need to tell the collector that it needs to listen to your application and start storing the data.

This is one of the few things that you cannot do in JDeveloper. You can only register a fully deployed WebCenter Portal application to the collector.

> This recipe can be used for both WebCenter Portal applications as for WebCenter Spaces.

Getting ready

For this recipe, you need a WebCenter domain running on a WebLogic server and at least a single WebCenter Portal application deployed to it.

How to do it

1. Browse to the Enterprise Manager of your WebCenter domain (default is `http://<hostname>:7001/em`).
2. Log in with an administrator.
3. Open the **Farm** node.
4. Open the **Application Deployments** node.
5. Select your WebCenter Portal application:

Chapter 14

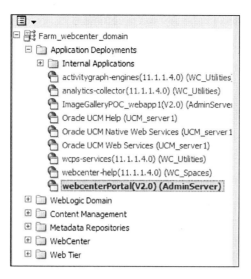

6. Open the **Application Deployment** menu on top of the screen.
7. Select WebCenter.
8. Click on **Service Configuration**.
9. Click on **Analytics & Activity Graph**.
10. Press the **Add** button to create a new connection.
11. Specify a **Name** for the connection.
12. Check the **Active Connection** checkbox.
13. Check the **Enable WebCenter Event Collection** checkbox.
14. Set the **Collector Host Name** to the host name of the Analytics server.
15. Set the port to the port of the collector (by default this is **31314**):

WebCenter Analytics and Activity Graph

16. Press the **Test** button to check if the parameters you entered are correct.
17. Press **OK** to save the connection.
18. Restart the managed server were the WebCenter Portal application is running.

How it works

The WebCenter Analytics collector runs as an application in the `WC_Utilities` managed server. This is so by default, when you create a WebCenter domain.

By default the collector listens on port 31314 and this is what we configure in the connection section for our application.

By registering the application to the collector, the collector will read the log files of the server and gather the data. The data you will see in the analytics taskflows are not real time data. That's why you need to schedule the collector so it runs once in a while so the data gets updated.

Manually running the Gathering Engine

The Gathering Engine is the heart of the WebCenter Activity Graph component. The Gathering Engine will gather the data and usage for each user, so it can compute recommended resources and do recommendations.

Getting ready

For this recipe, you need to have a fully installed WebCenter domain on a WebLogic server.

How to do it

1. Browse to the activity engine web application. By default this is `http://<host>:8891/activitygraph-engines/`.
2. Log in as an administrator (the same used in Console / EM).
3. Select **Run once** now.
4. Select **Full Rebuild**.
5. Press the **Start** button:

Chapter 14

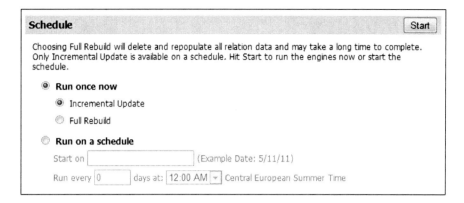

How it works

When you press the start button, you will get some feedback below the schedule section:

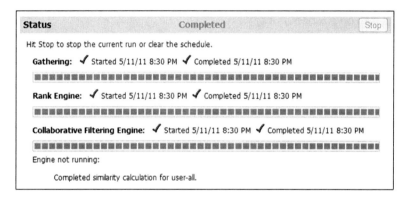

Depending on the size of the log files, this process can take quite some time.

That's also a reason why there is a separate managed server for WebCenter Analytics. You don't want your users to wait longer for their content while the gatherer is processing the log files.

When you run the gatherer, you have two options:

- **Incremental Update**: This is best suited for situations where you have already run the gatherer in the past. This will only process the new entries in the log files since the last run of the gatherer.
- **Full Rebuild**: This option will completely rebuild the gatherer index. This process can take a long time if you have large log files, but can sometimes be needed when the data of the gatherer gets corrupted.

Scheduling the Gathering Engine

It is a good practice to schedule the Gathering Engine. By doing this, you do not need to run the gatherer manually. By choosing a good time of the day you minimize the impact on the performance of your site.

Getting ready

For this recipe you need to have a fully installed WebCenter domain on a WebLogic server.

How to do it

1. Browse to the activity engine web application. By default this is http://<host>:8891/activitygraph-engines/.
2. Log in as an administrator.
3. Select **Run** on a schedule.
4. Specify a date to run the gatherer.
5. Specify the interval of days and time to run the gatherer.
6. Press the **Start** button to schedule the gatherer:

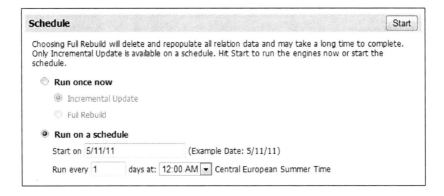

How it works

When you press the **Start** button, you will see in the status section when the next run is scheduled. This way you can see if the parameters you entered for the gatherer are correct.

For the Start on field, you need to specify a date in the format of month/day/year.

 The date format depends on the regional settings of the server where your managed server is running on, so the date format might be different in your environment.

By scheduling the gatherer, you don't have to bother to manually start the gatherer.

Creating a connection to the activities schema in JDeveloper

When you want to show reports from WebCenter Analytics, you need to create a connection to the proper schema. This schema should have been created when you run the RCU during the install of WebCenter.

Once the connection has been created in JDeveloper you can start adding the analytics taskflows to your page.

Getting ready

For this recipe, you need a WebCenter Portal application.

How to do it

1. In the **Application Resource** right click the **Connections** folder.
2. Select **New Connection** and **Database**.
3. Give your connection a name.
4. Specify the **Username** to your activity schema that has been created by the RCU.
5. Specify the **Password** for the activity schema.
6. Specify the **Host Name** and **SID** or **Service Name**.

WebCenter Analytics and Activity Graph

7. Press the **Test Connection** button to test the connection:

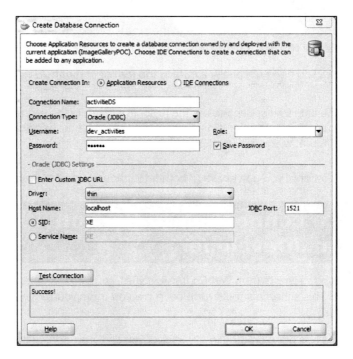

8. Press the OK button.
9. In the popup select ActivitiesDS and press OK.

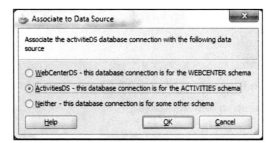

How it works

Almost every taskflow from WebCenter Analytics requires a connection to the activity schema. This is due to the schema that contains all the gathered data from the log files and the gatherer.

By associating the database connection to the ActivitiesDS, you tell JDeveloper to configure the connection so it can be used by the WebCenter Analytics taskflows.

Chapter 14

Using the WebCenter Analytics taskflows

WebCenter comes with a lots of out-of-the-box WebCenter Analytics taskflows. With these taskflows, you can easily integrate different reports, allowing you to analyze almost everything about your portal. From how many users have logged in to your portal to which portlets are being used.

In this recipe, I will show you how you can create a page that shows some of these reports.

I will give an overview of all the available analytics taskflows at the end of this recipe, so you know what is possible and which taskflow to use in which occasion.

Getting ready

For this recipe, you need a WebCenter Portal which is registered to the analytics service. If you don't know how to register the application to the analytics service then you should read the first recipe of this chapter.

How to do it

1. Browse to your WebCenter Portal application.
2. Log in as an administrator.
3. Go to the administration page.
4. On the **Resource** tab click on **Pages**.
5. Click on the **Create Page** button.
6. Specify **Analytics** as the **Page Name**.
7. Press **Create**:

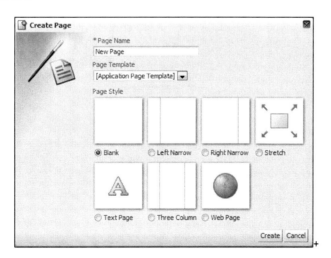

WebCenter Analytics and Activity Graph

 Before we will edit the page and add the analytics taskflows, we first need to add the taskflows to our resource catalog.

9. Select **Resource Catalogs** in the menu on the left.
10. Select the default resource catalog and select **Copy** from the **Edit** menu.
11. Specify a name for the new resource catalog.

 If you already have a custom resource catalog you can skip step 9 and 10 and just edit your custom resource catalog.

12. Select your resource catalog and select **Edit** from the **Edit** menu.
13. Press the **Add** button and select **Folder**.
14. Specify **Analytics** as the **Name**.
15. Press **OK**.
16. Select the **Analytics** folder.
17. Press the **Add** button and select **Add** from library.
18. Select **Task Flows** from the list on the left.
19. Select **Analytics - Page traffic** from the list on the right.

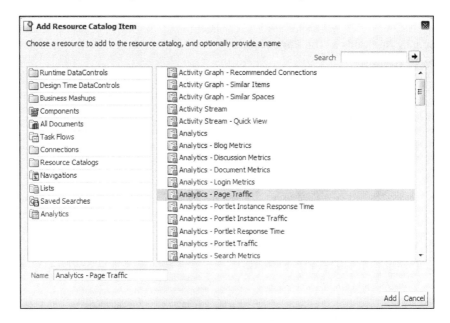

310

20. Press the **Add** button.
21. Repeat step 15 to 19 but select **Analytics - Login** Metrics in the right list:

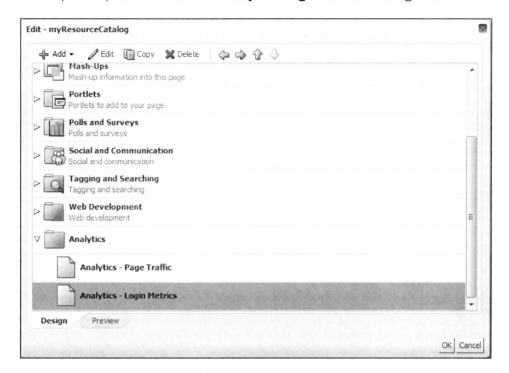

 If you want to know more about the resource catalog refer to Chapter 4.

22. Press **OK** to close the **Edit - myResourceCatalog** popup.
23. Open the **Configuration** tab.
24. Select your resource catalog from the **Default Resource Catalog** field.
25. Open the **Resource** tab.
26. Select **Pages** from the menu on the left.
27. Check the **Show Page** checkbox column for the **Analytics** page.
28. Click on **Analytics** to open the page.
29. Press *Ctrl+SHIFT+E* to go to edit mode.
30. Press the **Add Content** button to open the resource catalog.
31. Open the **Analytics** folder.

32. Press the **Add** button on the two taskflows available in that folder
33. Press the **Close** button to close the resource catalog.
34. Press **Close** in the top right corner to go back to view mode

Your page should look something like:

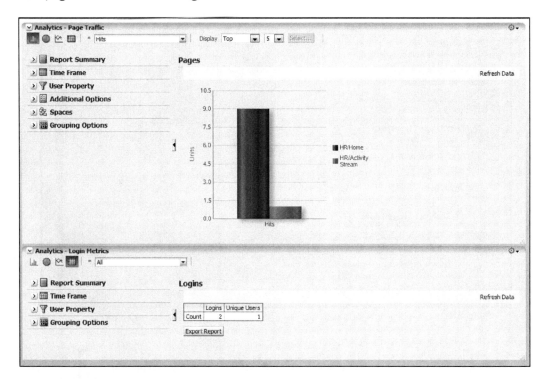

How it works

As you can see, both taskflows have some similar features. That is the same for all the analytics taskflows. If you know how one taskflow works, you can easily use the other ones as well.

On the left you can find different sections for filtering the data and on the right you can find the collected data itself.

Following section can be found on the left hand side:

- **Report Summary**: This section tells what the report shows in a readable sentence. It also gives an overview of all the filters that are applied to the data.
- **Time Frame**: Within this section you can specify the timeframe to view the data. You can specify a custom data range or a predefined one.

- **User Property**: Within this section you can filter the data based upon the profile of users.
- **Grouping Options**: With the grouping options, you can group data so you can aggregate data on the specified field.

When you have modified or added a filter you need to press the **Refresh Data link** so your changes will be applied.

Depending on the taskflow you can choose how the graph is displayed. On top of the taskflow you have a few buttons that will change the type of graph:

You have following choices:

- **Bar chart**: This graph will show the data in bars. The X-axis represents the different records while the Y-axis will be the amount of hits.
- **Pie chart**: Each record will get a piece of the pie. Depending on the weight of the record, the piece will be bigger.
- **Line Chart**: This chart will be enabled when you use the grouping options. This graph shows each group as a line.
- **Tabular data**: The last one is not really a graph. It actually shows the data in a table. By using this you can also export the data.

There's more

In this recipe, I have shown how you can use the taskflow for the page statistics and the login statistics. There are a lot more taskflows that can help you analyze the usage of your portal:

- **Blog Metrics**: This shows an overview of which blogs are more popular.
- **Discussion Metrics**: This shows which documents are most popular and how many views they have.
- **Document Metrics**: This shows which documents are viewed most often.
- **Login Metrics**: This shows an overview of the number of logins you had on your portal. You can also show the number of unique users that have logged in.
- **Page Traffic**: This shows the traffic per page. This way you can easily see which pages are popular.
- **Portlet Instance Response Time**: This shows an overview of the average response time per portlet instance. It can also show the minimum and maximum response times instead of the average.

- **Portlet Instance Traffic**: This shows an overview of the number of views per portlet instance as well as the unique visitors per portlet. This way you can see which portlets are used a lot.
- **Portlet Response Time**: This report shows the same data as the Portlet Instance Response Time; the difference is that this report will show the data grouped by portlet while the Portlet Instance Response Time report will show the data for each instance separately.
- **Portlet Traffic**: This shows the exact same data as the Portlet Instance Traffic but groups the data per portlet.
- **Search Metrics**: This shows an overview of the most used search strings.
- **Space Response Time**: This shows an overview of the average response time of a WebCenter group space. This taskflow is only available in WebCenter Spaces.
- **Space Traffic**: This shows the traffic for each space. This taskflow is also only available in WebCenter Spaces.
- **Wiki Metrics**: This shows the traffic for your wiki documents. This can tell you which wiki documents are popular.

Creating your own analytics report

In the previous recipe, you have seen all the out-of-the-box analytics taskflows. If you need more customized reports or you want a report with very specific data then you can create it yourself.

The idea behind creating your own report is just specifying the query for your data.

In this recipe, I will show how you can recreate the Page Traffic report so you know how you can build your own reports.

Getting ready

For this recipe, you need a WebCenter Portal application with a connection to the activity schema which has been described in the fourth recipe.

How to do it

1. Run your portal application or browse to the portal.
2. Log in as an administrator.
3. Go to the administration page.
4. From the **Resources** tab, select **Data Controls**.
5. Press the **Create** button.

Chapter 14

6. Select the connection that represents the activity schema.
7. Specify the **Password** for the activity schema.
8. Enter the following query in the SQL Statement field:

   ```
   SELECT  space.name_, page.name_, space.id, page.id, count(1), fact.page_, page.resourceid_
        FROM asfact_wc_pagevie_0 fact , asdim_wc_groupsp_0 space , asdim_wc_pages_0 page , asdim_wc_applica_0 app
        WHERE space.id = fact.groupspace_ and page.id = fact.page_ and app.id = fact.application_ and fact.occurred between to_date(:startdate, :dateformat) and to_date(:enddate, :dateformat) and app.name_ = :appname and page.personal_ = :ispersonal and space.name_ is not null and page.name_ is not null and space.id is not null and page.id is not null and fact.page_ is not null and page.resourceid_ is not null
        GROUP BY space.name_, page.name_, space.id, page.id, fact.page_, page.resourceid_
        ORDER BY count(1) desc
   ```

9. Press the **Enter** bind parameters values button to specify default values for the bind variables

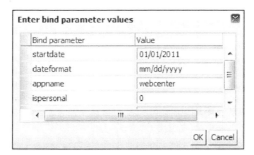

10. Specify a data in the **startdate** field.
11. Specify the **dateformat** you wish to use in the **dateformat** field.
12. Specify the **appname** (webcenter for WebCenter Spaces).
13. Specify whether you want personal pages to be included in the query. This only applies if the application is webcenter.
14. Specify the end data for the data.
15. Press the **OK** button to close the bind parameters popup.
16. Press the **Test** button to see if the query is correct.
17. Specify a name for the data control.

18. Press the **Create** button to create the data control:

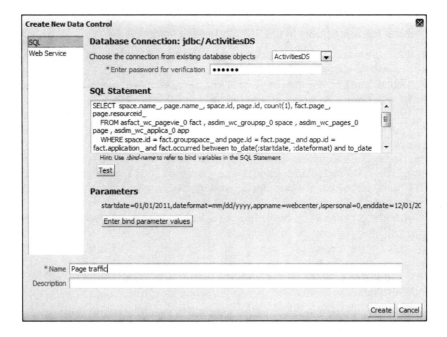

19. Select the data control.
20. Select **Show** from the **Edit** menu.
21. Now that the data control has been created, we can add it to our page as a graph.
22. Select **Pages** from the **Structure** section on the left.
23. Press the **Create** button to create a new page.
24. Specify **Report** as the name.
25. Press the **Create** button to create the page.
26. Select the **Report** page and select **Edit** from the actions menu.
27. Press the **Add Content** button to open the **Resource Catalog**.
28. Open the **Mash-Ups** folder.
29. Open the **Data** Controls folder.
30. Open your data control that you have created.
31. Press the **Add** button for your data control and select **Graph** from the context menu.

32. In the first step select **Bar** for the **Type** of graph.
33. Press the **Next** button.
34. Select **Bar** in the **Sub-Type** step.
35. Press **Next**.
36. Select a layout for the graph.
37. Specify X Axis for **NAME_1**.
38. Select Bars for **COUNT_1_**:

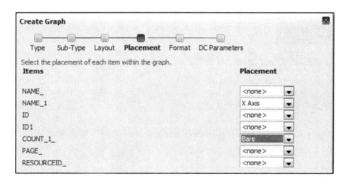

39. Press the **Next** button.
40. Press the **Next** button on the **Format** screen.
41. Specify the parameters for the query:

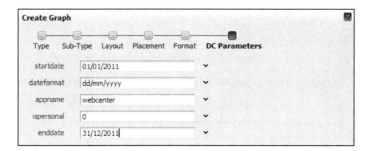

WebCenter Analytics and Activity Graph

42. Press the **Create** button.
43. Press the **Close** button in the top right corner to go back to view mode.

If everything went well, the report should look something like this:

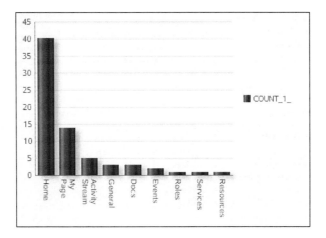

How it works

The data control we created will query the activities schema and return the data that you want to show.

The following tables can be used in your query:

- `asfact_wc_logins_0`: This contains data about the logins.
- `asdim_wc_applica_0`: This contains information about the application. You should always use this table to filter the data for your application. This table has a name field that you can use to filter the data of a specific application. Each other table has an `application_` field that contains the ID of the application.
- `asdim_wc_pages_0`: This contains information about pages.
- `asfact_wc_pagevie_0`: This contains information about events occurred on pages. It contains a link to the `asdim_wc_pages_0` table.
- `asfact_wc_groupsp_0`: This contains information about events occurred on WebCenter group spaces.
- `asdim_wc_groupsp_0`: This contains information about group spaces.
- `asfact_wc_portlet_0`: This contains information about events occurred on portlets.
- `asdim_wc_portlet_0`: This contains information about portlets.
- `asfact_wc_searche_0`: This contains information about search events.
- `asdim_wc_searche_0`: This contains information about search.

- `asfact_wc_doclib_0`: This contains information about events on the document service.
- `asdim_wc_documen_0`: This contains information about the documents.
- `asfact_wc_discuss_0`: This contains information about events occurred on discussions.
- `asdim_wc_discuss_0`: This contains information about discussions.

As you can see, each type of service or resource has two tables. One that contains the facts and one that contains the information about the resource itself.

Showing an activity stream on your portal

An activity stream is a component that you can add to your portal that shows the data gathered from the activity engine. With this component you can inform your users with the latest events that happened in the portal. You can show them the latest pages that have been created, newly uploaded document or documents that are updated, discussions that have new replies, and so on.

People can also personalize the activity stream so they see only the type of updates they want.

Getting ready

For this recipe you need a WebCenter Portal application that has been deployed to a standalone WebLogic server and that has been registered to the activity service, which is explained in the first recipe of this chapter.

You also need a connection to the activity schema, which is described in the fourth recipe of this chapter.

How to do it

1. Browse to your portal application.
2. Log in as an administrator.
3. Go to the page were you want to add the activity stream.
4. Press *Ctrl+SHIFT+E* to go to edit mode.
5. Press the **Add Content** button to open the **Resource Catalog**.
6. Open the **Alerts and Updates** folder.

7. Press on the **Add** button for the **Activity Stream** component:

8. Close the resource catalog.
9. Press the **Close** button on the top right corner to return to view mode.

That's it. When you add resources to your application like pages or documents or whatever resource from a service you have enabled, you should be able to track these changes in the activity stream.

For example in the following screenshot, you can see that I have created an event, a page, and a document:

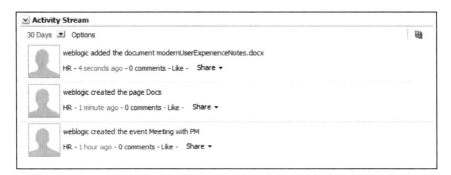

How it works

- The activity graph used the activities schema to request the gathered data about your application or WebCenter Spaces
- Every single entry will have a link to the user who created or updated the resource as well as a link to the actual resource
- The Activity Stream also has some social networking features such a 'Like' link and the possibility to add comments about the resource
- With the Share button, you can share the update with other people by sending them a link with the update

There's more

Beside the Activity Stream taskflow, you also have a quick view for the activity graph. The quick view is a lightweight version of the regular activity stream taskflow. It does not have the social network features and it also does not show the image of the user.

In the following screenshot, you can see how the quick view taskflow looks for the exact same situation as in the previous screenshot:

You can find this taskflow in the same folder as the activity stream taskflow.

Index

Symbols

#{node.createdBy} 144
#{node.createdDate} 144
#{node.isFolder} 144
#{node.modifiedBy} 144
#{node.modifiedDate} 144
#{node.path} 144
#{node.propertyMap['dDocName']} 144
#{node.propertyMap['dDocTitle']} 144
#{node.propertyMap} 144

A

activities schema
  connection, creating in JDeveloper 307, 308
activity stream
  showing, on portal 319-321
Add button 209
Add content button 20
additional pages
  enabling 252
  enabling, steps 252
  working 253
adf-config.xml file 74
ADFC Taskflow Metrics folder
  items 298
ADFC Taskflow request processing time folder
  items 299
Administration Console 11
af:xmlContent tag 113
af:pageTemplate tag 113
af:xmlContent tag 18
alias parameter 277, 278

analysis collector
  WebCenter Portal application, registering 302, 303, 304
analytics report
  creating 314-319
analyze tab 212
announcements
  adding, to portal 163-165
  creating 166
  creating, steps 166
  working 167
announcement service connection
  creating 240-242
application performance
  about 296
  active sessions 297
  Bean Accesses per minute 298
  Beans in use 298
  monitoring 296
  Request per minute 297
  request processing 297
  working 297-299
application server
  connection, creating 282
  in JDeveloper 282
  working 283
Apply button 127
asdim_wc_applicaa_0 318
asdim_wc_documen_0 319
asdim_wc_groupsp_0 318
asdim_wc_logins_0 319
asdim_wc_pages_0 318
asdim_wc_portlet_0 318
asdim_wc_searcha_0 318

asfact_wc_discuss_0 319
asfact_wc_doclib_0 319
asfact_wc_groupsp_0 318
asfact_wc_logins_0 318
asfact_wc_pagevie_0 318
asfact_wc_portlet_0 318
asfact_wc_searche_0 318
Associate Data Source popup window 195
attributes, portlets
  DisplayActions 36
  DisplayHeader 35
  DisplayScrollBar 35
  DisplayShadow 35
  Height 35
  partialTrigger 35
  Rendered 36
  RenderPortletInFrame 36
  Title 35
  Width 35
attributes, tagging button
  resourceId 178
  resourceName 178
  serviceId 178
Attributes tab 93
attrs collection 113

B

bar chart graph 313
blog metrics 313
browse button 135
business-based logic navigation resources
  filtering 68-71
business-based logic resources
  filtering 96-99
business-based resource catalog
  selecting 100-102
  working 102

C

catalog
  resource, adding at runtime 91, 92
  resource component, adding at runtime 93
  resource component, editing 93
CatalogDefinitionFilter 98, 99
catalogElement 99
catalogId attribute 88

Change Layout button 20
Close button 149, 199
CMIS (Content Management Interoperability Service) 132
component, adding to navigation model
  about 63
  steps 63
  working 64
component, adding to resource catalog
  about 88
  working 89
composer component
  about 19
  page properties, options 22
  pages, editing 20
  Reset Page button 22
  working 21
composerContext.inEditMode 109
Configuration Parameters 130
connection
  creating, to discussion service 154-156
connection, creating for poll service
  steps 194-197
connection management, Enterprise Manager
  about 287
  steps 287, 288
  working 288, 289
connection to content server
  creating 128, 129
  Set as primary connection for Documents service, working 130
content
  Link button, working 187
  linking 185, 186
content, organizing
  Activity Graph Service 172
  link service method 172
  search service 172
  tags service 172
content driven navigation model
  about 131
  content query, working 132, 133
  creating 131
Content List Template Def 147
content organization
  connection link, creating 172
  content, linking 185

discussion, linking to 190
document, linking to 187
related content, displaying 179
tag cloud, displaying 182
tagging functionality, enabling to pages 176
tag services, creating 172
content presenter
using, for multiple items display 137-140
using, for single item display 133-137
Content Presenter Configuration 137
content presenter template
creating, for multiple items 144-147
creating, for single item 140-144
content query, adding to navigation model
about 57
steps 57, 58
working 58
content server integration
connection, creating 128
content driven navigation model, creating 130
content presenter, creating for multiple item 144-148
content presenter, creating for single item 140
document service taskflows, using 148
multiple content item display, content presenter displaying 137
single content item display, content presenter displaying 133
UCM, preparing for remote connection 126
way 126
Content Template Def component 143
contextual wiring, of portlets
events, using 46-48
working 48
corporateTemplate.jspx 119
Create button 15, 213
Create Connection button 291
Create Page button 134
Ctrl+ N 24
custom content, adding to navigation model
steps 65, 66
working 66
custom content, adding to resource catalog
working 90, 91
customContent tag 66

custom folder, adding to navigation model
about 64
steps 65
working 65
custom folder, adding to resource catalog
about 89, 90
working 90
CustomfolderContextFactory 90
customFolder tag 65

D

default navigation model
specifying 74, 75
Delete button 286
design time
new template, creating 108-113
discussion
connection link, working 191
linking to 190, 191
Link to Existing menu 192
Link to New menu 192
discussion forums
adding, to portal 156-159
discussion metrics 313
discussion server
URL 242
discussion service
connection, creating to 154-156
taskflows 154
discussion service connection
creating 240-242
discussion services, taskflows
forums 154
popular topics 154
quick view 154
recent topics 154
watched forums 154
watched topics 154
Display Options tab 48
dname parameter 277
document
connection link, working 189
linking to 187-189
document metrics 313
document service connection
creating 242, 243

creating, steps 243
working 244
document service taskflows
  using 148, 149
  working 149-151

E

Edit icon 202
Edit Introduction Message link 210
Enterprise Manager
  connections, managing 287
  log messages, viewing 294, 295
  log messages, working 295, 296
  URL 245
enterprise portal 7
events
  ParametersChange 35
  using, for portlet contextual wiring 46-48
exportcert parameter 277
expression builder 44
external application
  adding, to portal 222-225
  registering, at runtime 220-222
  registering, in JDeveloper 218
  registering, steps 218-220
  registering 245
  working 220
external application, adding to portal
  about 222-225
  steps 223, 224
  working 224
external application, registering at runtime
  about 220
  steps 221
  working 222
external application, registering in JDeveloper
  about 218
  steps 218-220
  working 220
external content
  integrating, with Omniportlet 232
  integrating, with WebClipping portlet 227
external content, integrating with Omniportlet
  about 232
  Spreadsheet (CSV) 236

SQL 236
steps 233-235
Web page 236
Web Service 236
working 236, 237
XML 236
external content, integrating with WebClipping portlet
  about 227
  adding, steps 227-229
  working 230

F

factoryClass 86
file parameter 278
folder, adding to navigation model
  steps 53, 54
folder, adding to resource catalog
  steps 84, 85
  working 85
folder tag 54
forums
  creating 160
  creating, steps 160
  working 161
full rebuild option 305

G

Gathering Engine
  running, manually 304, 305
  scheduling 306
genkeypair parameter 277
goLink 117
goLinkPrettyUrl attribute 117
grouping options 313
group spaces
  creating 248
  creating, steps 249-251
  exporting 259
  exporting, steps 260
  importing 261
  importing, steps 261
  working 251, 252, 260, 261

H

hasSubpages attribute 77

I

identity store
  Oracle Identity Directory, using as 269-272
importcert parameter 278
includeInCatalog method 69
incremental update 305
Insert Folder Content checkbox 132
insertFolderContents attribute 58
Insert Tree popup 116
internal.jspx 264
internalUser 265
isUserInRole 99

J

JDeveloper
  connection to activities schema, creating 307, 308
  external application, registering 218
  JSR 286 portlets, building 24-26
  preparing, from WebCenter 8
  working 9
JDeveloper, preparing from WebCenter
  application templates 9
  requirements 8
  working 9
JSR 286 portlets
  building, in JDeveloper 24-26
  working 26, 28
JSR 286 portlets building, in JDeveloper
  additional steps 28
  working 26, 28

K

keyalg parameter 277
keypass parameter 277
keystore parameter 277, 278

L

line chart 313
link, adding to navigation model
  steps 54, 55
  working 55-57
link, adding to resource catalog
  steps 85
  working 86
Link Button 188
link connection
  creating 172-175
Links Detail Button 186
lists
  creating 254
  creating, steps 254-256
  working 256, 257
login metrics 313
Log Messages screen 295

M

MDS metrics folder 299
Movable Box title bar 21
multiple content items
  displaying, content presenter used 137-148

N

navigation attributes
  AccessKey 51
  description 51
  IconURI 51
  subject 51
  target 51
  title 51
  tooltip 51
navigationId attribute 63
navigation model
  about 50
  component, adding 63, 64
  content query, adding to 57, 58
  creating, at design time 50-52
  creating, at run time 52

custom content, adding 65, 66
custom folder, adding 64, 65
default model, specifying 74, 75
existing model, importing 73, 74
exporting to 71-73
folder, adding to 53
link, adding to 54-56
page hierarchy, adding to 59, 60
referencing 61-63
navigation model, creating at design time
about 50
steps 50
working 51, 52
navigation model, creating at runtime
about 52
steps 52
working 53
node.goLinkPrettyUrl 110
node.title 110
node attribute 147
nodeStamp facet 117

O

o_w_s_l_LoginBackingBean bean 112
OHS
URL 244
OK button 204
Omniportlet
about 230
external content, integrating with 232
registering 230
registering, steps 231, 232
WC_Portlet 230
working 232
oracle.adf.rc.component.ComponentFactory interface 64
oracle.adf.rc.component.XmlComponentFactory 63, 88
oracle.adf.rc.spi.plugin.catalog.CustomContentProviderV2 65
oracle.adf.rc.spi.plugin.catalog.CustomContentProviderV2 interface 90, 91
Oracle Identity Directory
using, as identity store 269-272

Oracle Universal Content Management 126
Overview Metrics folder
general metrics 299

P

page
poll service, adding to 200-202
page bindings 34
pageDef tag 77
page hierarchy
managing 75, 76
used, for securing pages 264-266
working 77
page hierarchy, adding to navigation model
steps 59, 60
working 60
page parameters 41
Page Properties button 22
pages
securing, at runtime 266-268
securing, page hierarchy used 264-266
tagging functionality, enabling 176, 177
pages, WebCenter portal
access rules 16
actions, performing 16
error.jspx 12
home.jspx 12
login.jspx 12
managing 13, 14, 15
moving 15
securing 15, 16
page style
af:pageTemplate tag 123
creating 121
creating, steps 121-123
page definition 124
working 124
page traffic 313
panelBorderLayout 109
panelGroupLayout 109
panelStretchLayout 116
ParametersChange event 35
Parameters tab 44
partialTrigger 42

pie chart 313
Poll Id dropdown list 202
poll service
  about 193
  adding, to page 200-202
  connection, creating 194-197
  creating 197-199
  scheduling 209, 210
  template, applying to 214-216
  working 199
poll template
  creating 212-214
  working 214
portal
  activity stream, showing 319-321
  announcements, adding 163-165
  discussions forums, adding 156-159
  external application, adding 222-225
portal:preferences tag 74
portal, WebCenter
  about 12
  Administration Console, tabs 11
  creating, steps 10, 11
  navigations 13
  page hierarchy 13
  pages 12
  page templates 12
  resource catalogs 13
  working 11, 12
portal default start page
  modifying 66
  modifying, steps 67
  working 67
portlet-class entry 28
portlet.xml 27
portlet class 28
portlet instance response time 313
portlet instance traffic 314
portlet producer
  registering 247
  registering, steps 247, 248
  working 248
portlet response time 314

portlets
  consuming, at design time 33
  consuming, at design time 34-36
  consuming, at runtime 36
  interoperability 38
  managing 23
  wiring together, at design time 38-43
  wiring together, at runtime 43-45
portlets consumption, at design time
  about 33
  property inspector, using 35
  steps 34
  working 34, 35
portlets consumption, at runtime
  about 36
  properties popup, tabs 38
  property inspector 37
  starting with 36
  working 37
portlet traffic 314
processAction method 28
producer registration, at design time
  PDK portlet producer 29
  starting with 29, 30
  WSRP producer 29
  WSRP producer, working 32
producer registration, at run time
  about 32
  requirements 32
  steps 32
  working 33
producer registration, in design time
  steps 31
production environment
  changes, propagating to 289-291
  working 292, 293
Propagation tool 292

Q

questions
  managing 204-208
  types 208
  working 208

R

related content
  displaying 179-181
  working 181
Related Links 180
rendered attribute 112
rendered parameter 111
render method 28
report summary section 312
Reset Page button 22
resource
  catalog, adding at runtime 91, 92
  catalog component, adding at runtime 93
  catalog component, editing 93
resource catalog
  about 80
  creating, at design time 80-82
  creating, at runtime 82-84
  custom content, adding to 90, 91
  custom folder, adding to 89, 90
  existing component, adding to 88, 89
  existing resource catalog, adding to 87
  exporting 103, 104
  folder, adding to 84, 85
  importing 104, 105
  link, adding to 85, 86
  securing 95, 96
resource catalog, creating at design time
  steps 80-82
resource catalog, creating at runtime
  steps 82-84
ResourceCatalogSelector interface 103
Resource Library
  about 93
  managing 94
  working 94, 95
result
  analyze tab, working 212
  analyzing 211
role-based resources
  filtering 96-99
runtime
  external application, registering 220
  pages, securing at 266-268

S

search metrics 314
sections
  managing 202-204
SecuringPages 264
SecurityContex 99
securityContext.authenticated expression 110
Servlet/JSP Metrics folder 299
Show Metric Palette 298
single content item
  displaying, content presenter used 133-137
space response time 314
space template
  creating 257
  creating, steps 258, 259
  working 259
space traffic 314
SSL
  enabling, for WebCenter portal application 273-278
storepass parameter 277, 278
subspaces
  creating 253
  creating, steps 253, 254
  working 254
survey service. *See* **poll service**

T

tabular data 313
tag cloud
  additional functionality 184
  Cloud / list view 184
  displaying 182, 183
  Refresh button 185
  Sort options 184
  working 184
Tagging Button 176
tagging functionality
  enabling, to pages 176, 177
  working 177-179
tag service connection
  creating 172-175

Target tab 93
taskflows
  securing 278
  securing, steps 279, 280
  working 280
template
  applying, to poll 214-216
  corporateTemplate.jspx 119
  creating, at design time 108-113
  creating, at run time 113, 114
  runtime editing, enabling 118-121
  working 120, 121
template, creating at design time
  af:pageTemplate tag 113
  af:xmlContent tag 113
  attrs collection 113
  composerContext.inEditMode 109
  node.attributes['Target'] 110
  node.goLinkPrettyUrl 110
  node.selected 110
  node.title 110
  o_w_s_l_LoginBackingBean bean 112
  panelBorderLayout 109
  panelGroupLayout 109
  rendered attribute 112
  rendered parameter 111
  securityContext.authenticated expression 110
  steps 108, 109
  working 109-111
template, creating at run time
  steps 114
  working 114
templates, WebCenter portal
  pageTemplate_globe.jspx 12
  pageTemplate_swooshy.jspx 12
Test Connection button 128, 283
time frame section 312
topics
  creating 162
  creating, steps 162
  working 163
tree navigation
  creating 115
  creating, steps 115-117
  goLink 117
  goLinkPrettyUrl attribute 117
  Insert Tree popup 116
  nodeStamp facet 117
  panelStretchLayout 116
  working 117, 118

U

UCM, preparing for remote connection
  about 126
  intradoc server, working 127, 128
  steps 126, 127
Upload button 190
url tag 56
user property section 313

V

validity parameter 277
variableIterator 34, 41
view attribute 147
visible attribute 55, 71

W

WC_Portlet 230
WebCenter
  applications, managing 281
  JDeveloper, preparing 8
  navigation model 50
  portal, creating 10
  resource catalog 80
  WSRP producer 29
WebCenter 11*g* PS3
  features 125
WebCenter Analytics taskflows
  creating 309-313
WebCenter portal
  customizing 17
WebCenter portal, customizing
  steps 17, 18
  working 18, 19
WebCenter portal application
  about 283
  deploying 283, 284

registering, to analysis collector 302-304
SSL, enabling for 273-278
undeploying 286, 287
working 285
WebCenter Space environment
URL 253
WebCenter Spaces
about 239, 240
URL 252
WebClipping portlet
adding, steps 227-229
registering 225
registering, steps 225-227
used, for integrating external content 227
working 227, 230

WebLogic console 174
When responses count reach checkbox 210
wiki document
creating 167
creating, steps 167
editing 168
editing, steps 168, 169
working 168-170
wiki metrics 314
WSRP producer
about 29
context root 30
default format, URL 30
endpoint 30

Thank you for buying Oracle WebCenter 11g PS3 Administration Cookbook

About Packt Publishing

Packt, pronounced 'packed', published its first book "*Mastering phpMyAdmin for Effective MySQL Management*" in April 2004 and subsequently continued to specialize in publishing highly focused books on specific technologies and solutions.

Our books and publications share the experiences of your fellow IT professionals in adapting and customizing today's systems, applications, and frameworks. Our solution-based books give you the knowledge and power to customize the software and technologies you're using to get the job done. Packt books are more specific and less general than the IT books you have seen in the past. Our unique business model allows us to bring you more focused information, giving you more of what you need to know, and less of what you don't.

Packt is a modern, yet unique publishing company, which focuses on producing quality, cutting-edge books for communities of developers, administrators, and newbies alike. For more information, please visit our website: `www.PacktPub.com`.

About Packt Enterprise

In 2010, Packt launched two new brands, Packt Enterprise and Packt Open Source, in order to continue its focus on specialization. This book is part of the Packt Enterprise brand, home to books published on enterprise software – software created by major vendors, including (but not limited to) IBM, Microsoft and Oracle, often for use in other corporations. Its titles will offer information relevant to a range of users of this software, including administrators, developers, architects, and end users.

Writing for Packt

We welcome all inquiries from people who are interested in authoring. Book proposals should be sent to `author@packtpub.com`. If your book idea is still at an early stage and you would like to discuss it first before writing a formal book proposal, contact us; one of our commissioning editors will get in touch with you.

We're not just looking for published authors; if you have strong technical skills but no writing experience, our experienced editors can help you develop a writing career, or simply get some additional reward for your expertise.

Web 2.0 Solutions with Oracle WebCenter 11g

ISBN: 978-1-847195-80-7   Paperback: 276 pages

Learn WebCenter 11g fundamentals and develop real-world enterprise applications in an online work environment with this book and eBook

1. Create task-oriented, rich, interactive online work environments with the help of this Oracle WebCenter training tutorial
2. Accelerate the development of Enterprise 2.0 solutions by leveraging the Oracle tools
3. Apply the basic concepts of Enterprise 2.0 for your business solutions by understanding them completely

Oracle 10g/11g Data and Database Management Utilities

ISBN: 978-1-847196-28-6   Paperback: 432 pages

Master 12 must-use Oracle Database Utilities with this book and eBook

1. Optimize time-consuming tasks efficiently using the Oracle database utilities
2. Perform data loads on the fly and replace the functionality of the old export and import utilities using Data Pump or SQL*Loader
3. Boost database defenses with Oracle Wallet Manager and Security

Please check www.PacktPub.com for information on our titles

EJB 3.0 Database Persistence with Oracle Fusion Middleware 11g

ISBN: 978-1-849681-56-8   Paperback: 448 pages

A complete guide to building EJB 3.0 database persistent applications with Oracle Fusion Middleware 11g tools with this book and eBook

1. Integrate EJB 3.0 database persistence with Oracle Fusion Middleware tools: WebLogic Server, JDeveloper, and Enterprise Pack for Eclipse
2. Automatically create EJB 3.0 entity beans from database tables
3. Learn to wrap entity beans with session beans and create EJB 3.0 relationships

JDBC 4.0 and Oracle JDeveloper for J2EE Development

ISBN: 978-1-847194-30-5   Paperback: 444 pages

A J2EE developer's guide to using Oracle JDeveloper's integrated database features to build data-driven applications with this book and eBook

1. Develop your Java applications using JDBC and Oracle JDeveloper
2. Explore the new features of JDBC 4.0
3. Use JDBC and the data tools in Oracle JDeveloper
4. Configure JDBC with various application servers

Please check www.PacktPub.com for information on our titles

Lightning Source UK Ltd.
Milton Keynes UK
176265UK00002B/58/P